P9-DEA-573

THE
BLACKBOARD
AND THE
BOTTOM LINE

THE BLACKBOARD AND THE BOTTOM LINE

Why Schools Can't Be Businesses

LARRY CUBAN

Harvard University Press

Cambridge, Massachusetts, and London, England · 2004

Library of Congress Cataloging-in-Publication Data

Cuban, Larry.
 The blackboard and the bottom line : why schools can't be businesses / Larry Cuban.
  p.   cm.
 Includes bibliographical references and index.
 ISBN 0-674-01523-1 (alk. paper)
 1. Business and education—United States.   2. Public schools—United States.
 3. Education change—United States.   I. Title.

LC1085.2.C83   2004
371.19′5—dc22   2004052312

For Larry Kowitch, 1929–2004

A dear friend whom I loved and admired for his intelligence, compassion, and playful wit

CONTENTS

THE
BLACKBOARD
AND THE
BOTTOM LINE

INTRODUCTION: BUSINESS AND SCHOOL REFORM

To the renowned social reformer Jane Addams, business leaders' self-interest and what children were taught in public schools converged. Addams told a meeting of the National Education Association in 1897: "The business man has, of course, not said to himself: 'I will have the public school train office boys and clerks for me, so that I may have them cheap,' but he has thought, and sometimes said, 'Teach the children to write legibly, and to figure accurately and quickly; to acquire the habits of punctuality and order; to be prompt to obey, and not question why; and you will fit them to make their way in the world as I have made mine.'"[1]

Two decades later, the ardent progressive school reformer and Stanford University professor Ellwood Cubberley went further than Addams in describing the links between U.S. businesses and public schools: "Our schools are, in a sense, factories in which the raw products (children) are to be shaped and fashioned into products to meet the various demands of life. The specifications for manufacturing come from the demands of twentieth-century civilization, and it is the business of the school to build its pupils according to the specifications laid down."[2]

And in 2003 U.S. Secretary of Education Rod Paige, appointed by President George W. Bush to help reform the nation's public schools, in softer but no less direct language reaffirmed Cubberley's view: "Henry Ford created a world-class company, a leader in its industry. More important, Ford would not have survived the competition had it not been for an emphasis on results. We must view education the same way. Good schools do operate like a business. They care about outcomes, routinely assess quality, and measure the needs of the children they serve."[3]

Addams, Cubberley, and Paige, reformers all, clearly saw business and education as interrelated in school goals, curriculum, organization, and outcomes. And they were not alone. Because public schools have long supplied the nation with future workers, customers, and citizens, business and civic elites have seen education and the economy as interdependent ever since tax-supported public schools began nearly two centuries ago. On more than one occasion, reformers have launched ambitious efforts to make schools more businesslike.[4]

While most teachers and principals see teaching and learning as complex activities intertwined with what children bring to school, and think of schools as places where children become literate and well behaved, learn to display solid character, and get connected to their communities, many corporate leaders (along with some educators like Paige) see schools as places producing a product—such as academic achievement—and sorely in need of marketplace moxie. Business leaders and other critics often accuse teachers and district administrators as inefficient and interested in avoiding accountability for academic results.[5]

The belief that crisis-ridden public schools need business-led resuscitation gets renewed periodically when the media report that young people from other nations are outscoring U.S. students on international tests, and when employers and professors complain about high school graduates who cannot put together coherent sentences or listen to directions for more than five seconds. Such criticism often makes beleaguered educators feel that school reform is being done *to* and *for* them rather than *with* them.

Not all school reformers from the business world equate schools with businesses, and some find their opinions changing as they work with educators. Consider the case of the former CEO Jamie Vollmer, who recounts an epiphany he experienced in the 1980s:

> "If I ran my business the way you people operate your schools, I wouldn't be in business very long!"
>
> I stood before an audience filled with outraged teachers who were becoming angrier by the minute. My speech had entirely consumed their precious 90 minutes of in-service training. Their initial icy glares had turned to restless agitation. You could cut the hostility with a knife.
>
> I represented a group of business people dedicated to improving public schools. I was an executive at an ice cream company that became famous in the middle 1980s when *People* magazine chose its blueberry flavor as the "Best Ice Cream in America."
>
> I was convinced of two things. First, public schools needed to change; they were archaic selecting and sorting mechanisms designed for the Industrial Age and out of step with the needs of our emerging "knowledge society." Second, educators were a major part of the problem: they resisted change, hunkered down in their feathered nests, protected by tenure and shielded by a bureaucratic monopoly. They needed to look to business. We knew how to produce quality. Zero defects! Total Quality Management! Continuous improvement!
>
> In retrospect, the speech was perfectly balanced—equal parts ignorance and arrogance. As soon as I finished, a woman's hand shot up . . . She began quietly. "We are told, sir, that you manage a company that makes good ice cream."
>
> I smugly replied, "Best ice cream in America, ma'am."

"How nice," she said. "Is it rich and smooth?"

"Sixteen percent butterfat," I crowed.

"Premium ingredients?" she inquired.

"Super-premium! Nothing but triple-A." I was on a roll. I never saw the next line coming.

"Mr. Vollmer," she said, leaning forward with a wicked eyebrow raised to the sky, "when you are standing on your receiving dock and you see an inferior shipment of blueberries arrive, what do you do?"

In the silence of that room, I could hear the trap snap. I knew I was dead meat, but I wasn't going to lie.

"I send them back."

"That's right!" she barked, "and we can never send back our blueberries. We take them big, small, rich, poor, gifted, exceptional, abused, frightened, confident, homeless, rude, and brilliant. We take them with attention deficit disorder, junior rheumatoid arthritis, and English as their second language. We take them all! Every one! And that, Mr. Vollmer, is why it's not a business. It's school!"

In an explosion, all 290 teachers, principals, bus drivers, aides, custodians, and secretaries jumped to their feet and yelled, "Yeah! Blueberries! Blueberries!"

And so began my long transformation.

Since then, I have visited hundreds of schools. I have learned that a school is not a business. Schools are unable to control the quality of their raw material, they are dependent upon the vagaries of politics for a reliable revenue stream, and they are constantly mauled by a howling horde of disparate, competing customer groups that would send the best CEO screaming into the night.[6]

Vollmer's confession often brings I-told-you-so smiles to the faces of educators who question the involvement of business leaders in school reform. His conversion from caustic critic to stouthearted advocate of education practitioners remains an exception, but his story illustrates the century-long prickly relationship between educators and business leaders over school reform and their contrasting assumptions about what is needed to improve schools.

Policymakers and others who set out to overhaul schools encounter a fundamental paradox: teachers and principals who block changes sought by reformers are supposedly the problem, yet these very same educators—almost three million strong—are the people who connect with more than fifty million children daily and do the essential work of schooling. Inescapably, therefore, they also have to be the solution. The paradox of distrusting teachers and principals for having created the problem and then turning around and demanding that they solve the problem they created has flummoxed school reformers in the past. As a result, reformers then and now have pressed for curricular, managerial, governance, and organizational changes to give them more control over the behavior of teachers and principals.

The history of business participation in public schools contains many examples in which reformers have exerted various degrees of control over teachers. From aggressively applying business principles to school districts (with affirmation from superintendents and school boards but loud dissents from classroom teachers), to lobbying elected officials to pass legislation establishing academic standards, to donating money and equipment to beleaguered schools (garnering ardent thanks from teachers and principals), private-sector leaders have influenced school reform. The history of their efforts also reveals their distrust of educators' expertise and willingness to change.

Business leaders' suspicions of educators have been small but colorful strokes in the larger portrait of business-inspired school reform. It is that larger picture, spanning more than a century, that I present in this book. Six questions frame the book, with a chapter devoted to each question:

- What is the logic of business-inspired reforms?
- How have business leaders influenced schools?
- Why have public schools adopted business-inspired reforms?
- What are the limits to business influence?
- Are public schools just like businesses?
- Has business influence improved public schools?

Tying together all these questions is the special status of public education in the minds of generation after generation of reformers: the tendency to expect the schools to provide solutions to pervasive national problems. Or as one reform-minded clergyman put it in 1895: "One way to bring better times, better civilization, better men, better women is education." Basically, relying upon public schools to solve the nation's problems amounts to deferring direct political, economic, and social action to the next generation, a pattern that has been evident repeatedly in American history.[7]

Late nineteenth-century reformers viewed public schools as a social melting pot for converting the ore of polyglot immigrants into the tempered steel of 100 percent Americans. Subsequent generations of reformers drafted schools to help the country prevail over foreign enemies in two world wars and the Cold War. In the 1960s reformers focused on social justice, seeking to eliminate segregated schools and reduce the huge learning gaps between poor minority and white middle-class children. If there has been one constant refrain over the decades, it has been the reliance on public schools as a future cure for national ills. As the Boston superintendent of schools told the National Education Association in 1898, public schools were "the salvation of the American Republic."[8]

I will examine two extended periods—from the 1880s to the 1930s, and from the 1970s to the present—in which business-inspired reformers looked to schools to help solve severe national economic problems. As in earlier movements for reform, business leaders and their allies in civic elites magnified schools' defects and bashed educators for mediocrity. In their criticism they discounted the effects of eroding public trust in educators, and they underestimated the hard, complicated work of changing school cultures and teaching practices.

Business leaders were confident that the sound principles that guided their companies, if applied to public schools, would provide employers with skilled workers and thus would increase economic productivity, contribute to national prosperity, and help U.S. firms carve out a larger market share of international trade. Believing that public schools would profit from imitating high-performing, efficient businesses and the market system, they formed broad-based coalitions of civic officials, union heads, foundation administrators, parents, and educators to concentrate on improving the schools and, through that improvement, to help solve serious economic and social problems. They saw public schools as an active arm of the U.S. economy. The six questions that structure this book are derived from this long-held belief in strong ties between the economy and education, and from the recurring tendency to turn to public schools for help during national crises. The answers to these questions are embedded in the following argument.

Between the 1880s and the 1930s, many business leaders actively participated in school reform. They were seldom the sole intellectual or political force behind efforts at reform; instead, they worked with progressive civic and educational leaders interested in improving schools. They did so because of an agitated concern that Germany and Britain were outstripping the United States in competition for global markets. These business-minded reformers believed that Germany, in particular, had surged ahead because its workers had benefited from school-based vocational training.

Accordingly, leaders of large and midsized manufacturing firms, progressive reformers, and educators—each for different reasons—promoted school-based vocational programs that would equip students with new skills fitted to an industrial workplace. By the end of World War I, the progressive-business coalition had made the preparation of workers a goal of U.S. secondary schools, established vocational programs in urban public schools, and secured federal aid for high school industrial courses. Moreover, business leaders' political alliances with civic and educational progressives had broadened the schools' traditional academic role to include social and medical services for children and families, while also applying corporate practices to make school governance and organization more efficient.

This successful early twentieth-century coalition of business and civic leaders operated from two assumptions. First, reformers assumed that schooling urban youth for an industrial workplace would end the skill deficits among entry-level workers, raise economic productivity, and increase the social stability of crime-ridden and poverty-stricken cities, thus contributing to a growing, globally competitive economy. Second, they assumed that businesses and schools were kindred organizations, and thus that the schools, which were rife with political appointees and suffered from gross inefficiencies, could be substantially improved by the application of sound business practices. By 1930 the broad-based coalition of reformers had transformed the goals, curriculum, governance, and management of public schools. These changes remained in place until the last quarter of the twentieth century.

By the mid-1970s, in response to an economic recession, increasing crime and poverty in largely minority-populated cities, and deep concerns over Japan's growing share of automobile, electronic, and other international markets, corporate leaders again attributed national problems to underperforming and inefficient schooling. Now the accusation was that the U.S. educational system was failing to prepare students to enter a post-industrial labor market. As before, a broad coalition of corporate and government officials blamed the schools and mobilized support for their restructuring. A presidential commission distilled the mounting criticism of schools into a report entitled *A Nation at Risk* (1983), which blasted public schools for shoddy performance. Across the nation, this searing attack triggered state-mandated reforms aimed at improving the academic performance of all students.

In the 1980s and 1990s business and civic leaders learned through trial and error how hard it was to raise academic performance, especially in big cities. From corporate partnerships with individual schools in the 1980s, to whole school reform and charter schools in the early 1990s, to lobbying state officials for top-down systemic reform in the late 1990s, business-minded reformers allied with elected officials and educators stumbled from one strategy to the next in trying to improve schools and influence classroom teaching and learning.

Late twentieth-century business and civic leaders, along with most educational policymakers, scorned the type of vocational education promoted by the earlier generation of progressive reformers. In their view, the best type of "vocational education" would be a rigorous academic program designed to equip all students with broad knowledge, cognitive skills, and attitudes suitable for jobs that required cooperative decisionmaking, creative problem solving, and finger-snapping flexibility. To move toward tough academic schooling for all students, educators imitated business practices. They set high standards, tested students frequently, and initiated strong accountability policies. They expanded parental choice and sought diverse ways of getting schools to compete for students and become more innovative. These different approaches converged as policymakers in state after state sponsored systemic reform.

In systemic reform, governors and legislatures mandate the goals and curriculum standards that educators and students must meet. States then require students to take tests to determine whether they have learned the requisite knowledge and skills and met the standards, disregarding the judgments of teachers and principals about individual students. To ensure high performance on these tests, state officials hold students, teachers, and administrators accountable, giving rewards for success and exacting penalties for failure. States also offer help to teachers and administrators to ensure that the standards are understood and put into practice. Finally, some states abolished geographical boundaries for attendance, encouraged charter schools, and allowed parents to use vouchers to send their children to private schools.

The two assumptions that drove the earlier business-inspired school reform movement—that school-based vocational programs would improve schooling, society, and the economy; and that education and business were basically alike so that business principles could improve inefficient schools—also heavily influenced the thinking of late twentieth-century reformers, although the assumptions were modernized to fit a different workplace. And government officials and business leaders, deeply concerned about a workforce drawn increasingly from cities, added a third assumption aimed specifically at urban students: that systemic reform, choice, competition with clear incentives, and rigorously enforced sanctions would provide equal educational (and later economic) opportunity for poor and minority youth. All students, regardless of background, would be able to go to college and get high-paying jobs. By 2000, most national, state, and local policymakers, corporate executives, media leaders, educators, and parents took for granted all three assumptions.

National, state, and local policymakers found it relatively easy to implement these business-inspired reforms in schools for several reasons. First, the belief that a good education would lead to individual financial success, higher personal status, and the benefits of a flourishing economy had become largely unquestioned by the late twentieth century. Moreover, economists and other scholars had given a quasi-scientific gloss to education as an investment by dubbing it "human capital" and placing it on an equal basis with the other ingredients essential for economic growth.

Second, in a decentralized system of tax-supported schools in which voters determine who holds public office, the level of taxation, and the allocation of monies, elected officials are responsive to well-organized, well-financed constituencies (such as business groups). Given the widely accepted belief about the cash value of education and its benefits to the public good, many voters wanted reforms to ensure that schools prepared their children for college and the workplace; and given a political system in which elected officials depend upon voters, officeholders were likely to accept or even push for such reforms.

There is a third reason for the broad acceptance of these reforms: the tendency in the United States, as mentioned earlier, to regard more and better public education as the solution to many of the nation's social, economic, and political problems. Generations of reformers have delegated public schools to solve such national problems as racial segregation, poverty, lack of patriotism, and even alcohol and tobacco abuse; they have pushed changes in schooling that, they believed, would prepare students to handle these social issues better than their parents did. As we have seen, reformers also looked to schools to solve the problem of lagging global economic competitiveness in the 1890s and the 1970s. This pattern of expecting education to solve national problems is deeply embedded in the nation's social and economic structures.

As successful as these business-inspired reforms have been in altering school goals, curriculum, governance, and organization, there are (and have been) definite limits to business influence in schools. Business-oriented reforms past and present, endorsed often by the Republican Party and other critics of public schools—such as separately funded vocational schools, site-based management, merit pay for teachers, for-profit schools, and school vouchers—have conspicuously failed to secure popular support or widespread changes in policy. Furthermore, classroom instruction in academic subjects has been largely impervious to the pedagogical reforms and commercial ventures promoted by these business-inspired coalitions.

The limits of business influence on public schooling, along with reformers' constant finger pointing at public schools, suggest that the widely accepted "truths" about the relationship between the economy and education may be seriously flawed. Moreover, the frequently heard claim that schools are dominated by business interests may be exaggerated. In addition, business leaders have made assumptions and implemented strategies that were both confused and contradictory, especially the assumption that businesses and public schools are essentially alike.

Surface similarities do exist between businesses and public schools (leadership responsibilities, organizational responses to top-down changes, managing personnel, purchasing, budgeting, planning, and so on). Moreover, schools socialize children to be punctual, work hard at tasks, and be literate, all outcomes that employers welcome in entry-level workers.

Still, their purposes, authority, and outcomes differ in fundamental ways. An employer's goal of seeking profits, for example, is very different from the social, political, and academic goals of school boards, such as ensuring that schools make students literate, build character, get involved in civic work, and appreciate productive labor. Corporate earnings reports and published test scores may appear to be equivalent signs of efficiency and productivity, to cite another example, but they differ enormously in what they measure and what the two types of institutions seek to achieve.

To note dissimilarities between business and public education is not to dismiss the substantial gains accruing from business influence on school reform, such as increased efficiency in school operations and the bringing together of leaders and citizens from many sectors of a community to solve civic problems. But losses have also accrued from business influence: the narrowing of broad civic purposes of schooling to mere preparation of workers, the growth of a one-best-school model that has the singular goal of steering every child to college, and the belief that only what can be counted is worthwhile in judging success.

The history of active business involvement in schools contains both shining triumphs and awful blunders. Although myths have been cultivated about the victories and mishaps have been ignored, business leaders have appeared—more often than not—as unflinching heroes crafting intelligent and muscular solutions to tough educational problems. I write these words after several years of corporate scandal, recession, and a federal budget surplus vanished to be replaced by enormous deficits. Nevertheless, even if the current surge of public anger toward corporate greed temporarily dampens interest in applying business-based methods to create high-performing schools, I predict that another generation of business and civic leaders will again scold educators for low-performing schools and will turn, as before, to those very educators to solve national social, economic, or political problems.

Why am I so confident in the continuing involvement of business leaders in school reform? For one thing, after more than a quarter-century of aggressive participation by business leaders in contemporary school policymaking, even at a time of corporate implosions, many practitioners and most policymakers accept business influence without question. The application of business-crafted solutions to public schools (better managers, getting the incentives right, choice, market competition, accountability) has become so thoroughly embedded in policymakers' thinking about improving schools, particularly in urban districts, that these policies are taken for granted and often seen as "common sense" rather than as having been borrowed from the corporate closet.

Furthermore, business influence in public schools stems from a pervasive ideological climate supported by law, political institutions, and social structures since the late nineteenth century, a climate in which a market economy, freedom, and democracy are considered indistinguishable. Within that milieu, business leaders have drawn continuing political support, initially from Republicans, even when business reputations plummeted during attacks on corporate greed after World War I and during the Great Depression of the 1930s. Time and again in the last half of the twentieth century, strong support for profit-seeking firms, distrust of government intervention, and anticipation of individual gains in earnings from getting an education garnered applause among conservatives in both political parties, as well as from the general public, for business-inspired school reform.[9]

The influence of business on schools has to be judged fairly. Too often, writers and pundits either laud business-minded reformers as altruistically seeking the public good or blast them as using public schools to pay corporate training costs for entry-level workers and imposing crass market values onto vulnerable children and financially struggling schools. The literature on the subject of business involvement in school reform is largely polarized, reflecting the writers' sharply differing values about the purposes of public schools and for-profit firms, the disciplines in which they write, and their experiences in (and with) both types of institutions. Drawing on my quarter-century of experience as a practitioner and then my two decades as a historian of education and a policy researcher, I want to avoid these extremes and make balanced judgments in describing and analyzing historic patterns of business influence on school reform.[10] An even-handed analysis of how and why business leaders prompted and in some instances led coalitions of reformers to revamp U.S. schools (and the surprising results of those determined efforts) may help policymakers, educators, and parents make sense of business-inspired school reform when it next occurs. And it will.

1

THE LOGIC OF THE REFORMS

In 1909 a report by the Teachers Association of Brooklyn, New York, aimed a stark question at students:

> DOES EDUCATION PAY?
> [Annual] Salaries in the New York Bridge Department
> In positions demanding only reading, writing, and arithmetic . . . $982.00
> In positions demanding high-school and commercial courses . . . $1729.00
> In positions demanding high-school and two or three years of college or technical education . . . $2400.00
> Which position are you preparing yourself to fill?
> IT PAYS TO CONTINUE YOUR EDUCATION[1]

Before and since 1909, the cash value of getting an education has been an oft-repeated theme. From the efforts of evangelical school reformers like Horace Mann in the mid-nineteenth century to present-day civic- and business-sponsored placards on buses and televised public service advertisements that urge young people to stay in school, the message has been that education will pay off in dollars and cents. The appeal to youth to stay in school reflects the sturdy popular belief, shared by parents and corporate leaders, that those with more education reap more financial gains.[2]

An equally long held belief is that education creates not only individual benefits but also collective benefits that flow to the government and the national economy. In 1899 the southern educator Charles Dabney put it bluntly:

EDUCATION INCREASES PRODUCTIVE POWER
Massachusetts Gave Her Citizens 7 Years' Schooling
The United States Gave Her Citizens 4.4 Years of Schooling
Tennessee Gave Her Citizens 3 Years of Schooling
Massachusetts Citizens Produced Per Capita $260 Per Year
Citizens of the United States Produced Per Capita $170 Per Year
Tennessee Citizens Produced Per Capita $116 Per Year
IT PAYS THE STATE TO EDUCATE[3]

How Dabney arrived at these figures is of less interest than his conviction, shared with other promoters of public education in his day, that both individuals and society stood to gain economically from continued schooling. According to advocates, students who stayed in school contributed far more to the economy than those who ended their education at around age twelve and moved from one dead-end job to another. And not all the gains were economic. The director of school guidance in Oakland, California, said in 1918 that school leavers followed a "common trail" from "educational misfits to vocational misfits, to social misfits, to antisocial feeling, recklessness, and crime." Staying in school was believed to benefit the social order.[4]

Believers in the economic virtues of more and better schooling were drawn from corporate boardrooms and from immigrants' crowded apartments. Business leaders saw schooling as linked to workbench productivity, national economic prosperity, and less social alienation and crime; immigrant parents saw continued education as the path to higher status and living standards for their children. The individual and collective advantages of what a later generation of economists would trumpet as investment in human capital have been made explicit many times.[5]

In 2002, for example, newspaper headlines across the country describing a U.S. Census Bureau report sent a message that readers a century earlier would have found familiar. A *Salt Lake Tribune* reporter told Utah readers: "Listen up kids—your parents are right. The amount of money you earn in life will be an almost direct result of how educated you are. Now more than ever." And the *Washington Post* summed up the report in dollars and cents: "The average lifetime earnings of a full-time, year-round worker with a high school education are about $1.2 million, compared with $2.1 million for a college graduate and $3.4 million for those with doctorates. Workers with professional degrees command $4.4 million, while high school dropouts earn about $1 million."[6]

Arguments in favor of longer and better schooling, however, went beyond individual financial gains. Education has long been seen as important to the economic and social health of the nation. Had advocates produced a bumper sticker, it would have read: GOOD SCHOOLS = STRONG ECONOMY AND STRONG NATION. What originated in the mid-nineteenth century as a theoretical claim by promoters of public schools—that schooling has individual and collective economic benefits—had become by the late twentieth century an accepted "truth," on the basis of which reform coalitions were mobilized, new goals established, and new programs put into schools. Two beliefs held by business, political, and educational leaders, that schooling could solve national problems and that it was the key to individual financial success, had become conflated into one powerful ideology that fueled business-inspired school reforms.

The power of this ideology is evident in opinion polls, which reveal that parents assign high importance to staying in school, as well as in the dramatic rise over the past century of the percentage of students going to postsecondary institutions. It is also indicated by the business endorsement of the federal No Child Left Behind law (2002), which calls for higher academic standards, testing, and district accountability as ways of making schools more productive.[7]

Business and civic leaders eventually had to forge a broad political consensus among diverse groups to define what is known as a "theory of action"—to specify the nature of the problem to be solved, the strategies to be used in solving the problem, and the criteria by which to judge success. Their shared assumptions about the individual and collective benefits of schooling shaped the designs for reform they developed and the policies they proposed, policies that they believed would yield desired results in schools.[8]

And yet, although leaders' assumptions may shape their agendas for improving schools, the logic of any given reform is a work in progress. More often than not, what begins as policy doctrine becomes political compromise as assumptions are tested in actual settings, found wanting, and reconfigured. As reform coalitions compete with one another, the one that triumphs may adopt items of the opposing coalition's agenda. There is no inexorable straight-line march toward a particular strategy or outcome. Inevitably, zigzag lines map the trajectory of a policy's theory or logic of action as the policy's advocates encounter unexpected events, varied contexts, and unpredictable individuals.[9]

Ideas and beliefs seldom determine specific behaviors, but they do offer both direction and justification for actions taken, and examining the ideas and beliefs behind a policy—its logic—is a way of holding policymakers accountable. Public trust comes from political accountability. In a democracy in which elected and appointed officials formulate policy, make decisions, and allocate resources in ways that directly affect the public, disclosure of policymakers' reasons for their decisions is essential to sustaining public faith in government. The assumptions driving the policies officials choose, and the short-

and long-term outcomes they seek, deserve close public scrutiny because human costs and benefits accompany those policies put into practice.

One Policy's Logic of Action

The introduction of computers into schools and classrooms offers an illuminating example of the reasoning embedded in a popular reform. Because every school reform is initiated as a solution to some problem, every logic of action carries within it the policymakers' views about which problems are important to solve now rather than later.[10]

Beginning in the early 1980s, business and civic leaders, along with a smattering of academics and educators, identified low test scores (which they equated with low productivity) in schools, out-of-date methods of teaching and learning, and a failure to prepare students for an information-based workplace as salient problems to be solved. Business leaders, parents, and some educators considered the desktop computer a tool for improving workplace productivity that could easily find a home in the classroom. Hardware and software vendors and public officials predicted that computers and software applications would boost the productivity of both teachers and students: teachers would be able to convey far more knowledge to students in far less time. According to the national Business Roundtable, an organization whose members are CEOs of leading U.S. corporations, one feature of a successful school system was "the creative use of technology to broaden access to knowledge, to improve learning and productivity, and to achieve student expectations."[11]

For those who advocated moving away from traditional styles of teaching (lectures, worksheets, homework from and readings in textbooks) to student-centered practices (independent research, teams of students working on interdisciplinary real-world projects, small-group work), new information technologies offered a bonanza of novel ways of teaching and learning. "Students don't have to be tethered to a desk at all times," said Steve Case, who was then chairman of America Online.[12] Widespread use of computers in schools was expected to prepare young people to enter a changing workplace, ending the mismatch between high school graduates' skills and employers' needs. High-paying jobs in the future would require technological knowledge far different from anything earlier generations had learned in school. With a well-prepared workforce, the U.S. economy could compete with any nation in the world.

Because of the various groups—civic and business leaders, parents, educators—behind the push for more technology in schools, divergent goals (for example, increasing teacher and student productivity, making both teaching and learning exciting, preparing students for the workplace) evolved into a policy logic justifying the introduction of computers and other devices into schools on a mass scale. In 1996, at the national Educational Summit, state governors, corporate leaders, and federal officials heard President Bill Clinton speak about the importance of standards-based school reform and technology in schools. The policy statement issued by the Summit nicely summarized the three goals driving a reform coalition of business leaders, vendors, elected officials, and educators: "We are convinced that technology, if applied thoughtfully and well integrated into a curriculum, can be utilized as a helpful tool to assist student learning, provide access to valuable information, and ensure a competitive edge for our workforce."[13]

But how were these goals to be reached? The dominant strategy was to make more machines and more software available in schools. Once schools were wired and equipment was in place, policymakers assumed, teachers and students would use the information technologies regularly in classrooms, and once computers were used regularly in schools, the desired outcomes, divergent as they were, would naturally follow. In short, access to technology would lead to instructional use, and use would lead to achievement of the goals.

The astonishing swiftness with which schools were wired and hardware and software were purchased (aided considerably by state and federal legislation), especially during the 1990s, made personal computers nearly ubiquitous in public schools. Home purchases of equipment by teachers and parents further widened access, albeit unevenly across socioeconomic classes. Deployment of the equipment in schools has varied from placing machines in classrooms, computer labs, and media centers to giving each student and teacher a laptop. Training for teachers to integrate the new technologies into their daily routines and technical support to help them cope with the inevitable breakdowns have been supplied across the country but differ considerably from place to place within the decentralized national system of schooling.

Have the desired goals been achieved? Not yet. After nearly a decade in which computers have been widely available in schools, no body of evidence demonstrates clearly that students learn more, faster, or better by using computers. Nor is there a body of evidence that documents the shift in classroom practice envisioned by promoters of information technologies: from largely teacher-centered forms of instruction to classrooms where students work in teams on real-world projects, cross subject-matter boundaries, and do independent research. Finally, the goal of producing computer-literate graduates qualified for high-paying jobs in knowledge-based industries has yet to be fulfilled in an economy where increasing numbers of high-tech jobs are being sent overseas or lost rather than created.[14]

This blemished record of unreached goals may well be due to flaws in the assumptions and strategy contained within the policy's logic of action. While access to computers in schools certainly did increase, so that new technologies became generally available to both students and teachers, regular use of the equipment for classroom instruction did not automatically follow. Studies have shown (and more need to be done) that teachers' use of information technologies is erratic and that students tend to use the equipment for word processing, Internet searches, and other low-level tasks. Most teachers have yet to integrate the technology into their daily lessons. More-over, teachers maintain conventional forms of teaching rather than shifting to the methods envisioned by promoters of the new technologies. Even in settings where professional development and technical support are available, use of computer technology by teachers falls far short of expectations. Strikingly, some evidence indicates that teachers and students who have access to school computers and also have ones at home use those at home more than the ones at school.[15]

In spite of such evidence, even skeptics who doubt the usefulness of computers in classrooms would agree that information technologies remain popular among parents, employers, and educators. Ideologically, getting computers into schools to solve divergent problems has been a stunning success, according to opinion polls and district purchases. Practically, however, new technologies have been bought and installed but their use is fragmented, unimaginative, and still far from solving the original problems that prompted the goals for technology in classrooms. Thus the key assumption, that increased availability would lead to increased classroom use, and the strategy to which that assumption was tied are deeply flawed.

This example reveals how perceptions of problems, assumptions, strategies, and outcomes are grounded in a logic of action. Although ideas seldom directly determine action, given that many factors come into play, policy reasoning is more than an abstract notion of little import in the practical world. The ideas behind the policy of placing computers in schools led to the devotion of much money and effort to that policy—and yet the goals embedded within the logic of action have not been achieved.

Business-Inspired School Reform

What, then, has been the logic behind the business-inspired coalition to reform public schools? To parse out that logic in detail, I focus on the more recent of my two historical periods: from the 1970s to the present.

Framing the Problem

After the longest stretch of prosperity in the history of the nation in the quarter-century following World War II, the economic downturn of the 1970s caused great turmoil among U.S. opinion leaders, the corporate community, and growing numbers of disillusioned workers. Between 1974 and 1981, annual growth of the Gross National Product (GNP) averaged only 2.2 percent, down from an annual average of nearly 5 percent between 1964 and 1972. Inflation that averaged just below 5 percent in the late 1960s rose to an annual rate of 9.3 percent between 1974 and 1981. Unemployment, which had risen to 5.2 percent in the recession of 1974 (with the figure for out-of-work youth more than double that and three times higher among minorities), went to 7.5 percent in 1981 and plateaued at 9.5 percent during the recession of the following two years (with unemployment of youth, especially among poor minorities, again at double these rates). The growth of labor productivity, which had averaged 3 percent per year between 1947 and 1973, was just 1 percent after 1973. The U.S. share of the world market for manufactured goods declined by 23 percent in the 1970s. By then, Japanese and German automakers had captured 22 percent of American car buyers.[16]

By 1980 one economist said that the United States had the "highest percentage of obsolete plants, the lowest percentage of capital investment, and lowest growth in productivity of any major industrial society other than Great Britain." A pollster tried to sum up the national mood: "The state of mind of the public is worried sick and in a panic . . . people know that there is something wrong." In the summer of 1980, *Business Week* editors concluded that "the decline in the U.S. economy has advanced so far that the public as a whole has begun to sense a need for change."[17]

But what should change? A search for causes of slow economic growth, low worker productivity, high unemployment, and escalating inflation triggered intense examination of national social, cultural, and educational trends. For decades, economists and policymakers had elaborated and refined the human capital argument, reaffirming expert and popular beliefs in education as the engine for economic growth, higher standards of living, increased productivity, social stability, and global competitiveness. During the recessions and social instability of the 1970s and early 1980s, corporate leaders, economists, and public officials, as in the past, turned their attention to the quality of public schooling.[18]

Employers' criticism of high school graduates unprepared for the workplace, violence in urban schools, and the flight of white middle-class families from decaying and racially volatile cities to suburbs made it easy for faultfinders from both the left and the right to blame American public schools for economic and social problems. A sampling of typical one-liners points to schools as inadequate for preparing the next generation of workers and citizens:

A semi-literate population cannot support a productive economy. (Chester Finn, Assistant U.S. Secretary of Education, 1987)

Poverty and ignorance cause shortages of qualified workers and threaten America's stance in a global economy. (Committee for Economic Development, 1987)

If we don't keep them in school and do a better job of educating them, who will do the work that enables the US to compete successfully in the global marketplace? (Business Roundtable, 1988)[19]

Business and civic elites and academic critics did not merely assert that public schools were failing; they repeatedly pointed to various types of evidence to confirm their claim. Test scores from achievement exams such as the Second International Math Study, Trends in Math and Scientific Studies, and the Scholastic Aptitude Test, data from the National Assessment of Educational Progress, and the *Nation at Risk* report (1983) were used time and again to demonstrate that faulty schooling left American youth unprepared for a changing workplace and caused low labor force productivity. In 1989 President George H. W. Bush summoned all state governors to the first education summit, held in Charlottesville, Virginia, to draft six national goals for U.S. public schools. In 1996 a joint statement from CEOs who headed the Business Roundtable Education Task Force, the U.S. Chamber of Commerce, and the National Alliance of Business reaffirmed the corporate community's commitment to school reform in what had become familiar terms:

> As organizations representing American business and employing 34 million people, we are concerned that the graduates of America's schools are not prepared to meet the challenges posed by global economic competition. Our nation's future economic security, and our ability to flourish as a democratic society, demand a generation of high school graduates with solid academic knowledge, world-class technical skills, conscientious work habits, and eager, creative, and analytical minds. Despite some encouraging recent gains, business continues to have trouble finding qualified workers. The time has come for business to participate far more actively in generating high achievement.

Plainly, a medley of civic and business leaders actively identified deficient schooling as a national problem to be solved. Amplified by the media, other political and social constituencies voiced their dissatisfaction with schools and joined the chorus of school critics. These events and statements offer further evidence of a developing consensus among potent civic and business elites, journalists, parents, and educational policymakers that public schools were the culprits in the nation's economic and social deterioration.[20]

Occasionally, lone voices would object to blaming schools and propose alternative ways of framing the problem. For example, some observers pointed to patterns of poor corporate investments, mismanagement by CEOs, and top managers' failure to stay abreast of technological changes. Others noted the importance of oil boycotts and U.S. fiscal and monetary policies during the Vietnam war (1964–1975), suggesting that both had played major roles in causing recessions in which swelling unemployment and inflation occurring simultaneously. Those who offered alternative ways of framing policy problems were ignored, even muffled, and seldom moved opinion leaders to consider other causes for economic downturns and cultural changes than the shortcomings of the public schools.[21]

Core Assumptions

As the problem became defined as poor public schooling, the broad political alliance of corporate leaders, public officials, and educators came to share several key assumptions. Jamie Vollmer, the former executive of an ice cream company I quoted in the Introduction, summarized the assumptions he had held when he was a member of the Iowa Business Roundtable and a vigorous critic of the schools: "The first was that schools were terribly flawed. The second was that teachers, administrators, and support staff in the system were the obstacles to fixing it. The third was that if we would just run schools like businesses, they would work."[22]

These were not the only key assumptions behind the reform coalition; several others can be discerned. The first three assumptions in the following list deal with the relationship between the economy and the schools; the last two presume a fundamental congruence between businesses and schools, applying strategies and metrics borrowed from one to measure success in the other.[23]

- Strong economic growth, high productivity, long-term prosperity including a higher standard of living, and increased competitiveness in global markets depend upon a highly skilled workforce.
- Public schools are responsible for equipping students with the knowledge and skills necessary to compete in an information-based workplace.
- All public schools are doing a poor job of preparing high school graduates for college and the workplace, with urban schools doing the worst job of all.
- Schools are just like businesses. The principles that have made businesses successful can be applied to schools to produce structural changes that will improve academic achievement as measured by standardized tests, end the skills mismatch between jobs and entry-level workers, and increase public confidence in schools.[24]
- Higher test scores in school mean better performance later on in college and the workplace.

These beliefs did not spring full blown from corporate brows; they were shared among elected officials, many parents, and educators. They evolved unevenly across the country from diverse economic, social, demographic, and political contexts that business and civic elites faced in their states and companies. Occasionally these premises were stated explicitly, but for the most part they remained implicit in the framing of the problem as failing schools and in the strategies proposed to solve the problem. These taken-for-granted assumptions—occasionally contested in academic journals and by isolated voices in op-ed columns—became the basis for ways to improve schools.

Strategies to Improve Schools

Acting on these core beliefs, U.S. presidents, governors, and corporate leaders promoted diverse changes intended to solve the problems afflicting public schools. A bipartisan agreement emerged that called for more centralizing of federal and state authority over school policies, with local districts remaining the primary agents to deliver education to students. States increasingly took over local funding of schools, and given the vital importance of schooling for the economy, culture, and future of the nation, the consolidation of state authority over education was viewed as politically reasonable.

Through U.S. Supreme Court decisions and legislation to correct perceived inequalities arising from segregation, poverty, and racial, ethnic, and gender discrimination, federal authority over education has increased substantially since the 1950s. Although the passage of the Civil Rights Act (1964) and the Elementary and Secondary Education Act (1965) made federal authority a presence in state and local school decisions, it was the No Child Left Behind legislation (2002) that cast the federal government as an active decisionmaker in local school affairs. U.S. Department of Education officials now reached down into every classroom across the nation to determine whether a qualified teacher was present and whether each child was improving his or her academic achievement.[25]

Beginning in the late 1960s with increased federal funding and accelerating swiftly after the early 1980s, state control over educational policy also increased across the nation, albeit at a uneven pace, given the differences in political cultures in such places as New York, Vermont, Minnesota, Georgia, and California. Two decades after the *Nation at Risk* report, most states had assumed far greater control over local funding, curriculum, testing, governance, and classroom in-

struction than they had exercised in 1983. By the end of the twentieth century, few questioned that schools needed close and continuing scrutiny by state and federal lawmakers.

With an increasing concentration of policymaking authority at the
state and federal levels, and through close working relationships between policymakers and corporate leaders, varied strategies for improving schools emerged, some of which relied upon market principles that not only the business community but many educators and
parents endorsed. Throughout the 1980s, corporate chiefs and writers boasted of firms that had gone from bankruptcy to high performance. Innovative companies crowed about their achievements. In
the depths of the auto slump, the Saturn Division of General Motors,
in a merger crafted by General Motors and the United Auto Workers union, established high standards (zero defects in finished cars),
measured workplace performance continually, delegated authority to
make decisions to teams of workers (including those on the assembly
line), and linked pay and job security to results. The governor of Delaware, Pierre S. du Pont IV, at a 1989 conference sponsored by the
Heritage Foundation and entitled "Can Business Save Education?"
told corporate participants that fixing public schools in the 1990s
would depend on putting into practice the "tried and true principles
that have helped each of your businesses prosper over the years."
Going beyond business partnerships, state mandates to stiffen academic requirements, and implementation of whole school reform,
civic and corporate leaders promoted reshaping the national system
of schooling to make it more businesslike.[26]

Educators borrowed from the corporate closet innovations that
industrial leaders claimed had turned around Ford Motor Company,
General Electric, and other major firms. Not only did many superintendents and school boards mimic business practices such as managing by objectives, strategic planning, restructuring units, participatory management, holding mid-level executives responsible for
achieving goals, and linking salaries to outcomes, they used the vo-

cabulary of customer satisfaction, efficiency, and productivity. Educators wanted schools to be more like successful businesses that had learned how competition, choice, and "participatory management and leadership to empower employees can lead to far greater productivity." Traveling this path, they believed, would produce results that would renew public trust in schools.[27]

A popular formula for school reform evolved during the 1980s and 1990s among policy entrepreneurs and public officials who laid out experienced-tested truths drawn from business sources:

- Set clear organizational goals and high standards for everyone.
- Restructure operations so that managers and employees who deliver the services decide what to do.
- Reward those who meet or exceed their goals. Shame or punish those who fail.
- Expand competition and choice in products and services.[28]

These prescriptions crossed political party lines. Beginning in the early 1980s, state governors and legislatures from both Democratic and Republican parties, heavily lobbied by business leaders, moved swiftly to implement what is often called systemic reform: to establish curricular standards, impose tests, and hold teachers and administrators responsible for student outcomes with such devices as cash payments, expanded parental choice, and the taking over of failing schools and districts.[29]

Broad political coalitions, made up of practitioners, union officials, policymakers, researchers, business leaders, and elected officials, offered a public face of agreement but often glided over conflicting strategies to improve schools. Free market advocates among coalition partners, for example, wanted vouchers; others believed in providing broad choice within public schools by means of charters and intra- and inter-district transfers; efficiency-driven critics wanted ex-CEOs with managerial moxie to lead school systems and contract out tasks to the private sector. Corporate leaders and elected officials wanted more and faster systemic reform (and computers as well) and less sluggish school-by-school change. Despite such conflicts, the model of systemic reform initially pushed by business leaders—standards-based reform, tests, accountability, and parental choice—was largely adopted by states and districts in the 1990s. Except for vouchers, standards-based reform became de facto national policy in the No Child Left Behind Act.[30]

Surely much of the strong push for computers, academic standards, competition among schools, wider parental choice, and accountability came from business leaders, but their agendas quickly embraced other reform-seeking constituencies inside and outside schools. As the merged agendas were adopted by states and districts and put into schools, business leaders slipped over to the sidelines, where they eased into cheerleading and lobbying roles rather than remaining as central participants.

Determining Success

Given that school improvement has become politicized, and that strategies to revamp schools reflect both politics and abiding value conflicts, it should come as no surprise that the question of how to judge whether or not a particular reform is succeeding is another focus of contentious debate. No consensus as to what constitutes success yet exists. What business leaders may take as evidence of success often conflicts with criteria that teachers, parents, academic researchers, journalists, and educational administrators consider important.

The primary standard being used for such judgments is whether a program's intended goals have been achieved. Has it done what it was supposed to do, and is there evidence to prove it? In a society where corporate bottom lines, football wins and losses, box office receipts for films, and vote counts matter, quantifiable measures of outcomes are often equated with success. This *effectiveness standard* has been widely accepted. More attention has been paid to quantifiable results than to questions of what caused those results and what strategies worked.[31]

Starting in the mid-1960s, the effectiveness standard tilted decidedly toward economic models of schooling, emphasizing quantitative measures. Reflecting the business community's strong belief in results, it slowly spread among researchers and public officials; by now it has been applied to most reforms. Thus policymakers subjectively set desired goals and choose measures to determine success—measures such as test scores, dropout rates, and rates of college attendance. These measures are assumed to bear a strong connection to students' later performance in the workplace.

A second common yardstick used to measure success is how closely actual changes in governance, organization, curriculum, or instruction mirror what reformers intended. This *fidelity standard* aims at assessing the fit between the initial design, the formal policy, the subsequent programs it spawns, and its implementation.

For corporate executives accustomed to depending on research and development, creating and testing prototypes before moving into full production, fidelity and quality control are synonymous. They may ask: How can an effectiveness standard ultimately be applied if the reform departs from the blueprint? If a corporate partner with a school district, for example, funds a program that has proved to be effective elsewhere—say a program to encourage teachers to use computers to integrate math curriculum into classroom lessons —teachers will be expected to follow the program's original design, on the assumption that if they deviate from it they will not achieve the desired goals. Faithfulness to design is important because it reduces guesswork in attributing causality: if the program succeeds it is because the design was put into practice.

The effectiveness and fidelity standards for judging success of policies derive from the rational view that organizations are instruments for solving problems through formal structures and employees (such as administrators and teachers) who act as agents with technical expertise to fulfill their task: to achieve the results intended by policymakers.[32] Yet effectiveness and fidelity compete with another standard, one that few researchers and CEOs consider seriously but that matters to elected officials, journalists, and school district administrators: *the popularity of the reform.*

For example, in 1965, President Lyndon B. Johnson and Congress adopted the Elementary and Secondary Education Act (ESEA), in which one section of the law, known as Title I, funded, for the first time, programs to help poor children improve their academic achievement. Under Title I, billions of dollars have been spent in urban and rural schools, on Head Start as well as on programs in reading, math, and so on, to help mostly poor minority children do well academically. Nearly every district in the nation has received Title I funds.

Early evaluations of these funded programs in the states revealed very little improvement in the academic performance of children from poor families. Initial studies of Head Start four-year-olds, for example, showed that cognitive and social gains from the program faded away in the early years of elementary school. By 1998 nearly 70 percent of all fourth graders in high-poverty schools had reading skills below the basic fourth-grade level. Subsequent studies of Title I and Head Start effectiveness did not quiet the faultfinders. Conservative critics who questioned the right of federal policymakers to tell local school officials how to spend the monies they received had plenty of ammunition to use in arguing against the continuation of Title I.[33]

Yet unpromising test scores and critics' scornful attacks were insufficient to overcome the Title I program's attractiveness to voters, legislators, and educators. Each U.S. Congress and each president since 1965—including George W. Bush—has used the program's widespread popularity to allocate funds to needy students in schools across the country. If the effectiveness and fidelity standards derive from organizational rationality, the popularity standard derives from the political nature of public institutions.

As an example of the use of the popularity standard by elected policymakers, administrators, and journalists, consider the managerial innovation known as total quality management, touted by business leaders as a productivity-enhancing tool that worked wonders in corporate settings. A few business-oriented superintendents in a metropolitan area introduced the novel idea to their principals to use with teachers. The innovation won the approval of parents, business leaders, school board members, and administrators as an ingenious way to improve the quality of decisionmaking and communication. Few from these groups questioned the escalating outlays of funds to release education administrators to attend meetings and work more closely together. After all, business leaders said the program worked and many other districts were putting it into practice. Even if little or no evidence existed to support the claim that total quality management increased productivity, administrators and board members viewed the program as a business-certified way of coping with workplace demands and the educational needs of children.[34]

Careful readers will note that I have made few references to classroom practitioners in discussing the dominant standards used to judge policy success and failure. Do teachers use the same criteria? No, they do not.

Practitioners bring to their classrooms strong moral and service-oriented values inherent to teaching. These overlap with but nevertheless differ from the technical values of policy elites, corporate leaders, researchers, and administrators. Experienced and thoughtful practitioners accumulate detailed knowledge about students, broaden their repertoire of teaching skills, and gain deeper understanding of the content they teach, forms of expertise that few researchers, policymakers, or CEOs lacking classroom experience can fathom. From these teacher values and types of expertise emerge standards for judging success and failure that diverge considerably from those described above. Of course teachers seek improvement in students' academic performance, but teachers tend to consider scores on standardized achievement tests as less significant than students' attitudes, values, and behavior on both academic and non-academic tasks inside and outside of classrooms. One teacher from Brush Prairie, Washington, made this point in an article entitled "Letter to a State Test Scorer," which offered the scorers a tad more information about Lindsey, one of his fifth-grade students:

> Lindsey left quite a few of the . . . questions unanswered. Reading has never been easy for her, and she sometimes goes off on a tangent when she has to follow written instructions on her own. But you should see Lindsey during our class discussions—when I'm explaining how metamorphic rocks are formed or how diabetes affects people. She's like a sponge soaking up information—and she remembers what she hears. That's the way she learns. Lindsey doesn't say much, but when she raises her hand, I frequently hear a question or a comment that's full of insight. Last fall, our class built rubber-band-powered go-carts. When other students became exasperated by the technical problems of finding ways to increase wheel diameter or rubber-band engine power, Lindsey was the one with ideas and persistence who got things going again . . . I believe Lindsey has a future as a mechanical engineer.[35]

What is especially important to teachers facing policy change is a quality we might call *adaptiveness*: whether and how they can put their personal signature on the mandated policy and make it work for their students. To most policymakers, business leaders, administrators, and researchers, however, teachers' alterations of their designs and variations in practice are signs of failed policies. Teachers, meanwhile, view the very same modifications as healthy signs of inventiveness, active problem solving, and as preconditions for determining effectiveness—as they define it. To policymakers the end product is everything; to practitioners, the process of getting to the end product is as important as the outcome. This practitioner-derived *adaptiveness standard* becomes an essential prior condition for other criteria to be applied.[36]

But why is the adaptiveness standard seldom invoked by policymakers, corporate executives, administrators, journalists, and researchers? The question boils down to one of power and status: Whose criteria count the most? CEOs and policymakers hold strong views about efficient and effective organizations, use research findings to bolster their decisions, and have access to media so they can place their weight behind particular policies. Legitimacy (and power) in making changes rests with those at the top of the organization, not those at the bottom, who have different organizational views, experience, influence, and values. Without the cachet of scientific expertise, access to top officials, or easy entrée to the media, individual teachers are unable to promote their service-oriented and moral values in public policy arenas.[37]

Collectively, teachers have organized into unions and asserted their political muscle in taking explicit policy positions. Yet in the areas of standards-based reform, accountability, and parental choice, unions have played a peripheral role except occasionally at the state level. Thus when individual teachers do choose to adapt or modify policies, they do so unobtrusively or, in some cases, in concert with like-minded principals, or they engage in guerrilla warfare against administrators.

Effectiveness, fidelity, popularity, and adaptiveness, then, are four criteria that policymakers, corporate leaders, researchers, practitioners, journalists, and informed parents use to judge success and failure of policy changes aimed at improving schooling. Imperfections and contradictions mar each criterion. Figuring out what caused what to happen is not easy. Determining whether the reform was even implemented is difficult since the labels applied to reforms—

such as "Success for All" or "Coalition for Essential Schools"—seldom capture which parts of the program were actually put into schools and classrooms.

In spite of these shortcomings, these conflicting standards are worth our attention. My point is a simple one. Because many different groups contribute to an agenda for school reform, they are unlikely to agree about which standards should be used to judge success. They are also unlikely to have the same opinions about how standards lead to results, or to publicly state why the standards they prefer should be used. Few members of reform coalitions openly acknowledge the undeniable fact that most policy changes entering schools undergo adaptation by teachers. And even among the occasional policymakers and CEOs who do recognize the inevitability of classroom adaptations, few figure out how to determine whether the new policy itself, teachers' modifications, some other factor, or a combination of all of these produced the desired (or undesired) outcomes. Until officials who make policy, advocates of reform, and researchers who evaluate policy openly state their criteria, justify them, articulate the desired chain of cause and effect, and come to terms with the reality of how policy changes percolate downward into classroom practice, the words "success" and "failure" will remain contested.

This persistent contentiousness becomes worrisome when policy decisions have to be made regarding which strategies produce the outcomes that matter most. This is why expressly knowing policymakers' logic of action is essential. If some outcomes—say, reducing the gap in test scores between minorities and whites—are unconnected to the strategies or assumptions embedded in the policy's reasoning, then determining success or failure becomes not only impossible but also damaging to the faith children and their parents have in schools and teachers.

Today, in the first decade of the twenty-first century, a broad consensus exists that the effectiveness of a reform is determined by achievement test scores and similar measures. While most policy-makers, administrators, parents, journalists, and CEOs would accept such numbers as strong evidence of a policy's effectiveness, most teachers, many researchers, and many parents would not. When irate parents boycott state tests, when academic journals are filled with admonitions against using test scores to determine whether students receive diplomas, when instances of cheating become more frequent, when methods of establishing cut-off scores for passing and failing are politically determined, and when test companies must confess errors in computing scores—then the effectiveness standard is weakened as a legitimate measure of school success.[38]

In these conflicts over the metric of success and failure, causality is largely ignored. Exactly what happens after high standards are put into place? Which strategies (testing? accountability? professional development? choice?) and combinations of strategies are most powerful in reaching into classrooms? Seldom do policymakers—or researchers, for that matter—explicitly trace the causal chain of thinking about policy. Often no one knows for sure. And that is a major problem when children's futures, practitioners' careers, and huge sums of money are at stake.

2

HOW THE REFORMS HAVE CHANGED SCHOOLS

As we have seen, between 1880 and 1930, and again starting in the 1970s, business leaders allied with civic elites, educators, union officials, and parents to reform U.S. public schools. On the basis of widely held assumptions about the relationship of education to the economy and about the similarity of schools and businesses, they believed that improving the schools would solve major national problems—by, for example, boosting economic growth, increasing the productivity of the labor force, and reducing crime and unemployment among youth in urban slums. These reform-seeking coalitions magnified the defects of public schools, intensified popular belief in the link between education and the economy, and succeeded in altering the purposes, governance, organization, and curriculum of public schooling. I now examine what sorts of changes business leaders and their allies introduced into the schools.

Better Workers, Better Citizens

In the half-century following the Civil War, millions of Europeans immigrated to the United States, many Americans left farms to seek jobs in cities, and industrialization brought factories to provide those jobs. During this period the United States changed from a largely rural, agricultural nation into an increasingly urban, industrialized society marked by concentrations of wealth and power.

Entrepreneurs used the newly invented corporation to gain control of railroads, oil, meat packing, sugar, steel, and other industries. In the process, a revolution in the organization of large businesses produced a managerial capitalism characterized by bureaucratic hierarchies, technical experts, and a new professional class. By 1920 the top 5 percent of all industrial corporations accounted for almost 80 percent of total corporate income. In spite of regional differences (between, say, the largely rural South and the industrialized Northeast) and periodic depressions (such as those in 1873, 1893, and 1907), by the last decade of the nineteenth century the United States had become a major exporter and an avid seeker of foreign markets.

The concentration of wealth intensified. For example, in Massachusetts, by 1880 the top 8 percent of families owned 90 percent of the wealth. Nationally, in 1890 more than half of all wealth was owned by 1 percent of families, much of that wealth generated by commercial and industrial growth. Since then, these inequalities in the distribution of income have only slightly ebbed.[1]

Even with these stark differences between the rich and the poor, by the end of the 1920s the popular image of industrial leaders (partly thanks to a corporate focus on public relations) had become transfigured from heartless Robber Barons to community leaders and corporate "good neighbors." As Gerard Swope, president of General Electric, put it in 1927, "My conception of industry is not primarily for profit but it is for service."[2]

But in the years leading up to World War I, public relations and corporate status in the community took a back seat to U.S. competition with Great Britain and Germany. Already industrialized and possessing navies to protect their far-flung interests, these two nations had staked out global markets that American manufacturers envied. U.S. industrialists feared that the United States, though blessed with natural resources and a growing domestic market for their products, would fail to keep pace with European competitors in the wider world.

The shortage of skilled workers and the breakdown of the traditional apprenticeship system in the United States led to a shortage of welders, bookkeepers, machinists, carpenters, and engineers to meet employers' needs, and industrialists turned their attention to public schools as the cause of the undersupply of skilled workers. In 1905 the Committee on Industrial Education of the National Association of Manufacturers reported: "A contracting firm in New York City employed 4,900 skilled mechanics direct from Europe, paying them fifty cents per day above the union rate, because it was impossible to secure such valuable workmen in our greatest industrial center. We must not depend on Europe for our skill; *we must educate our own boys.*"[3] In a 1908 survey of Chicago employers, the City Club found that 75 percent of the companies had difficulty in finding and training foremen and 88 percent of the employers said that "industrial schools" would be valuable to them. The City Club report concluded, "Nearly ninety percent believe that industrial schools of different types for the years between fourteen and eighteen would be of value."[4]

When American businessmen traveled to Germany to determine how the country had so quickly become a world trade rival to Great Britain, they were favorably impressed by German technical schools, which graduated highly skilled workers. Theodore Robinson of the Illinois Steel Company warned educators in 1910: "This country has been sleeping a self-complacent sleep of confidence, born of stupendous resources. Meanwhile old nations like Germany are rapidly becoming new by industrial education, while our new world will become old unless we awake." Industrial leaders became convinced that Germany had surged ahead of the United States because its government had recognized the connection between national economic growth and school-based vocational training to equip workers with skills useful in a fast-changing industrial workplace. Manufacturers and other business leaders plunged into school reform, giving direction to an emerging movement.[5]

Criticism of U.S. public schools as traditional and impractical also came from other directions. Progressive reformers drawn from corporate, civic, religious, and union leaders argued that schools should do more than teach literacy and civic responsibilities. Schools should reduce poverty, Americanize immigrant families, and, of course, turn out graduates equipped with skills needed by industries. They should, as Samuel Gompers told the American Federation of Labor in 1909, "make better workers of our future citizens, better citizens of our future workers." "Do you not see how the whole battle with the slum," said the passionate urban reformer Jacob Riis in 1902, "is fought out in and around the public school?" "The kindergarten, manual training, . . . experiments in their day, cried out as fads by some, have brought common sense in their train. When it [progressive reform] rules the public schools in our cities . . . we can put off our armor; the battle with the slum will be over."[6]

In the first decade of the twentieth century, leaders from large and mid-sized manufacturing firms (but few from small businesses outside the growing industrial sector) joined other progressive reformers in scolding schools for hewing to their traditional academic curriculum and rigid teaching practices, ignoring the workplace, and persisting in inefficient governance while doing nothing about the obvious problems of urban slums, crime, and the need to turn immigrants into Americans.

Business leaders and philanthropists (sometimes one and the same), driven by both altruism and self-interest, started kindergartens and after-school programs for children of immigrants, hired doctors and dentists to care for children, built playgrounds next to schools, and provided food for hungry children. A few founded private schools to do what the public schools could not or would not do. J. P. Morgan, for example, endowed the New York Trades School with $500,000 at the turn of the twentieth century. Some urged educators to add vocational continuation schools for young people aged fourteen to sixteen. H. E. Miles, president of the Wisconsin State Board of Industrial Education, wrote emphatically in 1913 that vocational schools were "THE BUSINESS MAN'S SOLUTION OF THE SCHOOL PROBLEM—TO ORGANIZE EDUCATION SO THAT GOOD VOCATIONAL TEACHING COSTS ONLY $10 PER YEAR PER CHILD." Delaware's Pierre S. du Pont used his sizable personal fortune to modernize the state's rural and urban schools, build better schools, and increase public spending for schools to make the state competitive in preparing its own workforce and attracting newcomers. Humanitarian business leaders and other progressive reformers wanted to expand the mission of the eighth-grade grammar school beyond the three R's and character building to encompass the obligations that they felt many families neglected.[7]

When business and civic leaders turned to the high school, they also found much to criticize. To critics, late nineteenth-century high schools, which enrolled small percentages of youth and required applicants to pass entrance exams, were impractical and out of touch with the gritty realities of an ever-changing workplace.

Echoing earlier criticisms of these institutions, business leaders wanted more from these tax-supported schools. A Massachusetts woolen manufacturer in 1872 answered the U.S. Commissioner of Education's question about whether he would hire a high school graduate with blunt words: "Don't think we could operate our mills with such a class of help, as we could not run it by algebra." An industrial publisher from Philadelphia over a decade later told legislators: "Too much education of a certain sort, such as Greek, Latin, French, German, and especially book-keeping, to a person of humble antecedents, is utterly demoralizing in nine cases out of ten, and is productive of an army of mean-spirited 'gentlemen' who are above what is called a 'trade' . . . The 'high school' of today must . . . be supplanted by the *technical school* with possibly 'shops' connected with it."[8]

Beyond an impractical elementary and secondary curriculum isolated from the workplace, other progressive critics despised traditional classroom practices of having children give "sing-song concert recitations" and do "pure memorizing" of textbook paragraphs without a glimmer of understanding. Joseph Rice, a physician who visited scores of schools in the early 1890s, described a teacher who lined up children to recite a lesson. They were "perfectly motionless, their bodies erect, their knees and feet together, the tips of their shoes touching the edge of a board in the floor." He heard the teacher ask a small boy: "How can you learn anything with your knees and toes out of order?" Such classroom stories gave faultfinders further ammunition with which to blast public schools.[9]

Other critics, including business leaders, noted the waste of public money when mayors controlled school boards and their political machines hired cronies and relatives as principals, teachers, and janitors. If using a school district as a political feeding trough angered efficiency-minded reformers bent on making school governance nonpartisan and effective, they were irate over the waste of taxpayer funds in keeping overage students in the same grade year after year. Leonard Ayres's *Laggards in Our Schools* (1909) listed the costs of failing students repeating a grade in urban elementary schools and then later dropping out at age eleven or twelve. He created an "Index of Efficiency" and ranked thirty-one cities' schools to show "the relation of the finished product [children finishing elementary school] to the raw material [those entering elementary school]."[10]

Progressive reformers drawn from business and civic elites, academics, and the ranks of newly professionalized school superintendents provided a bonanza of data documenting corruption, inefficiencies, and waste in public schools. At the deepest level, these reformers had absorbed, in the words of one historian, "the goals and values of a business-oriented culture [that] established the rules of the game: how men were expected to act, what they strove for, and what . . . achievements were rewarded."[11]

By the first decade of the twentieth century, an extraordinary progressive reform coalition included such diverse figures as James Van Cleave, president of the National Association of Manufacturers, Jane Addams, founder of Chicago's Hull House, Samuel Gompers, president of the American Federation of Labor, Charles Eliot, president of Harvard University, George Strayer, professor of education at Teachers College, Columbia University, and Ella Flagg Young, a teacher and administrator in the Chicago public schools. They called themselves "progressives" and generally agreed that the problem to be solved was a tradition-bound, wasteful system of schooling, vulnerable to corrupt local politicians and staffed by mediocre teachers teaching a curriculum horribly out of touch with a rapidly changing economy and society. If they agreed on the problem, they differed substantially among themselves over solutions.

One group, the "administrative progressives"—mostly university academics, school superintendents, and a smattering of business leaders—believed in a science of education that could yield solutions to problems such as inefficient school organization, operation, and governance. They admired industrial leaders and drew inspiration from corporate reorganization and consolidation. These reformers, borrowing the language and policies of corporate leaders, donned the mantle of expert and the title of educational engineer.

In the decades bracketing World War I, administrative progressives applied the principles of Frederick Taylor's "scientific management." They reorganized school system governance by creating small, nonpartisan, corporation-like school boards that hired professional managers to gather facts and monitor system activities. They worked to professionalize classroom teaching and school administration. They created junior high schools and large comprehensive high schools. In these secondary schools, they installed newly developed academic and vocational curricula that offered different destinations for students once they graduated. They used scientifically constructed ability tests to place students in classes with those of similar aptitude. They designed and administered achievement tests to determine exactly how much of the academic and vocational curricula students had absorbed. They compiled test scores that compared students from one district to those from another so that taxpayers would know whether or not their monies were being spent efficiently.

Three leaders of these administrative progressives were Ellwood P. Cubberley, a Stanford University professor and textbook author, Edward Thorndike, a professor at Teachers College, Columbia, and Frank Spaulding, a school superintendent in Newton, Massachusetts. These men, and scores like them, borrowed from successful business practices and used findings from the latest scientific studies, and had an enormous influence on public school governance, organization, staffing, and curricula.[12]

A second group, "pedagogical progressives," agreed with administrative progressives that education was a science and believed that traditional schools had to be changed. They had different ideas, however, about what needed to be done. Drawing heavily from John Dewey's ideas, and seldom turning to corporate leaders for advice or models, pedagogical progressives concentrated on what teachers taught and how students learned. Solutions to urban poverty, crime, unemployment, and social instability, they believed, could be found by modernizing curricula, moving away from age-graded schools, and establishing teaching practices aimed at developing the intellectual, emotional, social, and physical dimensions of each child to meet the demands of the increasingly complex world outside the schoolhouse door. Their concept of the "whole child" merged easily with the concepts of student-centered classrooms and multi-age groups where children, guided by teachers, decided on interdisciplinary projects that engaged students' intellect and interest.

Among the many leaders of these pedagogical progressives were William H. Kilpatrick, a professor at Teachers College, Columbia, Caroline Pratt, founder of the City and Country private school in New York City, and Carleton Washburne, superintendent of schools in Winnetka, Illinois. Although pedagogical progressives succeeded beyond their highest hopes in spreading their ideology, especially the vocabulary of the "whole child" and "learning by doing," they underestimated the complexity of altering the age-graded school and actual school practices, and thus they had much less influence on reshaping classroom teaching and learning.[13]

In the years prior to World War I, the loose coalition of administrative and pedagogical progressives promoted new courses of study, system-wide testing, student-centered forms of teaching that reached the "whole child," corporation-like governance of school districts, and efficient organizational procedures to reduce waste. Eventually administrative progressives joined corporate leaders seeking closer links between industries and schools and union leaders who wanted industrial courses in public rather than in private employer-run schools. These allies were eager to strengthen the U.S. share of international trade by drafting schools to end the deficit in industrial skills among American workers. By 1910 the merger of disparate reformers was complete and had become the vocational education movement.[14]

After extensive lobbying of federal officials by promoters of vocational education, the Smith-Hughes Act of 1917 sent subsidies to states to fund courses in industrial arts, home economics, and agriculture (only later did legislation include commercial education, which enrolled mostly young women). In the next two decades a clearly designated vocational curriculum expanded to become a permanent fixture of the modern high school (with vocational guidance in the lower grades).[15]

By 1930 the coalition of business and civic elites, labor leaders, and educational progressives had transformed public schools' purposes, size, management, curriculum, and organization. They created the three-rung schooling ladder that gave students access to a public-financed education from ages six to sixteen in elementary school (grades one through six), junior high school (grades seven through nine), and senior high school (grades ten through twelve). Variations of these configurations throughout the country included separate vocational schools for boys and girls (and in certain regions, for blacks and Hispanics). By the early years of the Great Depression, almost half of all U.S. young people aged fourteen to seventeen were attending high school. No longer a small selective place for a tiny elite, the high school was becoming a mass institution for youth. Its primary purpose had shifted from training the young to be responsible citizens to training the young to be workers first and citizens second.

Progressives also had created the junior high school and the large comprehensive high school, offering access for all American youth (albeit segregated and underfunded in black and Spanish-speaking neighborhoods). The late nineteenth-century ideal of equal access to a uniform and academic secondary curriculum that would prepare all students for admission to college and civic obligations gave way to another version of equal education promoted by administrative progressives. In this definition, an equal education meant secondary schools that offered multiple curricula for youth and tests to distinguish the small minority of students who should prepare for college from those who would best fit into industrial, commercial, or general courses of study.[16]

Yet as reformers vocationalized the public school—that is, shifted the primary goal from preparing students to assume adult civic obligations to preparing workers—junior and senior high school students in the 1920s and 1930s hardly flocked to industrial, commercial, and other vocational courses. In most instances, no more than 10 percent of high school students enrolled in vocational curricula, although much higher percentages took individual vocational courses. Even more surprising to advocates of vocational education was the lack of solid evidence that graduates prepared in specific trades and occupations earned more money than workers who had less education or lacked vocational training.[17]

Evaluations of vocational education pointing out these shortcomings, however, seldom curbed business and civic leaders' enthusiasm for work-oriented curricula in secondary schools. Even when evidence surfaced that school guidance officials and administrators were assigning students who failed academic courses to vocational tracks or separate vocational schools—a process called "dumping"—the practice drew little public criticism. Preparing students for the labor market was so important that legislators dismissed data challenging the effectiveness of vocational curricula and cheerfully endorsed more funds for vocational education. By 1930 vocational education had become a permanent part of the secondary school.[18]

Finally, the hopes of administrative and pedagogical progressives that "learning by doing" or a project-based approach in vocational classrooms would spread to academic courses were dashed in subsequent decades. Stunning victories by promoters of vocational education—in adding a specialized course of study in the high school curriculum, installing vocational testing and guidance in elementary and junior high schools, reorganizing the age-graded school, and making a priority of job preparation alongside the historic purpose of civic preparation—failed to spill over into the typical classroom.

Teaching practices enshrined in the rhetoric of the "whole child" and "learning by doing," embedded in practical vocational courses, did find a solid foothold in private nursery schools, kindergartens, and the early grades of elementary school. But project-based teaching, collaborative learning, and other student-centered innovations championed by pedagogical progressives seldom made it past the doors of secondary school subject-centered classrooms except at some private schools. The "whole child" and "learning by doing" made fine one-liners at conventions of progressive educators but were seldom practiced in most classrooms.[19]

*   *   *

Neither the first nor the last time that a generation of reformers concerned about national economic, political, and social problems turned to public schools for solutions, this early twentieth-century coalition, initially led by business leaders seeking industrial training for schoolboys, proceeded from two assumptions. First, progressives assumed that schooling urban youth for an industrial workplace would end the skill deficits among job applicants, decrease youth unemployment and crime in poverty-stricken cities, improve worker productivity, raise standards of living, and thus contribute to social stability and a growing, globally competitive economy. Second, they assumed that businesses and schools were kindred organizations. Since the governance and management of school systems were both inefficient and ineffective, they believed, applying successful business practices to school board governance, the superintendent's office, and even the first-grade teacher's classroom would considerably improve the quality of U.S. education.

By the 1920s, business leaders were no longer in the forefront of school reform, but they could see the triumph of these core assumptions across the nation in new public school goals, reshaped governance, efficient organization, and differentiated curricula. Not even during the Great Depression, when business leaders' reputations plummeted, were serious objections raised about the kind of schooling inspired by an earlier generation of private-sector leaders. Occasionally challenged in subsequent decades, these assumptions about the relationships between education, the economy, and a stable society, and between business and schools, were generally unquestioned beliefs that shaped the thinking of business leaders, public officials, journalists, educators, and parents for the remainder of the twentieth century.[20]

After the 1930s, active business involvement in schools was intermittent until the mid-1970s. Beginning in that decade, another burst of national reform, also intended to solve serious economic and social problems by improving public schools, again drew sustained participation by national, state, and local associations of business leaders, along with other critics of K–12 education. As before, critics spotlighted school shortcomings (such as falling test scores and poor preparation of graduates for jobs) to arouse public support while minimizing the tough work of altering school and classroom practices. Business leaders again mobilized civic officials, parents, union leaders, and voters to pay attention to school improvement—this time not through vocational education but through tough academic standards, testing, accountability, and efficiency measures.

Thinking of Students as Workers

In the 1970s, as in the past, economic woes turned business leaders' attention to figuring out which problems needed to be fixed in order to stimulate domestic prosperity and global competitiveness. Business executives, civic elites, union leaders, grassroots reformers, and media pundits discussed many issues, including poor corporate management, low capital investment, CEOs' tardy acceptance of new technologies, the lack of adequately skilled workers, and federal economic policies. The same problem that had occupied an earlier generation of business-driven reformers—that is, the shortage of workers with the skills required by a changing economy—appeared on the agendas of policy elites in the recession-prone 1970s as a vital problem that needed solving. In this instance, can-do business and civic leaders concurred that more skilled workers were needed to manage the transition from a factory-dependent industrial economy to a knowledge-based postindustrial one.[21]

Of course, turning to schools to solve national problems was hardly new by the 1970s. Progressives had done so with the vocational education movement at the beginning of the twentieth century. In the Cold War years after the Soviet government launched *Sputnik,* school reforms were swiftly introduced to enable the nation

to catch up with an enemy that had forged ahead in space exploration. And a few years later national business and civic officials agreed
with civil rights leaders that poverty, unemployment, inadequate
housing, and health service problems could be solved by better education in poor urban and rural schools. "The answer for all our national problems," President Lyndon B. Johnson said in the mid-
1960s, "comes down to one single word: education."[22]

By the mid-1970s, however, critics from the political left and right
claimed that schools were still failing. From the left, critics objected
to the racist organizational, curricular, and teaching practices embedded in largely white-staffed urban public schools. They pointed
to reluctant policymakers and school officials who were stalling over
desegregation. Moreover, critics on the left faulted these same bu-
reaucrats for perpetuating self-serving school organizations in big
cities and failing to turn over schools to parental and community
control. Finally, some critics condemned the "mindlessness" of dull,
regimented classrooms that killed children's natural "joy of learning."[23]

From the political right, angry pundits pointed to major increases
in spending for both urban and suburban schools with nothing to
show for the additional funding but schools so infected with the
counterculture that had emerged in the late 1960s that teachers and
students were wearing jeans and dashikis in class. They saw ineffec-
tual suburban school authorities floundering amid rising drug use.
They watched administrators capitulating to fad after fad, including
open-space schools and open (or neo-progressive) classrooms. Fewer
high school students took three years of math, science, and foreign
language. Steep declines in Scholastic Aptitude Test (SAT) scores
worried both business and civic leaders since the best and the brightest were supposed to go on to college and become scientists, engineers, and company CEOs. When a "back-to-basics" movement for
more traditional elementary schools appeared, conservative critics
applauded but called for more such programs. Schools were sup-

posed to be the bulwark of society, transmitting core community values to the next generation, and they were failing miserably.[24]

Critics from both left and right saw mediocre public schools as causes of the nation's problems. An emerging political consensus among business and civic elites, drawing on a deep popular faith in the collective and individual economic benefits of education and amplified by the media, called for giving more resources to educators only if they reformed school structures to focus on high academic standards and raising student achievement. According to its advocates, the political bargain of giving more money to educators in exchange for school reforms would once again enable the United States to raise worker productivity, lower youth unemployment, and enhance standards of living, economic growth, social stability, and individuals' chances to become financially successful.[25]

The Committee for Economic Development, a national business organization of more than two hundred top executives, concluded in the 1980s: "Tomorrow's workforce is in today's classrooms; the skills that these students develop and the attitudes toward work that they acquire will help determine the performance of our businesses and the course of our society in the twenty-first century." Even larger social benefits accrue to the nation, the report concluded. More highly educated people invest in better health care and experience lower mortality rates; they are efficient consumers; they save more and plan better for the future. And, the report reminded readers, "Violent crime is reduced by an increase in education."[26]

Beginning in the mid-1970s and for the next two decades, business leaders working closely with their national associations' local affiliates, public officials, teacher unions, and parent groups designed, amended, and stumbled through a series of strategies aimed at mobilizing federal, state, and local authorities to improve schools. In the 1980s partnerships between large, mid-sized, and small businesses and individual schools across the country poured money, staff, and equipment into programs and classrooms. Toward the end of that decade, most top business leaders concluded that far more than local partnerships was necessary. Albert Shanker, president of the American Federation of Teachers, said in 1988: "We must start thinking of students as workers, which means we've got to deal with the same issues business does." "The system," said the president of Chevron USA, Willis Price, "is bad. American industry has got to join with education, parents, and government to institute drastic, systemic reorganization [of schools]."[27]

Building on the elementary school "back to basics" campaign of the early 1970s, civic leaders, educational policymakers, and state business roundtables prodded legislatures to demand more of schools. By the end of the 1970s, two-thirds of the states had mandated minimum-competency tests for high school graduation to make educators accountable to the public. In California in 1983, CEOs of forty-seven major corporations supported passage of a major increase in state spending on education to pay for an omnibus reform package promoted by the newly elected state superintendent of schools. Chicago's business community, fed up with teachers' strikes, unemployable youth, and annual budget deficits, took over the fiscal management of the city's schools. In Boston business leaders signed a compact with school officials that promised jobs to high school graduates if educators raised academic standards.[28]

The *Nation at Risk* report (1983) capped over a decade of constant carping about public schools. Comparing U.S. students' test scores with those of students in other countries crystallized the business community's unease about public schooling. In the same year, a report from the National Science Foundation pointed out that typical Japanese students spent three times as many hours in science classes as their U.S. counterparts did. "Our children could be stragglers in a world of technology," the report warned, vowing that "we must not let this happen; America must not become an industrial dinosaur." A longtime critic of schools and former assistant secretary of education, Chester Finn, explicitly linked academic subjects, achievement,

and the economy, asserting that "faltering academic achievement between 1967 and 1980 sliced billions of dollars from the U.S. gross national product." The link between Americans' mediocre scores on national and international tests and low worker productivity and lack
of competitiveness in the global marketplace became a virtual cliché
in subsequent national discussions.[29]

After the *Nation at Risk* report, state after state, often at the urging
of business associations, went beyond mandating minimum competency tests to increasing high school graduation requirements,
lengthening the school year, and requiring more tests. In an unprece-
dented act, President George H. W. Bush convened the fifty state governors in 1989 to develop a list of national educational goals. They
called for six goals (later expanded to eight by President Clinton), of
which one was that American students would rank first on international tests in math and science by the year 2000.[30]

Lamar Alexander, secretary of education under the first President
Bush, hired David Kearns, former chair of the Xerox Corporation,
to develop national academic standards. "What schools needed was
what businesses had to go through," Alexander said. "We had to
turn schools upside down." Federal officials also created a privately
funded initiative, the New American Schools Development Corporation, to design extraordinary schools that would be twenty-first century models of whole school reform for the nation. Business leaders
drawn from all segments of the private sector and political leaders of
both parties endorsed the creation of a National Skills Standards
Board as part of the Goals 2000 legislation and later, during the
Clinton administration, the School-to-Work Opportunities Act. As
the chair of IBM put it: "Education isn't just a social concern, it's a
major economic issue. If our students can't compete today, how will
our companies compete tomorrow? In an age when a knowledgeable
work force is a nation's most important resource, American students
rank last internationally in calculus and next to last in algebra."[31] All
of these efforts from the late 1980s through the 1990s were "an easy

sell," according to a top U.S. department of education official during the Clinton years, because staff in each Republican or Democratic administration told business leaders that "our agenda is your agenda."[32]

That agenda was not only for schools: conservative critics identified schools as part of the larger problem of an inefficient, underperforming government. Both political parties sought to improve state and federal performance through market-inspired principles. Vice-President Al Gore wrote in the first National Performance Review of "our twin missions to make government *work better and cost less,*" which would reduce the "trust deficit." President George W. Bush called for a "bold strategy for improving the management and performance of the federal government." What matters most, he said, "is performance and results."[33]

In urban schools, academics and practitioners had already mobilized an "effective schools" movement that concentrated on raising students' academic achievement one school at a time. By the early 1980s these researchers and reformers had identified a handful of big-city elementary schools enrolling large numbers of low-income minority children whose students scored higher on standardized achievement tests than would have been predicted by socioeconomic status. They extracted certain factors from these schools that they believed accounted for the students' better-than-expected performance: clearly stated academic goals, principals' instructional leadership, concentration on basic academic skills, safety and order in the school, frequent monitoring of academic achievement, and connecting what is taught to what is tested. Effective schools advocates such as Ron Edmonds shared four key principles: all children can learn and achieve results that mirror ability, not family background; top-down decisions wedded to scientifically derived expertise can improve individual schools; measurable results count; and the school is the basic unit of reform. By the early 1990s the effective schools movement had spread beyond urban schools. Reauthorizations of the Elementary and Secondary Education Act allowed federal funds to flow to states that used factors drawn from Edmonds and others in the movement to guide whole school reform. Suburban and rural schools as well as urban ones adopted these factors.[34]

Federal and state policymakers, believing in education as an engine of the economy and using effective schools research, sought a broader and speedier impact on the nation's schools than could be achieved with the slow school-by-school approach. They called for national goals, curriculum, and tests. The capstone of the effective schools movement was the No Child Left Behind Act (NCLB), passed in 2002, just a year after George W. Bush took office.[35]

George W. Bush, the first president of the United States to hold a masters degree in business administration, sought to extend the educational successes that he had seen in his home state of Texas, and appointed the superintendent of the Houston schools, Rod Paige—who carried a national reputation for working closely with the city's business community and raising test scores of African-American and Latino students—as his secretary of education. They rolled out legislation targeted at poor children but ultimately aimed at every student in the nation. Resolutely backed by national business associations and bipartisan to its core—Democratic Representative George Miller of California and Senator Ted Kennedy of Massachusetts helped draft the bill and move it through the Congress—NCLB required every child to be tested in grades three through eight.[36]

Business leaders applauded the changes introduced by both federal and state Republican and Democratic administrations. Louis Gerstner, Jr., a former CEO of IBM and one of the founders of Achieve, Inc., an organization of state governors and CEOs established to promote higher academic standards and accountability in schools, recalled the changes that had occurred since the early 1990s:

> You find a broad-based nonpartisan coalition that has come together to declare that reform starts with high academic stan-

dards, quality measurement, and real accountability . . . That sounds so simple. But it's taken enormous courage on the part of state governors. It's taken leadership from the business community, and it's required a lot of great educators to stand up and stand tall in the face of intense opposition. Today [2002], however, we have something that I wouldn't have imagined in the early 1990s: A broad national consensus about what we're going to do and how we're going to do it.[37]

Individual business leaders drew support for their efforts to reform schools from their well-financed and organized national associations such as the National Association of Manufacturers and the Business Roundtable. Small businesses and chambers of commerce, also represented by national associations, displayed similar positions on improving schools. Business leaders from companies of various sizes lobbied both political parties, governors, mayors, and school boards. They used sophisticated advertising campaigns and publicity that tapped the popular belief that better schools would enable students to get higher-paying jobs.[38]

Another wing of school reformers, located among political conservatives including business leaders, borrowed concepts from neoclassical economics and libertarianism to apply to schools. They wanted to convert public schools into markets and let individual consumers, that is, parents, choose the school, public or private, that would be best for their sons and daughters. Marketplace competition would prod schools to perform or fold. They were not the first to advocate parental choice, of course. The concept is rooted in the tension between public and private schools over religion and ethnicity in the nineteenth century and in a later generation of reformers in the 1960s and 1970s who pushed for alternative schools and vouchers to offer poor minority parents options inside and outside urban schools. In short, like the move to raise academic standards, the contemporary embrace of choice and competition has multiple origins beyond the business community.[39]

These choice-inspired reformers saw schools, particularly those in big cities, as overregulated, bureaucratic government organizations that needed a heavy dose of market competition. They believed that parental choice—through inter-district and intra-district transfers, vouchers, charter schools, and for-profit contractors—would create a sufficiently competitive environment to force school district leaders to make improvements. Although national business associations supported public choice through transfers, charter schools, magnet schools, and the contracting of schools to for-profit firms, they avoided endorsing vouchers.[40]

Yet vouchers that authorize public funds to be spent on private schools (including religious ones) have had great staying power as a market-based solution for low-performing schools. Even though voucher-supported referenda went down to defeat in California (1993, 2000), Michigan (2000), and other states, public support for vouchers has inched up. At present there are voucher experiments in Milwaukee, Cleveland, Florida, Colorado, and the District of Columbia that permit public funds to be spent in private schools.[41]

Much support for vouchers comes from fundamentalist Christians, Catholics, Orthodox Jews, urban African-Americans, and free-market libertarians. Astutely asking a simple question—If white middle-class parents can escape inadequate public schools by sending their children to private schools, why can't poor minority parents do the same?—Republicans have used a powerful colorblind equity argument to advance the cause of vouchers. Although they have been incorporated into GOP party platforms and have found support in legislative provisions and pronouncements from presidents Ronald Reagan, George H. W. Bush, and George W. Bush, vouchers have thus far remained at the margin of school reform—primarily because of the fears of suburban voters, who constitute solid majorities in both political parties and who are largely satisfied with their schools. Also, the suspicion that publicly financed vouchers would prompt poor minority students to leave their urban schools and enter suburban ones lingers in the background. In 2002 the U.S.

Supreme Court, by a vote of five to four, judged the Cleveland voucher program constitutional even though only religious schools in the city accepted vouchers but no suburban districts did. Other voucher cases are in the Court's pipeline and will be decided within the next few years.[42]

Since the late 1970s, then, corporate-inspired strategies for achieving success in U.S. public schools and libertarian claims about market choice and competition have moved from policy discussion to adoption and, finally, with private and public funding, into actual school programs. Foundations, including corporate ones, have also funded K–12 schools to advance these business-endorsed solutions. Although corporate and private groups account for less than 1 percent of the $370 billion spent annually on public schools, corporate giving to K–12 did increase from $18 million to $81 million between 1990 and 2000. These private monies, of course, are not in the same league as the federal allocation of $12 billion for Title I programs in 2003—which itself is just a few pennies out of every educational dollar spent in the nation.[43]

Federal, state, and district policymakers have instituted several changes consistent with business-minded prescriptions for improving schools:

- establishing rigorous academic standards that all students must meet,
- testing students often,
- rewarding staff members, students, and schools that meet standards; shaming and punishing the ones that don't,
- securing sharp managers who concentrate on raising academic achievement and trimming bureaucracies,
- telling parents and taxpayers exactly how their children and schools perform on tests by issuing periodic report cards,
- letting parents choose which schools their children will attend.

Together, these policies, endorsed by many business leaders, parents, and educators, have been called "systemic reform" or standards-based curriculum, testing, and accountability.[44]

Currently, forty-nine states have adopted standards of what their students should know and have established tests to assess their performance. The number of states that administer tests aligned with published standards in at least one subject climbed from thirty-five in 1998 to forty-one in 2000. Twenty-nine states rate schools primarily on the basis of test scores; twenty-two states have authorized their departments of education to close and take over low-performing schools. In nineteen states, students who fail the statewide graduation test do not receive diplomas. Ten more states have mandated that penalty to be enforced by 2008. In thirteen states (as of 2000), cash payments or awards flow to schools that meet their targets and show continuous improvement. Consistent with advice offered by business leaders—"You can't manage what you don't measure"—all fifty states (as of 2001) either produce or require local school boards to publish report cards that include data on students' test performance, attendance, dropout and graduation rates, school discipline, student-teacher ratios, and financial information. The swift adoption of standards, testing, and accountability, however, masks considerable variation from state to state in each of these categories.[45]

The No Child Left Behind Act takes the slogan "All children can learn," borrowed from the effective schools movement, and puts the full force of federal authority behind business-supported standards-based reform. The law requires all U.S. schools receiving federal funds to test every student in grades three through eight to measure their achievement in reading and mathematics and, by 2007, to test students in science at least once in grades three to five, six to nine, and ten to twelve. All schools are responsible for seeing that all their students make "adequate yearly progress" toward being "proficient" in state standards (that is, scores are disaggregated by ethnicity and race); by 2014, every student must be "proficient." NCLB also man-

dates that schools failing to meet targets for "adequate yearly progress" two years in a row will face "corrective action" and, ultimately,
"restructuring." If a child's school is identified as failing, the family
can choose to send the child to another school at the district's ex-
pense (but not across district lines to another school system). The
2002 law mirrors the business-driven focus on measurement, accountability, and market-based prescriptions of competition and
choice to spur better performance not only in schools but also in
government.[46]

Parental choice expanded in the 1990s. In many states and districts, students can now transfer easily to another school outside
their neighborhood. Alternative schools (for example, magnets established during rapid desegregation in the late 1960s, pedagogically
progressive small schools, continuation schools for dropouts) are
fixtures in urban, rural, and suburban districts. Private companies
have contracted with school boards to run public schools, offering
yet another type of choice. There are now more than 2,500 independent charter schools. A handful of state-designed experiments give
parents vouchers or checks that can be used in private schools. Busi-
ness-generated principles and practices, which also tap aspirations
and experiences of reformers outside the corporate community, have
become bipartisan education policy (with the exception of Democratic opposition to vouchers).[47]

The ubiquitous influence of business-inspired approaches to
schooling has brought many changes to schools in the past quarter-
century. Vocational courses, for example, enthusiastically introduced
by business-minded administrative progressives before World War I
and heavily subsidized since then by federal and state funds, dimin-
ished considerably in the 1980s and 1990s. The share of public high
school graduates taking three or more credits in vocational programs
went from 34 percent in 1982 to 25 percent in 1998, with the sharp-
est decreases in business and trade and industrial occupations.[48]

Contemporary reformers have turned the business-derived argument that an information-based economy requires youth to have more cognitive and social skills than they need in an industrial-based economy into an educational consensus that a college-preparatory curriculum (four years of English, three years of math and science, and so on) is the best way to prepare high school students for the world they will face after graduation. Forgotten has been a fundamental fact that has emerged from mass education in the twentieth century: students vary in motivation, interests, and academic capacities; some substantial percentage lack the desire to spend another four years sitting in classrooms or do not see academic studies as connected to their life after high school. Also forgotten is that this variation in students' interests and abilities prompted, in part, an earlier reform movement in favor of vocational education. Reformers forget high school students like Bobby Lindquist, for whom the "only thing that gets me up in the morning and gets me to come to school" is rebuilding a minivan at Marshall Academy, a career program in Fairfax County, Virginia. Such opportunities for Bobby and other students are rapidly shrinking and will shrink even further if the Bush administration succeeds in its policy goal of requiring vocational students to achieve higher scores on academic tests.[49]

Other business influences also have become obvious. School boards renamed superintendents CEOs and their deputies "chief operating officers" and "chief academic officers." Many urban school boards have inserted performance clauses in their superintendents' contracts that pay bonuses when students' test scores rise. Many districts have "outsourced" to private firms transportation, building maintenance, food services, security, purchasing, and, in some instances, entire schools. School policymakers and administrators (but rarely teachers) salt their vocabulary with such terms as "satisfying the customer," "benchmarking," and "marketing our services." District administrators have imported from the private sector such business mainstays as marketing studies, strategic planning and "total quality management." The Malcolm Baldrige National Quality

Award in manufacturing, service, small business, and health care—"the nation's premier award for performance excellence and quality achievement," established in 1987 by the U.S. Congress and named after a former U.S. secretary of commerce—added education in 1999. Three winners were selected in 2001 for their achievements in leadership, strategic planning, market focus, and organizational performance.[50]

U.S. schools now use information technology initially invented for the military in the 1950s, adopted by large businesses in the 1960s and 1970s, and now widespread in most workplaces. Desktop computers entered schools in the early 1980s. By 2001 the number of students per computer had dropped from over 125 to just over 4. For communication, compiling data for decisionmaking, and supporting teaching and learning, both administrators and teachers have largely adopted information technologies.[51]

Another influence of business can be seen in the increasing commercialization in schools, which raises the strong suggestion that particular businesses see children as future customers and public schools as profit centers. School boards and superintendents welcomed Channel 1 television, which is now in one-quarter of all high schools. In exchange for supplying the school with free electronic equipment, Channel 1 displays commercials that students watch in daily twelve-minute programs. Schools also now receive funds for signing exclusive contracts to sell soft drinks and advertising space.[52]

Missing from this inventory of business influences are teaching and learning. Have business approaches altered what routinely occurs in classrooms? Apart from the distribution of free corporate instructional materials, Channel 1 television, and classroom computers, it is hard to determine whether teachers now teach differently than they did before the late 1970s when the contemporary surge of private-sector involvement began its sweep across America's public schools.

The few studies that have been done on classroom teaching and learning before and after serious business involvement confirm the persistence of teacher-centered instruction, especially in secondary schools but less so in the lower grades where student-centered practices flourished. If anything, the impact of standards-based curriculum and accountability has weakened progressive teaching practices where they occur while hardening traditional classroom patterns. A movement to incorporate progressive practices such as portfolios, project-based teaching, performance-based assessment, and other student-centered approaches that blossomed from the mid-1980s until the early 1990s, for example, has since shriveled and gone underground under the unrelenting pressure for higher test scores. (I take up this puzzle of limited business influence on classroom teaching in Chapter 4.)[53]

In the decades after World War II, national and international events created problems that opinion-setting elites again attributed to underperforming public schools. From Soviet advances in space exploration to the *Brown* decision desegregating the schools to the economic boom-and-bust cycle of the 1960s and 1970s, critics blamed public schools for causing social, political, and economic turmoil or for not doing enough to solve these problems. Reform *through* schools inevitably meant reform *of* schools.

The war in Vietnam (not over for the United States until 1975, when the last troops were withdrawn) continued to divide the nation. The post-Watergate scandal that led to the first-ever resignation of a U.S. president fed a growing unease among Americans about trusting governmental authority. The unease was heightened by larger cultural changes in attitudes toward drugs and sex and a new questioning of authority that inspired (some say infected) youth, creating conflicts between generations.[54]

Coinciding with the social and cultural tremors, an economic recession in the early 1970s converged with weakened exports and Japanese and German inroads into key domestic markets in autos and electronics. As inflation and unemployment numbers rose in the 1970s, attention turned—as it has earlier in the century—not toward national debates over federal fiscal policies, corporate errors, or CEOs' tardy grasp of new technologies, but toward inefficient public schools that, according to critics, were producing graduates unequipped for a changing economy. Efforts to make schools more managerially efficient and accountable for results began in the mid-1970s and reasserted the important linkage of education to the economy. Public fears about social, cultural, and economic changes fused into a broad civic- and corporate-led movement to make schools, again, businesslike.

In these years, business leaders recognized that civic officials, union officers, parents, and educational policymakers shared their hopes for school reform. Company leaders used their resources to organize political coalitions, gain media access, and prod elected officials to do the right thing. Once the desired policies or approximate versions were adopted, business leaders' visibility receded.

The core beliefs that guided the business-inspired school reform movement earlier in the century were present in the waning decades of the twentieth century as well. Once again a stuttering economy was blamed on low worker productivity and employees' skill deficits, particularly among urban youth. Business and civic leaders from both political parties assumed that a college-preparatory curriculum, constant testing, and a coercive accountability would encourage youth to acquire cognitive skills marketable in a knowledge-based economy and would strengthen public trust in schools. Skilled and knowledgeable graduates would increase workplace productivity, reduce unemployment, boost standards of living, and make companies competitive in world markets.[55]

And, as before, the benefits of improved education were assumed to be more than economic. In 2000 the Business Roundtable's Education Initiative included the vow: "The Business Roundtable will continue the commitment CEOs made in 1989 to improve K–12 education in the U.S. The twin forces of technology and globalization mean that connections among an excellent K–12 education system for all students, the competitiveness of our workforce, the vibrancy of our communities and the future of our democracy have never been clearer."[56]

Reformers also assumed that businesses and schools (as well as government) were similar, and that since school systems' decision-making, management, and daily operations were inefficient and clearly ineffective—as measured by low test scores—they could be substantially improved by the application of successful business practices to administrative tasks and teachers' classrooms.[57]

A third assumption in this surge of business-oriented school reform was aimed specifically at urban students: the assumption that systemic reform, a college-preparatory curriculum, choice, and competition, with clear incentives and rigorously enforced sanctions, would provide poor and minority youth with marketable skills and an equal chance at financial success. Appropriating the slogan "all children can learn," political conservatives under presidents Reagan and Bush (father and son) waved high the banner of colorblind equity. They invited poor Americans of color concerned about the quality of schooling to join Republicans in promoting parental choice policies (including vouchers) and raising academic standards in big-city schools.

Beginning in the late 1970s, these assumptions slowly coalesced into a multilayered, trial-and-error strategy of business participation in school reform. In a flush of goodwill and altruism, business partnerships with individual schools and districts, with businesses donating cash, staff, and equipment, swept corporate boardrooms in various cities. Within a few years, however, business leaders saw that partnerships seldom transformed schools, much less districts and states. So some corporate executives adopted policymakers' lingo about whole school reform, choice, tests, and accountability that, they believed, would refurbish teaching and learning, school by school, across the country.

By the early 1990s, the strategy of systemic reform gripped business leaders. Its focus on performance, its mix of command-and-control decisionmaking and autonomy, efficiency values, and a way of thinking about systems, nicely mirrored the way company CEOs went about fixing botched enterprises in the private sector. Seeing these zigzag changes in direction over the past quarter-century, corporate leaders learned important lessons from their stumbling around in schools. That they worked closely with elected public officials and educational policymakers testifies to their multilayered influences. In 2004, business partnerships, whole school reform, and parental choice policies still dot the educational landscape. But systemic reform—packaged as standards-based curriculum, testing, and accountability, and heavily supported by corporate leaders—is now the dominant strategy of school reform.[58]

3

WHY SCHOOLS HAVE ADOPTED THE REFORMS

The abundant documentation of business influence on school reform prompts a simple question: Why did educational policymakers and practitioners working in tax-supported institutions aimed at achieving larger public goods (such as engaged citizens and graduates prepared to enter the labor force) so readily adopt prescriptions for success designed for private, profit-driven firms governed by market principles? The reasons are anchored in historic social and political beliefs about the relationships between education, the economy, and democracy.

First, the belief that more and better education leads to both individual and collective benefits—personal financial success and a prosperous, globally competitive economy—a notion initially promoted by business and civic leaders in the late nineteenth century, had spread to parents, educators, students, and voters to become an unquestioned assumption by the first decade of the twenty-first century. The pervasiveness of this belief, particularly in periods when corporate leaders were held in high esteem, gave business-inspired school reforms a particular sheen.[1]

Second, civic, business, and political leaders have habitually turned to schools to solve serious national problems. Time and again, solutions to serious social, political, and economic issues have been sought through dramatic reforms in the schools, with little public dissent from policymakers, practitioners, researchers, or parents. At first, educators welcomed the attention and the resources that flowed to them from being drafted to solve important problems and plunged vigorously into school reform. In time, however, public attention flagged, resources dwindled, educators tired, and criticism of reform work mounted as yet another national problem got stuck to the educational fly-tape.

Third, in a decentralized system of public schools in which voters determine tax rates and who gets into office, elected representatives respond to well-organized, well-financed constituencies such as business leaders. Elected officials are sensitive to media criticism and utterly dependent upon voters for their tenure in office. Hence, mayors who are in charge of district schools, local school board members—the largest single body of elected officials in the nation—state governors and legislators, U.S. presidents and congressional representatives invite public comment, react to questions from the media, and respond to constituents, especially business elites.

For those who see endless negotiations, inexorable tensions, and bargained compromises as democracy in action, the pushing and tugging between policymakers, administrators, practitioners, voters, and organized interests are natural parts of the terrain. Others, however, disdainfully characterize the same behaviors as nasty politics ever vulnerable to corrupt practices and hostile to good education. However characterized, the decentralized system is heavily participatory and, since the crescendo of civil rights movements of the past half-century, largely inclusive.

In elaborating on this tripartite explanation for school boards' and educators' accommodation of business-inspired school reforms, I will focus on one example of reform pushed by business leaders and others over the past quarter-century: the introduction of information technologies in general, and the personal computer in particular, into U.S. schools and classrooms.

Good Jobs, Good Schools

President George W. Bush, speaking in January 2002, crisply summarized the popular faith in what schooling promises for individuals and the nation when he said: "Good jobs begin with good schools." Poll results also suggest the pervasive strength of this idea; for example, when a Phi Delta/Gallup Poll conducted in 2000 asked, "In your opinion, which is more important for the schools—to prepare students for college or work, or to prepare students for effective citizenship?" 61 percent of public school parents chose preparing students for college or work. A close look at the rapid introduction of computers into the schools will illustrate the abiding interest of employers, parents, and educators in turning out graduates who are qualified to enter an information-based (rather than manufacturing-based) workplace.[2]

A toddler who happily banged away on the keyboard of her family's first personal computer (a TRS-80) in 1980, two decades later takes home over the winter break from college a four-pound laptop with memory, software, and functions that would have staggered the makers of that earlier machine. All of her classrooms are wired for access to the Internet. Even the "blackboard" is interactive, and the professor, writing on it, can call up a statistical display from his office computer. During the lecture, the student takes notes, contacts friends a continent away, gets the latest news about her favorite soccer team, and hears from her boyfriend about the film they will see that evening. In addition, she has a cell phone and a personal digital assistant (PDA), both of which can be downloaded to her laptop and dorm computer. She is wired. And these changes in information technology occurred in just over two decades. In the years ahead, change will come attached to a tachometer.

Historians have documented the larger story of Americans' infatuation with technology—the passion everyday folks displayed over the railroad, the telephone, flush toilets and electricity in the home, the automobile, and the airplane. The smaller story about computers within the larger one of fondness for machines begins more recently. During World War II, and accelerating swiftly during the early years of the Cold War, military demands for quickly gathered and accurate information, from artillery targeting to raw intelligence from airplane photos and advances in human-machine engineering, led to research into and development of automated and computerized processes. Some of these defense-related technological innovations promised higher productivity for business and industry as well as the military.[3]

By the early 1960s, heavy and light manufacturing, utilities, banking, communications, insurance, and service industries had adapted military hardware and software innovations to their own use to achieve greater efficiency and higher profits. From numerically controlled metal shaping machines, electronic control of production processes, and robotics in manufacturing to conversion from manual to automated processing of information in nonmanufacturing industries, computer-driven work eliminated old jobs while creating new ones and spread to a majority of firms. Global competition also altered the workplace in steel, autos, electronics, textiles, and other industries, gradually creating more jobs for "symbolic analysts" (such as technicians, engineers, lawyers, investment bankers, realtors, planners, consultants) while reducing the need for assembly-line workers.[4] Over the next four decades, these changes in the workplace touched millions of workers and their families, from CEOs to engineers to tool-and-die workers to tractor-trailer drivers. Meanwhile the departure of hundreds of thousands of manufacturing jobs to foreign shores, a huge explosion in well-paid professional and technical jobs, increased skill requirements for high-salaried jobs, and the importance of further education to get those skills became vivid lessons that the future had arrived. It was taken for granted that computerization enhanced labor productivity.[5]

As automatic teller machines, supermarket scanners, and desktop computers became commonplace, business and civic leaders and parents began asking why public schools were so slow in adopting the new technologies. Administrative and managerial uses of information systems had spread in higher education well before school boards adopted them for classroom use.

Veteran educators recalled policymakers' excitement in the early 1960s over computer-assisted instruction (CAI) in schools and universities. The innovation required students to sit in front of terminals connected to mainframe computers and press keys to move through sequenced software programs in math, reading, and certain other subjects. Programmed software (or courseware), such as that created by Computer Curriculum Corporation (CCC), spread in the 1970s and 1980s. Encouraging test results led to a flurry of corporations contracting with public school districts to teach reading and math to poor minority children in this manner. By the early 1970s, however, the pay-for-performance contracts that used CAI had largely disappeared after scandals revealed cheating by particular firms. Still, in the 1970s and 1980s Jostens Corporation and CCC marketed Integrated Learning Systems (ILSs), or CAI dressed up in educational jargon. ILSs steadily expanded its markets in the 1990s, particularly in high-poverty urban and rural schools. By 2001, CCC reported that its courseware was being used in sixteen thousand schools, with ten million students tapping out answers to computer-asked questions.[6]

Large employers in industries and businesses that had computerized their workplaces made clear—time and again—the crucial link between high-tech literacy and jobs. For example, the CEO Forum on Education and Technology, a five-year partnership between business and education leaders founded in 1996, issued policy papers on access and use in schools. A report from the CEO Forum did not mince words: "Information technology is transforming the global economy and drastically changing the way business and society operates. There must be a corresponding adaptation in education to ensure students have the necessary skills to thrive in the digital age."[7]

And entrepreneurs actively sought school markets. Apple Corporation's founder, Steve Jobs, lobbied for a federal bill in 1982 to contribute a computer to every school. The bill would permit hardware companies to donate machines to schools and write off taxes up to 200 percent of manufacturing costs—something that Congress had authorized the previous year for computer firms giving hardware to universities. The House of Representatives passed the bill but it died in the Senate. A year later, the California legislature passed a similar bill, the governor signed it into law, and nearly ten thousand schools in the state each received an Apple computer.[8]

Parents needed little convincing of technology's virtues when it came to their children working on classroom computers. In their workplaces, cars, and supermarkets, chips in machines were everywhere. As personal computers appeared for the first time, media stories on children and computers—such as *Time* magazine's 1982 cover story "Here Come the Microkids," about children using software to program—infiltrated suburban parents' conversations. A Michigan high school principal said: "Moms and dads are coming in and telling counselors they have to get their kids into computer classes because it is the wave of the future." In one 1998 poll, 79 percent of the respondents said computers would be "very helpful" in "teaching high-tech skills." When asked what they valued most about having computers in schools, 76 percent chose "students prepared for jobs" and 72 percent picked "students interested in learning." No surprise, then, that parents prodded their neighborhood elementary school principals to get machines and software into classrooms.[9]

Nor did educators need much nudging from parents and media to go beyond CAI. Teachers, principals, and superintendents were parents. They bought computers for their children and themselves. Moreover, the promise of additional funds flowing into schools led administrators (and parents as well) to chase after business support. They echoed employers' concerns about a skilled workforce and the need to make students computer literate. As with business leaders, educators' altruism and public service values easily got entangled with self-interest. At the New Technology High School in Napa, California, for example, founding principal Robert Nolan said: "We want to be the school that business built." Walls of the renovated elementary school sport huge banners from Microsoft, Lotus, Hewlett-Packard, and local business leaders. "This is not advertising," a New Technology High School administrator told a journalist, "this is a thank you from us to our partners."[10]

National leaders joined local employers, parents, and educators in the crusade for more technology in schools. With the end of the Cold War and the dismantling of the Soviet Union in the late 1980s and early 1990s, the triumph of market capitalism over command economies gave free-market promoters a decided lift. The massive shift in heavy manufacturing to other nations and the growth of knowledge-based industries made plain to presidents, governors, and other elected officials the direction in which both the economy and education would travel. The past three U.S. presidents styled themselves as "education" presidents and spent billions of federal dollars on wiring and hardware to make students technologically literate. "In our schools," President Bill Clinton said in 1996, "every classroom in America must be connected to the information highway with computers and good software, and well-trained teachers."[11]

Between the late 1980s and the early twenty-first century, school boards went on a buying binge (with help from corporate donations and federal dollars). A 1984 survey found that there were more than 125 students per computer in U.S. schools; in 2002 it was just below 4 students per computer. Schools wired for the Internet went from 35 percent in 1994 to 99 percent in 2002. Special high-tech schools multiplied across the nation. And families purchased new technologies as well: in 2000 more than 67 percent of students lived in homes with at least one computer.[12]

Averages, of course, mask variation in access to new technologies at home and school. In a 2000 survey, about half of employed Americans under age sixty with annual incomes less than $30,000 used a computer at work. For those earning more than $30,000 annually, four out of five used computers at work.[13]

While students' access is still affected by income, race, and ethnicity—the so-called "digital divide"—that gap has shrunk considerably. Nationally, the gap between students in poor and non-poor schools has nearly disappeared, although regional differences still occur. Public schools' responsiveness to reformers' determination to give students the latest technologies illustrates the iron-like grip of the popular belief that tying schools to the computerized workplace would yield both private and public benefits.[14]

Computers in schools made the point transparent about the bonds between education and economic success. In the words of John Pepper, then CEO of Procter and Gamble, "Students are going to know that outstanding performance in the classroom leads directly to better jobs and economic opportunity. That connection has been clear in the past. Our objective is to make it clear in the future."[15]

Yet why were public schools much slower in adopting new technologies than universities in the 1980s and 1990s? The reason is another deep-seated and widely shared belief in the power of public schools to solve national problems, especially when the opportunity arises suddenly.

Windows of Opportunity

The launch of a Soviet satellite a decade after the Cold War began and the accidental presidency of a brilliant legislator committed to civil rights and education after his predecessor's assassination are instances of when opportunities suddenly appeared for policy entrepreneurs to advance their reform agendas through public schools. An analyst who works for a lobbying group in Washington, D.C., describes the way would-be reformers look for such sudden opportunities:

When you lobby for something, what you have to do is put together your coalition, you have to gear up, you have to get your
political forces in line, and then you sit there and wait for the
fortuitous event. For example, people who were trying to do
something about regulation of railroads tried to ride the environment for a while, but that wave didn't wash them in to shore.
So they grabbed their surfboards and they tried to ride something else, but that didn't do the job. The Penn Central collapse
was the big wave that brought them in. As I see it, people who
are trying to advocate change are like surfers waiting for the big
wave. You get out there, you have to be ready to go, you have to
be ready to paddle. If you're not ready to paddle when the big
wave comes along, you're not going to ride it in.

We might also see the chances to advance new policies as windows of
opportunity. In less dramatic instances, these windows open slowly
but stay open sufficiently long for advocates of reform to exploit the
opportunity and shape new educational policies.[16]

In both of the two periods I examine in this book, business-inspired
reformers, working closely with others who also sought major
changes in schools, saw windows of opportunity open wide enough
to allow them to offer school-based solutions to national economic
problems. In both instances, the crafted solution to the problem was
to change the schools so they would produce graduates equipped
with the knowledge, skills, and behaviors required by the labor market: first for an industrial and later for an information-based workplace. When schools met the challenge, leaders believed, productivity
would rise, market competitiveness would increase, and personal
standards of living—economic prosperity—would spill over to
working Americans. In the process, public confidence in schools
would mount.

Policy windows at the end of the nineteenth century and in the
1970s, pushed open by international competition and deep disap-

pointment with traditional schooling, gave well-connected business and civic leaders chances to make better schools. These business-inspired critics blamed schools for sapping the nation's economic vitality and doing little to cure social ills. They enlisted public officials, union leaders, parents, and educators whose varied agendas intersected with business-designed reforms to sell vocational education in the early twentieth century and standards-based testing and accountability at the end of that century. In doing so, they harnessed the perceived national problems of insufficient global competitiveness and low labor productivity to the dreams of parents for their children, the hopes of reformers seeking social justice, and the yearnings of educators for more resources, serving the common good, and securing higher status.

The hitching together of education and the economy can be seen especially in the last third of the twentieth century, when U.S. uncertainty about world markets in a post-industrial society opened another policy window. Political leaders from both parties, influential CEOs, and opinion leaders in other sectors of society forged a basic agreement about the core problem and a preferred solution. A summary of their thinking, and the message they sought to communicate to the public, would go like this:

We are entering the Information Age. It is a time of change equivalent to the shift from an agricultural to an industrial society. The global economy is deregulated and bringing freedom and democracy to the rest of the world and technological marvels to America. But if Americans want to enjoy it, you will have to compete against six billion people out there, most of whom will work for lot less than you will. What you earn will depend upon what you learn. You should get all the technical training you can get, pack a computer on your back and get out there and compete.[17]

*   *   *

The linkage between education, technological proficiency, and economic prosperity is hardly opaque. The connections can be seen daily in newspaper ads, bus placards, and television news stories. Democratic and Republican policymakers at the federal and state levels, CEOs, business associations, union officials, and media opinion-setters have consolidated these ideas into an educational agenda with great appeal to parents and taxpayers: higher academic standards, college preparation for all, more testing, and tough-minded accountability. Interwoven in this mix of school reforms were new technologies, especially computers in schools.

Report after report from national and state business, civic, and educational leaders between the late 1980s and 2000 made the point that, in the words of one educator, "to use technology to promote school reform is like flying with a tailwind." Or as a state report entitled "Connect, Compute, and Compete" put it: "More than any other single measure, computers and network technologies, properly implemented, will bolster [our] continuing efforts to right what's wrong with our public schools." As had occurred in the past, critics exaggerated the defects of public schools, underestimated the hard work it would take to improve school and classroom practices, and oversold the reforms.[18]

A few typical examples confirm the point. California's elected state superintendent of instruction said in 1996: "Ninety percent of the jobs created from this moment on will require advanced technological training. To compete for these jobs, our children will have to be skilled in the use of information technology." Or, in the words of Louis Gerstner, then CEO of IBM and a tireless advocate of school reform: "Information technology is the single most important tool to help us get to where we need to be in reforming the public education system in America, if it is implemented into standards reform, measurement, accountability, [and] teacher training."[19]

What is remarkable about the spending spree on technology I described above is that it occurred in spite of the fact that research endorsing such federal, state, and local expenditures were, in a word, scant. Claims that advocates repeatedly made about new technologies, such as that they would advance school reform, increase student achievement, transform teaching and learning, and provide the skills graduates would need to compete in the workplace, lacked credible supporting evidence. Studies that showed positive results for such changes often were contradicted by other studies. Research methodologies were defective. All of this added up to a flawed policy, immensely popular with voters yet riddled with unanswered questions about the value of new technologies for teachers and students.[20]

If the claims of advocates for new technologies in schools are suspect, then why the spending binge in the 1990s? Part of the answer has to do with the political popularity and the symbolism of computers. By the late 1990s, the computer—like past mechanical marvels such as the steam engine or the radio—had become, among other things, a high-status symbol of power and modernity. Within mainstream American culture, past and present, being "modern" meant businesslike efficiency and innovation, both promising a better future. Just as a common synonym for computers is "high tech," the aura of prestige (as in high fashion or high class) surrounds the machines and their accoutrements.[21]

For local school officials to spend their severely limited funds building a technological infrastructure for teachers and students could be as much a symbolic political act as a technical one. Even with little evidence that investments in information technologies raise test scores or promote better teaching, most state and local school boards used the rhetoric of technological progress to secure additional funds, heighten their visibility as alert innovators, and bolster their legitimacy with their patrons and the private sector. Public and private support for these institutions depended on demonstrating to donors, legislatures, parents, and voters that schools were in step with current demands and traditional expectations. Woe to the school leader unable to show patrons and visitors rooms filled with machines. A "good" school came to be defined as a technologically equipped one.[22]

The deeply entrenched beliefs that more education leads to individual and collective economic and social benefits, and that better schooling can solve national problems, help to explain why Americans—including school board members, superintendents, administrators, and teachers—are predisposed to accept certain reforms. What is missing is the mechanism for adopting, managing, and implementing the reforms. This is where elected school boards and their agents (superintendents, principals, and teachers) enter the picture.

The Role of School Boards

School boards and superintendents depend on elites and various stakeholders for political and financial legitimacy and elevated social status. This dependency or, to put it more gracefully, this democratic responsiveness of school boards and educators to their constituencies brings me to the last part of my explanation.

Local school boards are creatures of the state. In the early nineteenth century, states created local school boards and delegated to these elected officials—most of whom, at the time, served rural districts—powers to raise funds, set policy, organize schools, establish curriculum, examine students, and hire (and fire) those responsible for schooling the young.

As the nation expanded after the Civil War and industrialization led to the explosive growth of cities, school districts changed as well. Chartered by the state, city school boards were initially controlled by political machines. The Progressive movement before World War I led good-government reformers to separate partisan politics from school affairs by borrowing the model of a corporate board of directors as an efficient, businesslike system. Smaller elected school boards with local business leaders and professionals making policy for educators became the ideal in the decades bracketing World War I.[23]

By the end of the 1920s, school boards in urban districts had thoroughly embraced the corporate model. They were smaller (usually five to nine members) and drew their members from middle- and upper-middle-income families. In 1917 Scott Nearing identified 967 board members in 104 cities, of whom 45 percent were businessmen, 34 percent were professionals, 9 percent were workers, and the rest were retired businessmen or wives of businessmen. A decade later George Counts found a similar skewed distribution among board members across the country. Subsequent studies of the social origins of school board members have confirmed time and again the pattern first noted by Nearing and Counts.[24]

By the end of the twentieth century, ninety-five thousand elected school board members served on nearly fifteen thousand public school boards in the United States. The majority of these board members lived in suburbs and small towns. The fifty largest, mostly urban, districts constituted 1 percent of all districts, but they contained over 15 percent of all students. National surveys found that 44 percent of all board members occupied managerial or professional posts and 13 percent owned companies. Moreover, 57 percent reported incomes at or above $60,000, with 23 percent claiming incomes higher than $100,000. In short, the hopes of progressive reformers at the beginning of the twentieth century to make all school boards smaller and draw from business, managerial, and professional classes had succeeded. Working-class and minority citizens were hardly represented on school boards, except in segregated, low-income districts.[25]

Does this substantial participation of business and professional groups mean that school boards were pawns of corporate interests? Some critics indeed assumed a connection between board members' occupations, their decisions as a school board, and what happened in classrooms. Because board members' occupations tilted toward business, managerial, and professional classes, these critics believed, school district policies and actions showed a similar slant. Don McAdams, a member of the school board in Houston, Texas, expressed this concern: "Public schools were in the middle of the political arena, and like elected officials at every level, school trustees were subject to the pressures of special interests. All board members were tempted to intervene in student discipline decisions, suggest personnel moves, or tilt toward a particular vendor." While there is some evidence that business elites mobilized political coalitions to change the composition of school boards and introduce governance and organizational reforms, the claim has yet to be sustained by research on the relationships between board policies and what happens in classrooms.[26]

Instead of being manipulated by interest groups, school board members drawn from business, managerial, and professional positions, more often than not, performed the civic roles for which they were elected. As elected officials they were expected to listen to the public, sift data provided by administrators, and make decisions to serve the public good, not private interests—not even the private interests of those who were well organized, influential, and friends of board members. Surely, in some communities business leaders secured hearings from the school board and lobbied for certain projects and policies. Surely, weekend golf matches and cocktail parties saw board members and Chamber of Commerce friends exchanging opinions. And, just as surely, some board members in some districts ignored their constitutional duties and represented private rather than public interests. On the whole, though, depending upon the place and the individuals involved, board members drawn from business occupations met their civic expectations.[27] One glimpse of this variation in responding to different groups appears in the story of how school boards adopted information technologies in the 1980s and 1990s.[28]

Computers and automation in the 1970s and 1980s came as no

surprise to school board members, superintendents, and teachers. They shopped, banked, read newspapers, watched TV news, and listened to wives, husbands, neighbors, and relatives talk about the computerization of the workplace. As parents themselves, many bought machines and software for their homes even before their schools did. So by the mid-1980s, when groups of reform-minded officials and corporate executives began to press state and local school boards, superintendents, and principals to buy the new technologies—not only to prepare the next generation to be computer-skilled for a changed workplace, but to revolutionize teaching and learning—school board members were already predisposed to act. Oiling the gears of school boards to move ahead with purchases and wiring were fervent technology advocates, vendors, and parents with visions of schools becoming high-tech workplaces. Few school boards and superintendents dug in their heels and resisted these pressures. After all, lay leaders and educators harbored the same beliefs about the linkages between the economy and education, and took little convincing from local business leaders to decide that computer technology was the "big wave" of the future.

A boom economy also accelerated school boards' embrace of technology. The only recession between 1982 and 2000 was brief, following the Gulf War of 1990–1991. A wave of prosperity and the New Economy bubble of the mid-to-late 1990s produced surpluses in state and federal treasuries that helped local school boards finance purchases of technology.

Spending on hardware, software, and wiring of schools escalated slowly in the late 1980s, accelerated after the recession of 1991–1992, and went to warp speed after the introduction of the Internet and generous federal subsidies in the mid-1990s. Parents, business leaders, school board members, administrators, and teachers in district after district sniffed out federal, state, and private funds to bring the new technologies into schools and classrooms. To cite one among many instances, in 2003 the superintendent of the Philadelphia schools, Paul Vallas, and Microsoft Corporation announced a partnership that would spend $46 million to build a high school filled with the newest technologies for teachers and students. For the first time, Microsoft would help build a high-tech high school from the ground up. Vallas explained the need for an entirely new type of school by saying: "We're preparing children for the economy of the future in the schools of yesterday." And another local official said: "This school is just preparing our work force to be competitive."[29]

A few typical examples illustrate the rush to establish technology in schools. South Carolina's Beaufort County school district began its efforts as a national technology pioneer in the mid-1990s when it began installing $10 million worth of new technology in its schools. Intent on bridging the local digital divide, the district provided individual laptops to middle school students, regardless of economic status. "Our community," according to Deputy Superintendent Steven Ballowe, "has continued to support our budget so we can provide new monies to update all of the infrastructure hardware and software."[30]

Or consider what the seven-member school board in Carterville, Illinois—a district with just three schools—did in 1996–1997 when it allocated $50,000 for a computer lab to be located in the junior high school building but shared by the elementary and junior high schools. The new principals enlisted volunteers to wire an additional lab and saved enough money to buy more computers for the media center and one junior high class. The board made technology purchases a line item in its budget and funneled monies from state and federal programs to each school. The elementary school's parent-teacher organization aggressively raised funds for classroom hardware and software.

The result? Every classroom now has at least one computer; over half have two or more. In addition, a set of AlphaSmart Pro portable keyboards gives students in a class complete access to equipment. Students may borrow these workstations overnight. The elementary school also has five scanners, six digital cameras, fourteen laptop computers for teachers, a CD-Rom tower, and a projection device. TV sets installed in classrooms also serve as computer monitors, and all classrooms have access to two large-screen TVs for presentations.

Teachers called "Trail Blazers" received training to use all of the equipment. To show the integration of the new technologies into daily instruction, teachers proudly recounted stories of students giving PowerPoint presentations, participating in pen-pal e-mails with students in Hong Kong, on-line projects involving dog-sled drivers in the Yukon, and a virtual trip to the Galápagos Islands.[31]

Yet there is vast variation among nearly fifteen thousand school boards, social demography, and the complexity of moving from adoption of a policy to seeing it realized in K–12 classrooms. Celebrations of technology in schools, as well as critics who accuse school boards of rolling over for vendors, business leaders, and organized parent groups, often ignore two glitches in the race by school boards to place hardware and software in schools. First, urban schools with large numbers of poor students have been a step behind in acquiring access to the new technologies and putting them into classrooms where teachers and students can use them regularly. Second, overall classroom uses of technology for instruction have been limited and irregular, and have often strengthened traditional forms of teaching, baffling promoters who expect these powerful machines to transform classroom routines.

The researcher Barbara Means and her colleagues, to cite one instance, examined six urban high schools in Detroit and Chicago in 1999–2000, when school boards made hardware and software available in varying amounts to these schools. To get a comparison they also examined two affluent suburban high schools in each of the metropolitan areas. They found in the six urban schools "that exciting and empowering instructional uses of technology are happening in some classrooms and some schools but that such applications are nowhere as frequent as one would wish." As for classrooms where teachers regularly use the new technologies, the picture in both urban and suburban schools is at best mixed, and at worst enough to give technology promoters and vendors severe migraines.[32]

These few examples illustrate the variety in the ways district boards of education translate the demands of their constituencies into educational policy. In general, across the nation, elected board members are responsive to organized constituencies, including business leaders, and to scattered groups of activists, but they are not pawns being manipulated by business or other interests.

To the question of why have public schools largely accepted business-inspired reforms endorsed by parents, elected policymakers, and educators (reforms such as vocational education and, later, computers in schools), I have offered a tripartite answer. First, the popular belief that more and better education leads to individual financial success and a productive, globally competitive economy spread from business and civic leaders in the late nineteenth century to become a taken-for-granted assumption by the end of the twentieth century.

Second, civic, business, and political leaders tend to turn to schools in times of national crisis, and twice since the 1880s, when concerns about U.S. competitiveness in global markets opened windows of opportunity for change, policy entrepreneurs linked national economic problems to the poor performance of public schools, blaming schools for failing to provide students with the skills needed in the workplace. Parents' wish for their children to succeed in life and educators' need for more resources and higher public visibility made the pitch for more skills and new technologies in schools attractive to both elites and voters. Policy brokers, amply supported by media hype about children and computers, were convinced that better schooling would make a stronger economy and enhance global competitiveness.

The steady dispersal of business-inspired reforms through the decentralized system of fifty states and nearly fifteen thousand school districts did not occur merely because the president of the United States gave a speech, the U.S. Congress passed a law, or governors and legislatures mandated changes. The spread of reforms happened because local school boards were (and are) acutely sensitive to parental and media criticism of poor performance, exceedingly aware of their civic responsibilities, and—particularly in cities and poor rural areas—underfinanced. Most important, the majority of board members and administrators believed in the worth of new technologies in schools on educational grounds.

My three-part explanation answers the question of why schools have adopted business-inspired reforms—but it inevitably simplifies a hugely complex reality. Local school districts are riddled with autonomous departments, independent school leaders, and teachers who close their classroom doors. State and district school systems are hardly command-and-control organizations. Moreover, districts vary within a state and across states in socioeconomic status, ethnicity, race, size, and capacities to improve. Finally, the quality of board members and their civic sensitivities vary. These internal and external variations account for widely different responses of district school boards to activist groups and organized interests such as local business leaders. Yes, elected school boards are dependent upon voters for political legitimacy, but this dependency has not led boards to operate as willing pawns for determined interest groups.

4

LIMITS TO BUSINESS INFLUENCE

Joel Herbst, principal of South Plantation High School in south Florida, looks forward to graduation in June. Not only will seniors "walk across the stage with a diploma in one hand," they will receive "something else" in the other hand. "Think of it," Herbst says, "as a supplementary diploma, proof positive that our students have skills and experience that decisionmakers in higher education and the workplace are really looking for."

The "something else" Herbst refers to is a paper certificate showing that a student has worked with high-tech Cisco's operating systems, is ready to step into a broadcast editing booth of a local communications company, or has benefited from a literacy initiative funded by Costco and Coca-Cola that engages mothers to help their children read at an early age.

With the cooperation of local and national businesses, Herbst has created partnerships that have brought his high school closer to the achievements that parents, faculty, and administration have long wanted for the students. As he explains:

> We're a large school facing the same kinds of financial challenges you might expect in an economically diverse community

. . . But we've always wanted—and expected—our [business] partners to do more than simply write a check. We want them to demonstrate on a daily basis the industry standards that future workers need to live up to. That means getting every corporate, nonprofit, and public partner that we work with to engage in a dialogue with our students. It means tapping in to their resources to drive and improve our curricula. And it means bringing them full-force into our world at the same time we venture into theirs.[1]

A Range of Participation

Business partnerships like the one Herbst describes for his Florida high school have been a mainstay of corporate and small business involvement with public education since the 1890s. Back then, companies agreed to employ students taking vocational and commercial courses a few hours a day and then hire them after they graduated. These and many other forms of partnerships have flourished in the ensuing decades, and have broadened considerably beyond school-to-work arrangements. By 1990 just over half of all school districts in the nation had school-business partnerships. A decade later, the figure was almost 70 percent. Volunteers in schools went from 2.6 million in 1990 to 3.4 million in 2000, with a value to schools of $2.4 billion. Of the businesses that were partners with schools in 2000 (keep in mind that schools had multiple business partners), three out of four were small firms, 61 percent were mid-sized, and 42 percent were large corporations.[2]

School-business partnerships, of course, are only one of many types of business influence on students and teachers. Other forms of business participation in schools have included direct lobbying of state and federal policymakers and private financing of whole school reform. In 1989, for example, the snack-food and cigarette maker RJR Nabisco announced a three-year, $30 million grant competition—"Next Century Schools"—to create "model schools of the future." Using a standard corporate strategy of creating new products, Next Century Schools would be the research-and-development phase of a transformation of the nation's schools. As the president of the RJR Nabisco Foundation, Roger Semerad, said: "I am more and more of a mind that reform of the American education system is only going to take place school by school and community by community."[3]

As the RJR Nabisco venture of whole school reform wound down, corporate and federal officials heavily involved in changing the nation's schools planned to build on the private initiative by launching the New American Schools Development Corporation (NASDC). Announced by President George H. W. Bush in 1992, NASDC was to be funded partly by the federal government and partly by businesses; the plan was to raise $200 million from corporate donors for 535 experimental schools. A former U.S. secretary of labor, Ann McLaughlin, who had served on the Next Century Schools advisory board, was appointed CEO of NASDC; Louis Gerstner Jr., CEO of RJR Nabisco, became NASDC's treasurer.[4]

As a firm of venture capitalists looking for first-rate school designs, NASDC selected the most promising proposals for new schools, helped the winners in implementing "break-the-mold" schools, and marketed the new designs to other districts as they became financially self-sustaining. James Jones, chairman of the American Stock Exchange and a NASDC director, claimed that the privately financed federal initiative to transform local schools would "take the shackles off" and would "think big to make education something that improves the productivity, the competitiveness, the quality of all the students going through the system."[5]

Business participation in school reform has marshaled partnership programs, jointly funded whole school improvement, district reform, and state and national policy changes. The rhetoric surrounding this array of involvement with schools reveals an abiding belief in the logical linkage between skilled workers, quality of schooling as defined by business leaders, and domestic prosperity. The involvement also displays businesses of all sizes engaging with civic life in local communities—a mix of altruism and hard-nosed strategies for cultivating future customers and preparing productive workers.

The Boeing Corporation is one example of a large firm ($58 billion in revenues for 2001) that has formed partnerships with schools while also using other forms of influence for nearly a quarter-century of school reform. Located in Seattle, Washington, Boeing contributed money, staff, and equipment for many years to Seattle and to suburban colleges and universities as part of its deep involvement in the community. Beginning in the mid-1980s, however, there was a shift toward statewide and local efforts to shape the direction and quality of public schooling. As Boeing's CEO and then-chairman T. A. Wilson put it: "We need a superior education system both to develop and to attract the skilled work force that will assure our state's continued prosperity. The talented people we try to attract want the best for their children, and a good education system is one of the significant factors in their decisions about where to live."[6]

Boeing altered its internal policies to permit direct donations of money and staff to local schools, and it developed K–12 partnerships across the Seattle metropolitan area. From collaborative programs to upgrade math and science teachers' knowledge and skills to internships for high school students to an "A Computer for Kids Contest" held in fifth-grade classes in a cluster of districts with personal computers awarded to the winners, Boeing funded a medley of programs.

Of equal importance was Wilson's membership in the Washington Business Roundtable, which he chaired in the mid-1980s. The Roundtable (thirty-two corporate leaders and two other citizens) identified state funding of schools, teacher salaries, academic standards, and statewide tests as areas that needed legislative action to improve Washington schools. State lawmakers eventually adopted versions of the Roundtable's recommendations. In 1993, for example, the state mandated "challenging academic standards" for all

Washington students. Subsequently, Boeing brought together other business groups in the Seattle area interested in improving schools and formed the Alliance for Education. The Alliance created networks of public, private, and nonprofit organizations concentrating on arts, technology, literacy, environment, and other school programs. More than five hundred businesses and organizations participated in these compacts. Having contributed over $1.5 million to the Alliance, Boeing urged other firms in the Seattle area to support education, and in 2001 more than five thousand donors gave $35 million.[7]

In 2001 Boeing stunned the Seattle community by moving its corporate headquarters to Chicago. A few months later, Boeing CEO Phil Condit served as "Principal for a Day" at Chicago's George Armstrong School for International Studies. He used paper airplanes to teach a seventh-grade science class how planes fly. "Our commitment to public education is an investment in our future," Condit told the students. "Our company depends on schools to help the next generation of engineers, scientists, and technicians take their first steps into a world-class workforce." After being "Principal for a Day," Condit joined Mayor Richard M. Daley to announce Boeing's gift of more than $1 million to fund Chicago education partnerships in training for urban principals, teacher development, and a charter school for women of color to prepare for college and become community leaders.[8]

Believing in these partnerships and referring to his prior experience with the Washington Business Roundtable, Condit said:

> At Boeing, our people are our competitive advantage and the educational capacity of our workforce is critical . . . But we are not paying for employees to learn to read well or to master basic algebra and geometry. Simply put, without strong academic preparation, a person couldn't get a job at Boeing in the first place. For this reason, our company . . . has been at the forefront of the movement to raise academic standards so that

all students—not just the brightest or most advantaged—reach higher levels of performance.

Condit pointed out that just setting standards is insufficient: "That's why business leaders have pushed for states to test students . . . to hold schools and students accountable for reaching standards . . . The accountability provisions attached to test results help us ensure that students are not stuck in poorly performing schools and that high-performing students and schools are rewarded . . . These ideas became the 'law of the land' last year with the passage of the No Child Left Behind Act."[9]

Thus, between the 1890s and the present, the influence of small, mid-sized, and large firms on the public schools has been a braided rope of many strands that included donating money, staff, and equipment, sponsoring whole school reform, building coalitions to support particular district policies and leaders, and lobbying governors and state legislatures, the U.S. Congress, and the White House. Business leaders at different times and in different settings endorsed, inspired, led, and/or actively supported school reforms. Accountable to their shareholders, business leaders believed that spending money on schools was an investment that would add luster to their company's image in the community and ultimately provide brand-name recognition to customers and a supply of entry-level employees. These intense decades of influence on schools have yielded broad changes in public school goals, curriculum, organization, and governance.

Reform Triumphant

As described in Chapter 2, the strenuous lobbying efforts of early twentieth-century progressive business and civic leaders for public schools to become engines for an industrialized economy transformed the nation's public schools. Added to the traditional goals of creating literate citizens and instilling moral values was a new goal: public schools must equip students with industrial skills for the workplace.

Vocational education came to include office work, machine trades, auto repair, and a wide array of technical courses allowing boys and girls to work in school and on the job. By the 1920s, most urban, suburban, and rural secondary schools offered vocational courses and work opportunities for youth.

A new goal and new curricula coincided with the reorganization of schools by efficiency-minded progressives to expand access to extended schooling and to preparation for the industrial workplace. Junior high schools (grades seven through nine) were created in the years before World War I and soon spread across the nation. Senior high schools (grades ten through twelve) became comprehensive institutions with many courses of study from which students could chose.

Well before business-inspired vocational courses were added to the high school and schools were reorganized, progressive reformers had adopted the emerging corporation as their model of efficiency and effectiveness in governing schools. When larger, politically appointed, and patronage-steeped boards were replaced by smaller, apolitical, businesslike elected school boards, civic-minded business leaders and professionals elected to the boards could set policy and appoint trained superintendents to implement new vocational curricula and reorganization. With only slight modifications, the extensive changes in school governance wrought by business and civic-minded progressives at the beginning of the twentieth century are still in place today.

Beginning in the 1970s, another surge of business-inspired school reforms swept across the nation, prompting state and federal officials in the 1980s and 1990s to establish high academic standards for all students and to reduce traditional vocational courses while imposing a uniform college-preparatory curriculum, instituting accountability measures fastened to standardized tests, and inserting market competition and choice into public schools.

In these years, business associations used various strategies to foster school reform. Corporate partnerships with local schools and lobbying for top-down state and federal measures to advance higher academic standards and accountability were matched by high-profile financial investments in bottom-up whole school reform. Boosted by RJR Nabisco in the late 1980s and embraced by President George H. W. Bush, the jointly federally and privately funded NASDC, with its "break the mold" schools, melded corporate monies with government support to advance school-by-school reform throughout the nation.

The federal government (under both Republican and Democratic administrations) pursued the same whole school or one-school-at-a-time reform by promoting the Comprehensive School Reform Demonstration Program, which was founded in 1998 and for which Congress appropriated $308 million in 2003.[10] Although continual battles were fought over vouchers, particularly when Republicans controlled the White House, the focus on whole school reform, and on corporate lobbying for states to legislate higher academic standards and testing, illustrates the mingling of private-sector and publicly funded strategies to improve school performance in the 1990s.

It seems, then, that changes promoted by progressive business and civic leaders well over a century ago, as well as the more recent business-driven school reforms, have altered the topography of public schools in substantial ways. This is a historically accurate judgment —but it is also important to note the substantial constraints upon business influence in schools that have emerged in the politics of reform and the institution of the school.

Reform Politics and Stable Teaching Practices

In Charlotte, North Carolina, in the early 1990s, the CEO of IBM shook hands with the district superintendent and agreed to contribute $2 million for four new high-tech schools to be built on land adjacent to the company's facilities. The handshake committed the superintendent to reserve a substantial portion of space in the schools for children of IBM employees. When parents in other parts of the district realized that their children would not be able to attend the new schools, they were outraged and protested to the school board.

IBM soon found out that the elected school board, not the superintendent, has the authority to approve deals. It turned out that the IBM executives, like any private or public group, would have to lobby board members, attend public hearings, and mobilize support for their plan. Months of public controversy over the agreement led to an embarrassed and chastened IBM renegotiating a contract with the school board.[11]

Political interest groups inside and outside public schools have halted, rearranged, and even mocked the idea that business-designed reforms would be welcomed into schools and classrooms. Before World War I, for example, union leaders in Chicago, San Francisco, and other cities successfully resisted business initiatives to establish private vocational schools that would graduate workers trained to take jobs in local companies. Union leaders, echoing the words of Samuel Gompers, wanted to "make better workers of our future citizens [and] better citizens of our future workers," especially if those private vocational school graduates might become strikebreakers.[12]

In fact, when one considers the muddled experiences of business-inspired ventures such as merit pay schemes since the 1920s, contracting-for-performance in the 1960s, and the devolving of decisionmaking authority to local school committees (site-based management) since the 1970s, the idea that business elites can do as they wish in reforming schools becomes comical. For example, the idea that good teachers should be awarded more pay than mediocre teachers derives directly from the private sector, where rewards and penalties for employee performance are common practice. Since the 1920s, most school districts have paid teachers on a uniform schedule depending on each teacher's credentials and years served in the system. Seniority, not performance, yields higher salaries. Even though, time and again, plans to pay teachers for superior performance were scrupulously designed—with principals evaluating teachers' classroom performance and, on occasion, even considering students' achievement—each plan eventually incurred the wrath of teachers' unions over perceived instances of unfair administrative judgments about effective teaching. The teachers' unions cannot be blamed for the defeat of these plans, since merit pay popped up and vanished in both union-dominated and union-free districts. Political battles over the lack of a suitable metric for judging effectiveness in classroom teaching and learning that was acceptable to both teachers and their supervisors led to either the dilution or the demise of merit pay plans throughout the twentieth century.[13]

If institutional cultures and unions constrain the application of commonplace business practices, larger forces also temper business influence. The hullabaloo surrounding the launching of the NASDC, for example, soon faded as the expected $200 million from corporate donations fell far short during the recession of 1991–1992. NASDC soon downsized into "New American Schools," scaling back its grants to only those schools that had won the design competition. Eventually (and ironically), the organization came to rely upon federal grants to become a provider of technical assistance to efforts at whole school reform.[14]

Conflicts within the business community have also dampened the influence of business on school reform, by killing federal legislation supposedly helpful to corporate interests. Tensions between large and small firms (about, say, application of tax laws and federal support for foreign exporters or importers), between multinational and local companies (over, for example, erratic versus abiding interest in community affairs), and between sectors of the economy (such as the stark differences between the manufacturing and telecommunications sectors over protective tariffs) have fragmented coalitions.

These splits mean that unified support for proposed state and federal legislation on, for example, school vouchers may occur for a time but eventually disintegrate. Internal strains over competing interests are most likely to tear apart national business coalitions during economic downturns or shifts in political coalitions.[15]

Reforming Teaching and Learning

The limits to business influence in school reform have been evident in many failed attempts to alter classroom practices. Popular support for major reforms in school governance, curriculum, and instruction made many business leaders into educational progressives a century ago. In those decades, corporate leaders, unionists, and public officials promoted classrooms in which students worked with both their heads and their hands on practical projects rather than copying lessons from textbooks and listening to teachers. Vocational courses promised major changes in teaching methods.

The stigma that came to be attached to vocational education—as a dumping ground for students doing poorly in academic courses, as a failed attempt to remedy youth unemployment, as segregated by gender, race, and ethnicity—makes it hard to appreciate the ardent belief of early twentieth-century progressive reformers in learning-by-doing pedagogy. These reformers, including prominent business leaders, passionately believed that vocational courses with students working on real-world projects, or what a later generation of progressive educators called hands-on learning, would rescue academic teaching and learning from the monotonous pattern of classroom lectures and textbook recitation that so often sapped students' motivation to learn. That fervent utopian faith in vocational curricula and progressive pedagogy was bound to the conviction that a well-trained industrial workforce was critical to the economic well-being of the nation.[16]

In Milwaukee, for example, the Merchants' and Manufacturers' Association raised money for the Trade School for Boys in 1906 and a year later the Milwaukee public schools took it over. The initial interest in the school came from prominent local manufacturers who needed young men with skills that could be used in their foundries to design, draft, and manufacture steam engines and machine tools. Pattern making, molding, and machinist trades became the core curriculum of the Trade School. Students learned to draft and interpret drawings. The math they did consisted of practical problems in arithmetic, algebra, and geometry connected to making patterns and creating molds. Students visited foundries to compare different methods of making molds. The machinist and tool-making shops had modern industrial machines and tools; students learned how to care for and use both. Teachers seldom lectured to students.[17]

At the Manhattan Trade School for Girls, established in 1902 as a private school by business entrepreneurs and taken over by the New York City public schools in 1910, hundreds of girls took courses in dressmaking, children's clothing, lingerie, lampshades, and millinery. They learned to operate machines making gloves and straw hats. They took home what they had made and brought into school ideas they had picked up at home and in the neighborhood.[18]

And in Muncie, Indiana, during the 1920s, two sociologists described how the curriculum for many students had become directly linked to the real world. "Actual conditions of work in the city's factories are imported into the school shops; boys bring repair work from their homes; they study auto mechanics by working on an old Ford car; they design and draft, and make patterns for lathes and drill presses, the actual casting being done by a Middletown factory."[19]

Beyond vocational schools and separate courses, business and civic leaders joined educational progressives to establish kindergartens, junior high schools, and comprehensive high schools to cope with increasing numbers of immigrant children, non-English-speaking students, and graduates unequipped to enter the industrial work-place. In time, educators embraced the ideas of progressive pedagogy at all levels of schooling, such as students planning activities with their teacher, sustained student participation in discussions, multi-age groupings within a school, cooperative groups working on proj-ects, and connecting curriculum to the real world. Progressives believed these ideas and practices would transform teaching and learning in all classrooms. By the 1930s, efficiency-minded and peda-gogical progressives had become the establishment and their lan-guage and ideas dominated educational talk.[20]

Yet except for kindergarten, the primary grades of elementary school, and vocational courses, progressive pedagogies in the 1920s and 1930s hardly entered the majority of classrooms. Within most secondary classrooms, teacher-centered—or what many efficiency-minded progressives sneeringly called "traditional" practices—con-tinued to dominate the student's day.[21]

A few examples illustrate the point. At the rural Shelton School in eastern Louisiana in 1924, the Fisk University sociologist Charles Johnson's research team visited the one-room schoolhouse that served sixty black pupils covering seven grades. The teacher passed out two half-sheets of paper to each student, saying, "It's got to do you all day, so be careful with it." She looked at one of the visitors and said: "We don't have no pencils; we don't have no books; we don't have anything." She turned to the class:

Take pages 45 to 50, seventh grade. Sixth grade, take pages 20 to 30. Now read this and tell me what you read when I come back . . . All right, fourth and fifth grade, spelling. The first word is *correspond*. It means to write people. Second, *instrument*—something you use. Do you know any *instrument* you'd like to play? Come on, talk up. Do you have a speller, Fred? No? Well, just sit and listen. You'll have to do without. Third, *examination*, sometimes we have *yes* and *no*—that's *examination*. Fourth, *ten*-

nis—that's a game. Fifth, *ninety,* counting from *one* to *ninety.* All right that's your spelling. Use them in sentences.[22]

In 1935 Thomas Briggs, a professor at Teachers College, Columbia, sent a graduate student into twenty-one high schools in suburbs of New York City to "observe the work of the best teachers of any subject." Principals selected 104 teachers to be observed. Briggs analyzed the data the student brought back and found that 80 percent of the teachers taught from the textbook for the entire period of instruction. The rest had classrooms where students participated in discussions and where teachers made strong links between current events and academic content. Nearly two-thirds of the teachers used "the conventional procedure of questions by the teacher on an assignment with answers by the pupils or of specific directions followed by board or seat work."[23]

In 1952 John Dewey looked back on progressivism in education and noted:

> There is a great deal of talk about education being a cooperative enterprise in which the teachers and students participate democratically, but there is far more talk about it than the doing of it. To be sure, many teachers, particularly in the kindergarten and the elementary schools, take the children into sharing with them to an extent impossible and inconceivable under the old system . . . In the secondary schools, . . . however, there isn't much sharing on the part of teachers in the needs and concerns of those whom they teach.[24]

I can add no gloss to Dewey's judgment.

In the early twenty-first century, the U.S. economy is no longer anchored in manufacturing but in the creation, production, and distribution of information and services. Corporate leaders now see academic courses—a general education—and standardized testing as essential to prepare students for twenty-first century jobs. English, history, literature, math, science, and foreign languages—once considered liberal arts courses—are viewed by employers as de facto vocational subjects since they equip high school students with the knowledge, attitudes, and skills needed in an information-based workplace.

Furthermore, the process has to begin early in a child's life. In 2003 federal officials mandated that all four-year-olds enrolled in Head Start, an anti-poverty program begun in 1965 under the original Elementary and Secondary Education Act, had to take a standardized test before entering kindergarten. A psychologist and professor advising federal policymakers about the test said: "If you were the head of any industry I know—automobiles, pharmaceuticals, take any product you would use—you have to have a quality assurance system in place to determine how your product is faring in terms of quality." Reform coalitions have pressed states and districts for higher academic standards, standardized testing, and accountability, changes aimed at graduating students with high school and college credentials that signal employers they have acquired the necessary workplace attitudes and skills.[25]

Business-inspired reforms since the 1980s, however, have been far less concerned about how teachers teach and students learn than their progressive forebears were. Beyond pedagogy, business-minded school officials have concentrated on setting standards, improving the quality of teachers, holding students and practitioners accountable for results, and, most important, raising test scores. A former New York City chancellor (and corporate lawyer), Harold Levy, crisply expressed this view: "That's the bottom line. Business has profit and loss. The school system has students and . . . there is nothing more important than our getting the children up to the levels of reading and math so that they can get through these exams and go on to successful careers. That's what this system is about. The minute we take our eyes off that we begin doing something wrong."[26]

By the late 1990s, there were far fewer progressive kindergartens, middle schools, vocational education courses, and academic teachers who sought greater student participation, active learning, deeper understanding of content, and democratic classroom practices. Kindergartens have become more like boot camps for the first grade; middle schools have become staging grounds for demanding high school academic courses; and there has been a steady decline in traditional vocational courses, as high schools have become increasingly college-preparatory and test-driven. An elementary school principal in Louisville, Kentucky, said in 2003: "Every chance we saw to return to a more traditional setting, we took it." Many of the progressive practices in kindergartens, middle schools, and vocational courses now being shunned were the very ones hailed by an earlier generation of business-minded reformers.[27]

Why have reforms sponsored by highly influential business and civic coalitions in the past century managed to establish new goals for public schools and alter their curricula, organizations, and governance and yet had marginal and unintended effects on classrooms? Part of the answer can be found in a tendency to confuse policy talk with policy action, both of which differ from policies being implemented in classrooms. Both promoters of reforms and critics of public schools often mistake words for actual changes in practice, an error also committed by reformers and journalists who report on reforms. The error is a major one because schools and districts are not command-and-control organizations in which words are swiftly converted into actions.[28]

The rest of the answer—and one that reveals clearly the limits of business-inspired reforms—can be found within the organizational and political web of connections that frame teaching and learning in classrooms. Few reformers, including very smart business leaders, have heeded the well-documented history of designs that went unimplemented or were adopted and only partially put into practice. A form of amnesia also afflicts reformers concerning how often well-intended efforts aimed at improving classrooms have had untoward outcomes. A brief journey through that history may help readers recall lessons that earlier generations of reformers learned.

Interventions to Change Classroom Practices

Policy researchers and historians have studied the relationship between reforms adopted by state and federal policymakers and what changes actually occur in schools and classrooms. Examining that history, including the past quarter-century of business-inspired reforms, prompts three questions:

- What happens in classrooms after policymakers adopt reforms?
- What do students gain from policies aimed at altering teaching practices?
- What have been the expected and unexpected consequences for administrators and teachers of implementing state, federal, and local policies of standards-based reform, testing, and accountability?

Answers to these questions are straightforward. At each link in the reform chain, from federal to state to local policy, adaptations have occurred that have had both intended and unintended effects on the conduct of schooling, classroom practices, and student outcomes. Rather than summarize the considerable literature, I condense its primary lessons.[29]

Policies Are Intentions, Not School Practices

Virtually every state has mandated standards-based reform. The federal No Child Left Behind legislation requires states to implement a complex set of conditions, including annual testing of students and benchmarks of adequate yearly progress on those tests. National associations of businesses have vigorously endorsed these state and federal laws. Yet quite different incarnations of standards-based reform and testing exist in states and districts although they share the same label. No generic factory-produced model of standards-based reform and tests has yet rolled off any federal or state assembly line. And that is because policy goals are intentions (some say, hypotheses), often inspirationally (and vaguely) worded, that policymakers seek to put into practice within a fragmented, decentralized system of schooling using a small set of blunt-edged tools.[30]

State and federal officials use mandates, incentives, technical assistance, court decisions, and sanctions (and mixes thereof) to spur local school boards, principals, and teachers to convert policymakers' aspirations into daily practices. District school boards have the same machinery at their disposal for schools. But business leaders, policymakers, and district school board members do not run schools or teach students. Practitioners do. Between top policymakers and teachers, there are many links in the causal chain between ambitious instructional aims and daily interaction with thirty students.

For policymakers, securing local compliance often trumps achieving desired goals. Title I of the Elementary and Secondary Education Act (1965) in the Act's first twenty-five years, for example, got most districts to target funds to poor children. Whether those funds produced the improved test scores sought in the law has been debated ever since. Far more important to practitioners than compliance with regulations, however, is whether teachers develop their knowledge and skills to implement the desired changes.[31]

Because principals and teachers are gatekeepers to school and classroom improvements, their perceptions, beliefs, knowledge, attention, motivation, and skills come into play when policies from state, federal, and district levels arrive at the schoolhouse steps. Many factors shape what happens to those policies once the classroom door closes. Consider how teachers and principals make sense of new policies in light of their pre-service education, classroom materials, actual tests students take, and professional help practitioners receive to expand their expertise. All of these in varied ways affect the implementation of policies intended to change routine classroom practices and produce student gains in academic achievement.[32]

Adaptations Reign

If policymakers expect from local educators flawless implementation of higher standards, except for particular efforts (see below), they engage in wishful thinking. Everyone's thumbprints smudge educational policies as they wend their way toward classrooms. State and federal officials interpret the legislation when they draft rules to govern local educators; officials seldom budget enough money to cover total costs of implementing the policy, so district board members drop those expensive parts for which they would have to pay—I could easily extend this list but will stop here. Novice, mid-career, and veteran teachers also filter the new instructional policy through their experiences and beliefs and decide what will work with their students. Thus determining whether a policy "works" depends upon specifying exactly what was put into practice when, by whom, where, and under what conditions.[33]

Context Shapes Implementation

States differ from one another in their history, political cultures, resources, and populations. A federal policy that officials expect to be implemented uniformly in both Rhode Island and Texas will yield disappointment. Within a state, Los Angeles Unified School District and Beverly Hills abut one another yet their differences in size, capacity to finance schools, and children's ethnicity, race, and social class mean that each district's students and practitioners will respond differently to state and federal policies aimed at their classrooms.

Even within the same district, say the city of Boston, Burke High School and Boston Latin have very different student demography, teachers, administrators, and available resources. When one adds in the professional community (or lack of one) in a school, the differences may be even greater. Consequently, each school and faculty (and each teacher) responds differently not only to district directives but also to those from the state commissioner of education.[34]

A specific instance illustrates these points. The state of California, with six million students taught by nearly three hundred thousand teachers in more than eight thousand schools in nearly a thousand districts, has introduced new policies on the teaching of reading three times in the past eight years. From the 1970s to the mid-1990s, state policy encouraged teachers to use the "whole language" approach. This approach to reading emphasized understanding text, integration of writing, reading, storytelling, and appreciation of reading; it deemphasized phonics, skills-based decoding of text, and similar methods. The role of the teacher was to guide students in making sense of what they were reading. Direct instruction in decoding and phonics was acceptable but not heavily emphasized.

In 1995 the legislature, under great pressure from parents, taxpayer groups, and business leaders who were outraged because California students performed poorly in reading on national tests, mandated a "balanced approach" to reading. The new law required fresh instructional materials that contained systematic instruction in phonics and professional development for administrators and teachers to use phonics. The state board of education and department of education adopted new reading textbooks, standards for reading, curricular frameworks, and tests that reflected this "balanced approach."[35]

Then in 1998 the state board of education issued an even more specific curriculum framework for reading that further narrowed instruction to prescribed skills taught in isolation rather than in context. The role of the teacher was to provide direct instruction in phonics, and students were to practice separate skills of reading. New state tests reflected this emphasis on reading as decoding text.

What happened in the classroom as these policy shifts occurred? Researchers who interviewed teachers and observed reading instruction in elementary schools found much variation in teachers' responses. Teachers adapted, combined, and even ignored these changing policy messages about how to teach reading. During and after the policy shifts, the teaching of reading varied from teacher to teacher as they made sense of the conflicting messages from the state capital. Overall, teachers' responses to these new laws and policy documents were shaped by the teachers' longstanding beliefs about students, about how to teach reading, and about prior teaching practices. To the degree that policy changes reinforced their beliefs and practices, no noticeable modifications occurred. When some teachers did make marginal changes in their approaches to reading in response to these policy shifts, such changes were negotiated through engagement with trusted colleagues and members of professional communities, not by teachers directly focusing on the new mandates, frameworks, or materials.[36]

Thus context shapes what happens to policies in classrooms. As classroom guardians, teachers determine individually to what degree they will accept, reject, or modify a mandate from their principal, superintendent, state legislature, or U.S. president. Teachers are, in the crisp phrase used by Andrew Porter and his colleagues, active "policy brokers." Determining how policymakers' intentions, teachers' adaptations, or other factors have influenced students' learning is an enormously complex task.[37]

Assessment Remains Primitive

For policies aimed at improving students' academic achievement, the criteria used to measure effectiveness (also ineffectiveness) have been severely narrowed in the past quarter-century to gains and losses on standardized test scores. Most federal and state policymakers are familiar with the strengths and weaknesses of the tests and the professional standards for judging whether tests are being properly or improperly used. Nonetheless, scores on state and national tests are used to evaluate whether standards-based reforms are successful.[38]

In equating academic achievement with test scores, business-minded reformers and policymakers ignore the critical assessment of whether the policy itself has been partially, moderately, or fully implemented. After all, without ample evidence of whether teachers are putting all, most, or even a smidgen of the policy into practice, the overall worth of the venture can hardly be judged accurately.

For example, if a new state policy called for teachers to teach math or reading differently, were teachers afforded multiple and extended opportunities to learn about the new approaches? Were special lessons and materials made available and demonstrated to teachers? Did teachers actually use the different ways of teaching math or reading in their classrooms? Were the tests connected to the policy's aims, professional development opportunities, and classroom materials?

Although some researchers have begun to construct measures that begin to answer these implementation questions, their work, sadly, remains on the periphery of most policy research. Instead, the easiest and least useful measure—test scores—dominates policymakers' judgments.[39]

Policies Have Unforeseen Consequences

If the concentration on test scores has emerged as a consequence of the implementation of standards-based reform and accountability, other unintended outcomes for administrators, teachers, students, and parents have also arisen in recent decades. Since the early 1980s, business leaders and civic-minded reformers have called for and eventually gotten a uniform academic curriculum stripped of traditional vocational courses and infused with more tests and coercive measures of accountability. If anything, these reforms have polished and buffed up the traditional age-graded school with its time schedules, curriculum divided by grades, tests, annual promotions, and teacher-centered practices. Within that framework, the grandparents of today's students would find familiar teacher practices including daily homework, lectures, completion of worksheets in class, pop quizzes, and chapter-by-chapter plodding through textbooks. Laptops and hand-held devices would surely strike grandparents as novel ways of learning, but the classroom routines, the teacher-centeredness of the class, and the end products the machines are used for would be easily recognizable.

Many elementary and secondary teachers complain that they have had to reduce their use of student projects and portfolios to assess work, and to make fewer connections between the content they teach and what happens in children's lives. They have been pressured to take time out from their already packed schedules to prepare students for tests that determine whether the school will receive an award (such as a cash payment or a certificate of merit) or a penalty (such as public notice of failing to perform adequately, probation, or being closed down). Such teachers have had to work out a subtle blend of the old and the new.[40]

What business-inspired reformers wanted for state and local curricula, tests, and "bottom line" accountability has largely been achieved at the cost of preserving orthodox school organization and conventional teaching practices that an earlier generation of business-led reformers severely criticized as both traditional and regimented. Now only one kind of "good" district, only one kind of "good" school, and only one kind of "good" teaching is considered correct.

According to current ideology, a "good" district improves its test scores, holds its principals and teachers accountable for raising academic achievement, and complies with state and federal mandates. A "good" school is age-graded, with all students moving from one level to another after thirty-six weeks. In a "good" school students take rigorous subjects, master content, use computers, score well on annual standardized tests, and go on to college. A "good" school is one in which teachers rely on textbooks, give lots of homework, and test students often to see if they are learning the prescribed content and skills. The pedagogy is largely teacher-centered and geared to getting students to do well on the required tests. Whether these versions of "good" schooling and teaching secure desired student outcomes remain an open question.[41]

I do not want to leave the impression that the success of the current reform coalition in shaping federal, state, and local policies to create one kind of "good" school has foisted an unpopular approach to schooling and teaching upon unaware or unwilling parents and taxpayers. On the contrary, the consensus among business leaders, policymakers, teachers' unions, and civic groups of what constitutes a "good" school and "good" teaching has converged with similar views that many parents and taxpayers have held for decades.

In reviewing public opinion polls since the 1940s, I have found time and again that respondents wanted safe public schools that ensured basic literacy, taught respect for authority, and instilled proper behavior in children. They also wanted age-graded schools to monitor students' academic achievement and give parents reports on how their children compare to others, both locally and nationally. They wanted "real schools." Repeatedly, Americans have told pollsters that they wanted their schools to prepare graduates to go on to college. For the past two decades or more, corporate executives and top public officials have been preaching sermons about educating children that most—but not all—parents and taxpayers already believed.[42]

In the steady push from business leaders for higher academic standards, more testing, and holding students and educators responsible for outcomes, policymakers (and parents) have endorsed a system of schooling that has hardened traditional forms of school organization and narrowed classroom pedagogies, giving them a legitimacy that progressive educators once held prior to World War II but now could only envy. Such effects on school organization and classroom instruction heighten doubts about whether teachers can (or should) teach for deep understanding of concepts, connect the world outside the school to schoolbook knowledge, integrate subject matter across disciplines, promote creative problem solving, and foster critical and analytic thinking skills.[43]

These six lessons that I have derived from the ample literature on state and federal interventions to improve classroom practices raise hard questions about the supposed virtues of business-inspired approaches, especially about the assumption that the adopted policies are implemented as intended and subsequently alter classroom practices. For those who yearn for silver linings to ominous clouds, glimmers of hope can be extracted from a few state and federal policies that have achieved intended results. There have been isolated instances in which state and federal policymakers, working in a decentralized system of dispersed power, have indeed cultivated local educators' capacities to innovate, gain knowledge and skills, and become committed to improving classroom practices and students' achievement.[44]

The federally initiated National Diffusion Network (1974–1985) helped local educators implement faithful replicas of school programs that were researched-based and proven in practice to improve academic achievement. Subsequent federal efforts along the same line can be seen in whole school reforms.[45]

Changing one school at a time is part of a tradition dating back to the late 1970s. At that time researchers, allied with federal and state reformers, identified urban elementary schools as "effective," that is, they found that those schools exceeded expectations by scoring higher on national standardized tests in reading and math than they were predicted to score given their numbers of poor and minority students. The effective schools movement throughout the 1980s spawned federally endorsed school-by-school reform and eventually led to many ventures including the jointly publicly and privately funded New American Schools Development Corporation

(NASDC), which, as I noted earlier in this chapter, changed its name to New American Schools. The movement to improve U.S. schools one at a time gained legitimacy from the federally funded Comprehensive School Reform Demonstration Program, which began in 1998. Districts and states now choose from many whole school reform models on federally approved menus of programs.[46]

Yet with nearly ninety thousand schools in the country, changing one school at a time makes policymakers impatient. Scaling up the process to transform hundreds of schools simultaneously gives them an adrenaline rush. Many states have pursued systemic reform in all schools, by legislating academic standards, adopting curriculum frameworks, and launching new tests to bring these reforms into closer alignment in the hope of raising student achievement across the entire state. In only a few states, however, have policymakers gone beyond gaining local compliance to mandates to render substantial assistance to principals and teachers. Kentucky and California offer instructive examples.[47]

Since the Kentucky state supreme court ordered a complete overhaul of the financing and operation of the state's schools, and since the subsequent passage of the comprehensive Kentucky Education Reform Act (KERA) in 1990, researchers have documented both compliance and capacity building with standards-based reform, testing, and accountability across the state's schools. School curricula are more sharply focused on state standards. Classrooms are better equipped, and teachers have received much professional development over the years. While much remains to be done, particularly in building practitioners' expertise and their commitment to classroom changes, researchers have concluded that increases in student test scores in the state's elementary schools can be attributed to KERA.[48]

David Cohen and Heather Hill capped a decade-long research effort to examine how California, one of the leaders in setting standards, built the capacities of math teachers to engage in deeper, more complex, and more ambitious teaching. They found that when curricular materials, tests, professional development, and teacher education were aligned closely and sustained, about 10 percent of the teachers who attended state-sponsored professional development sessions changed "their practices . . . appreciably and students' learning improved."[49]

Also, a small number of urban districts, building on state and federal mandates and receiving direct aid from the business community and foundations, have centralized control over instruction, provided strong school and classroom support, and prodded practitioners to develop school-level instructional coherence. In San Diego and Boston, for example, business leaders sought top-down changes in management, curriculum, and instruction, including instructional coaching arrangements that helped teachers and principals focus on literacy and math. Their policies of supplying teacher-coaches, reducing class size, intervening earlier with younger students, and aligning curricula have coincided with steady improvements in elementary (but not secondary) school scores on state tests.[50]

Business and civic leaders in Houston, using different managerial and instructional strategies, have also seen elementary school scores on state tests rise dramatically but had far less success in secondary schools. It is premature to suggest causal linkages for even limited test score gains in these and similar districts; careful and complex studies of whether teachers altered their practices to be consistent with state and district standards and whether those altered classroom practices led to students doing better on state tests must be done over five to ten years, but there are some flickers of hope in these big cities. These varied examples illustrate that some federal, state, and district policies, bolstered by explicit programs to enhance practitioners' knowledge and skills, can reach into classrooms to promote particular kinds of teaching and learning.[51]

Even with these hopeful glimmers, the overall weight of the evidence on federal and state policymaking to improve teaching and learning hardly incites confidence in the strategy of business-minded reformers pressing authorities into adopting their recommendations. The well-documented, failure-studded record of state and federal efforts to achieve intended outcomes in schools, and the repeated instances in which the value of seeking compliance has overwhelmed the value of building practitioners' skills, combine to darken the few rays of hope.

Let me sum up the reasons for this sorry record. First, because state and federal officials seek curricular and instructional uniformity, policy compliance takes on more importance than efforts to improve local educators' expertise, motivation, and commitment to change. No surprise here when considering conditions that state and federal policymakers face. Funds are often short. Constant turnover among elected officials is inescapable. Popular demands for swift outcomes are shrill. Local conditions are out of sync with the mandates. In most cases, the long-term political and financial stability that is essential for sustained improvement is missing. Such instability leads to symbolic compliance. State educators find it much easier to submit reports that adhere to the letter of federal requirements than to make the often difficult and expensive changes that might deepen policy roots in classrooms. Unsurprisingly, local educators also find it easier to submit perfunctory reports to state officials.[52]

Second, the promise of concentrating more authority in state and federal policymakers to secure higher-quality teaching and learning in classrooms has yet to be fulfilled because so much fragmentation and lack of coordination exist between and among the layers of governance and the private sector at all levels of schooling. Politics flourish in the crannies of the decentralized system of governing schools. Even new, web-like political relationships among business leaders, educators, and policymakers cannot fill the many holes in instructional, curricular, and managerial coordination between levels in implementing policies. So the quality of teaching and learning is too often left untouched.

Finally, contemporary business-inspired reformers, unlike an earlier generation of progressive-minded business leaders interested in improving classroom pedagogy, cared far more about complying with curricular standards, tests, and accountability than about teaching and learning. What happened in classrooms was far less important to these reformers than whether every teacher taught the required content and every single student was tested. The late twentieth-century tilt toward familiar approaches to teaching and learning was less of an intended outcome and more the unintended consequence of reformers' inattention to the importance of pedagogy in attaining desired student outcomes of intellectual engagement, deeper understanding of content, and analytic skills.

This brief look at the history of unimplemented policies, adaptations to policies, and unintended (even perverse) consequences of policies aimed at improving teaching and learning makes it clear that reform rhetoric often has little to do with classroom practice. The complexity involved in shaping federal, state, and district policies that will actually improve classroom practice mocks the simplistic reform solutions marketed by business and civic leaders who press to apply private-sector principles to schools. Although business-inspired reformers have had much influence in the form of critiquing underperforming schools and mobilizing political support for setting new goals, governing schools, and establishing new curriculum, when it comes to steering classroom instruction their record has been abysmal. Such accumulated evidence that business influence is strong outside the classroom but weak inside it requires a return to the logic of action that has driven this reform coalition, particularly the assumption that schools are like businesses.

5

ARE PUBLIC SCHOOLS
LIKE BUSINESSES?

When I was growing up in Pittsburgh, Pennsylvania, the idea of going into business for myself (as my older brothers had done) or working for a corporation (as some of my friends eventually chose to do) was missing from my picture of the future. As a son of immigrants and the first in the family to attend college, I believed in the American Dream. My hard-working father rented and then owned a truck and sold pickles, salami, and cheese to Mom-and-Pop stores in western Pennsylvania. He tried again and again to get a foothold on the lowest rung of the middle-class ladder, sometimes reaching a higher rung and then slipping back. He encouraged me, his youngest son, to go to college, and I lived at home and worked at part-time jobs for four years to pay tuition. I graduated in 1955, in the midst of an economic recession, with a degree in history and a license to teach.

As a teacher in ghetto schools between the mid-1950s and the early 1970s, I was preoccupied with getting by financially. My first job as a teacher in 1955 paid $2,000 a year. By 1962 I was earning $6,000 a year, an amount my Depression-scarred father had predicted would make my new family and me comfortable. He was wrong. My wife and I struggled to make ends meet.

I taught history in urban high schools for fourteen years and then moved on to different posts as an educator. My experiences as a practitioner, as a teacher-administrator for four years in a program preparing returned Peace Corps volunteers to teach in ghetto schools, as a district administrator in a large urban school system for two years, as superintendent of a small city district for seven years, and then as an historian of education and policy researcher for the past two decades have shaped my perspective on the questions of whether schools are like businesses and how private-sector leaders have influenced school reform. Although I was entrepreneurial in scrounging resources from superiors, foundations, and colleagues, I did it less to secure additional financial rewards than to strengthen my own teaching and help my students, my programs, and later, my district. The rewards teachers seek in their professional careers are much broader and less concrete than the corporate goal of making a financial profit.[1]

The job in which I had the most contact with business leaders was as superintendent of the public schools in Arlington County, Virginia (1974–1981), a period marked by two recessions, high unemployment, and staggering inflation. International corporations, national firms, and small businesses were heavily involved in Arlington, a county-city of over 160,000 people across the Potomac River from Washington, D.C. The extent of their participation differed little from that in other urban districts.[2]

The Arlington school board annually contracted for millions of dollars' worth of items and services from local banks, wholesalers, food suppliers, and construction companies. From buying Worcestershire sauce to paying retainers to legal firms to using pest control companies, the schools did business with local firms daily.

Young business leaders brought Junior Achievement programs into high schools each year. Local businesses contracted with the district's adult-education center to train and hire non-English-speaking and low-income residents. Each of the county's three comprehensive high schools had vocational education programs that sent hundreds of students into local firms to work a few hours a day. School supervisors hunted for jobs that placed high school students in government agencies, auto shops, and department stores. The district's career center enrolled students in grades ten through twelve in more than a dozen different programs that blended classroom and workplace training in construction, hospitals, motels, television studios, auto body shops, and beauty salons. Arlington realtors cooperated with the career center in finding a house for students to renovate. A network of contacts between businesses and schools throughout Arlington produced steady two-way traffic between classroom and workplace. The array of local and national companies directly involved with the schools was celebrated each June at luncheons to which I was invited to award prizes to top students and praise cooperating business firms.

There were also formal (and traditional) relations between school board and business leaders. The Chamber of Commerce, which I joined in my first year as superintendent, represented the small business, professional, and corporate satellites' concerns in the county. Their education committee included the school district's vocational supervisors, who helped with identifying and placing students in local companies. Each year members of the Arlington County Chamber of Commerce would appear at school board budget sessions to present their views on the next year's expenditures and revenues. Their recommendations seldom varied in my tenure as superintendent: cut administrators, raise class size, reduce proposed teacher salary increases, cut bilingual programs, and get rid of "frills."

For each of the seven years that I served, the Chamber of Commerce fought increases to the school budget, damned teachers' raises as being too high, and criticized programs for non-English-speaking children as costly extravagances. When the annual school budget came before the county's governing body—the county board—which decided how much money to allocate to the schools, the

Chamber urged budget reductions and lobbied the board to either cut the tax rate on property or keep it where it was. The Chamber did support particular improvements such as the career center and the introduction of economics courses that concentrated on the free enterprise system. After a few years of this pattern of treatment, I resigned from the Chamber of Commerce. To the best of my knowledge, the adversarial relations between the Chamber, the school board, and me had little effect on the richly textured relationship of the business community to the schools.[3]

Arlington's businesses were also indirectly involved with the schools through the individual service of civic-minded corporate managers. Business executives often sat on school board–appointed committees or served on advisory councils to neighborhood schools. Occasionally firms would release employees to help the district in tutoring programs and career days held in various schools.

My recollections of business involvement in the Arlington schools underscore three points about the links between businesses and schools. First, a school district is inevitably part of the business community as a corporate entity buying products and enlisting companies to provide services. Second, efforts to improve schools necessarily will involve key business leaders (beyond the local Chamber of Commerce) because of the school board's dependence upon the business community for tax-based revenues, expertise, and political support. Vital interests, however, often clash when school officials seek more revenues by urging higher tax rates that would affect business profits and property owners' finances. Third, businesses' involvement in schools may well arouse tensions simply because the two differ in fundamental values. While schools seemingly behave as business organizations in many respects and even perform business-like functions (managing people, planning, providing services, and budgeting), they nonetheless are expected to meet public obligations and are held politically accountable for their actions and student outcomes, a type of accountability absent from private institutions such as businesses (although market advocates might argue that vigorous competition and the duty company managers owe to shareholders hold companies far more accountable than schools).

One difference between education and business is the values that draw individuals into the two fields. What brings many young people into teaching is an ideal of serving the young. What keeps those who continue in their career as educators, however, is a complicated meld of private interests—job security, summers off, social status—and public values, one of which is the ethic of service in influencing the minds, character, and lives of the young.[4] Those who enter and stay in business are driven by different values—not better or worse, just different. Love of competition, the rewards of winning, of rising to the top of an organization, of successfully building a business and reaping its financial rewards and helping others—all enter into the mix of motives and values of those who pursue business careers.

I don't mean to draw too sharp a contrast: there are educators who start businesses or join firms in sales, marketing, or managing; and there are corporate employees who leave investment banking, marketing, engineering, or managing to become teachers. A teacher-recruiting advertisement on New York City subways, aimed at investment brokers, says: "Stop trading futures and start shaping them." Thomas Choate, to cite another example, after leading software teams for twenty-eight years at General Electric, left the company to become a computer teacher at a high school in Montgomery County, Maryland. "I'm an ex-Marine," Choate told a reporter, "but my first year in the job was the hardest thing I've ever done other than boot camp." A small two-way traffic between business and education careers exists precisely because some people hold both kinds of values, and when retirement creates new opportunities or a particular job becomes too unfulfilling, a person's moral center of gravity may shift.[5]

I have remained an educator for my entire adult life and have not pursued a business career; thus my core values reflect my experiences in schools and universities. Those values undoubtedly shape my analysis of the key assumptions held by business-inspired reformers.

Analyzing Assumptions

One of the core assumptions in the logic of action behind business-inspired school reforms asserts an unfaltering connection between a strong economy and public schools that produce a highly skilled workforce. The belief is that public schools, in failing to fulfill a primary obligation of preparing students for work, have caused wage inequalities, unemployment, low worker productivity, slow economic growth, and reduced global competitiveness—and therefore that the way to solve such serious national problems is to improve the schools. Another assumption is that public schools are like businesses—and therefore that time-tested market principles and practices can be applied to school operations to produce desired outcomes. Since these assumptions are taken for granted by opinion-leading elites and have been the basis of prolonged and intense criticism of public schools, examining them carefully and closely is an essential task.

Ties between Schooling and the Economy

By the end of the twentieth century, economists and policymakers, parents, educators, and taxpayers assumed two crucial causal links between education and the economy: that public investments in schooling produced both individual gains in lifetime earnings and collective benefits for the nation in the form of greater worker productivity, prosperity, a larger share of world markets, and social stability. Economists christened this belief in individual and collective gains accruing from schooling "investment in human capital." The popular belief and the technical phrase were different sides of the same tapestry with identical stitching, seams, and colors. Yet it was a cloth that had accumulated many ripped threads over the decades.

The tears in the cloth came from economists, social scientists, historians, and occasional contrarian policymakers who, citing research studies, contested whether the bonds between schools and the economy were as strong as popularly believed, particularly as inequalities in income rose and fell. The discovery of major flaws in the logic and evidence used to sustain the assumptions means that school policies anchored in these assumptions, at the minimum, can no longer go unquestioned.

Yes, there are obvious connections between whether students drop out of school early or stay to get a diploma and how much money they will earn in their lifetimes. President George W. Bush reminded us of this fact when he said, "Good jobs begin with good schools." Yet economists know that test scores, level of schooling completed, and family background explain less than one-third of the variation in earnings among individuals.[6]

Two different explanations for the variation in people's earnings turn up in study after study. The first is that, while there are other factors, skills are the dominant component in determining earnings. Those who use this explanation, however, point out that databases and studies measure only some of the skills—excluding important ones like interpersonal skills—that count in the workplace. If there were accurate data on a broad repertoire of skills, they claim, more of the variation in earnings would be explained. The other explanation is that earnings are basically determined by discrimination in labor markets, barriers to mobility, differences between unionized and non-unionized workplaces, and employees' preferences for different kinds of jobs.

Note that the two explanations have quite different policy implications. Policymakers adopting the first explanation, which was the dominant one in the twentieth century, push for improved schooling (including a wider range of cognitive, social, and technical skills and job training) as the best way to reduce wage inequalities. Policymakers adopting the second explanation press for energetic enforcement of anti-discrimination laws, better ways of matching workers with jobs, and vigorous labor unions. If economists differ over the reasons for the variation in employees' earnings, they also differ over the connections between education, economic growth, and the stability of the social order.[7]

I am certainly not arguing that schooling is a waste of time or that it doesn't matter. It does matter. I have gained from additional schooling. My wife and daughters have as well. In each of our cases, education plus background plus job opportunities plus luck combined to shape our careers. My point is that experts contest these ties between education and the economy. Another important point is that individual and collective benefits gained from schooling are not one and the same. Among policymakers and the general public, over the decades, the two have merged into one, strengthening the erroneous belief that simply getting more schooling not only enhances one's financial success but somehow magically makes for a stronger economy and society.[8]

There is no way to prove beyond a reasonable doubt that believers in human capital are "right" or "wrong." No scientific study can fully delineate the relationships between the economy and public schooling. Dueling economic studies only underscore the fact that connecting education to the health of the economy is a political, not a technical, issue. Republican presidents of the United States bring in their economic advisers to replace those hired by Democratic presidents. Federal tax and regulatory policies shift as administrations come and go. The economy grows and shrinks; jobs are created and jobs are lost. Tax cuts and tax hikes widen and narrow inequalities in the distribution of wealth. Business associations lobby for standards-based reform and No Child Left Behind legislation. So politics matter. Technical solutions in the form of brand-new tests or superbly crafted academic standards or ways of raising test scores cannot provide job opportunities, reduce inequalities in wealth, or enhance family life.[9]

What matters a great deal in forming public policy is to make clear to voters and opinion-setting elites that unquestioned articles of faith in close ties between education and the economy are suspect because they are often too narrowly focused on what schools can do while ignoring what other institutions contribute to economic growth and productivity. Moreover, the assumptions are contested by experts and need to be subjected to public debate so that fewer unexamined policies and cause-and-effect attributions will be sewn into the tapestry.

I examine the holes in the fabric by asking questions that probe at the causal assumptions embedded in policies that business and civic leaders have promoted for more than a century, particularly in the past three decades:

- Has the mismatch between employers' requirements and workers' skills in an ever-changing economy caused lower wages and higher youth unemployment?
- Does more education make workers more productive?
- Do increases in worker productivity increase the nation's global competitiveness?

The Skills Mismatch

Has the mismatch between employers' requirements and workers' skills in an ever-changing economy caused lower wages and higher youth unemployment? The president of the National Association of Manufacturers (NAM), speaking at the National Skills Summit in 2000, did not mince words about workers' lack of the skills required by employers:

Sixty percent of manufacturers reported in a recent . . . survey that they typically reject half of all job applicants as unqualified. Thirty-six million American adults lack high school diplomas. And, the fact that the annual, 12-month quota for highly trained foreign workers was met within just the first three months of the year speaks to the eagerness of American companies to find employees who can perform sophisticated, high-tech oriented tasks. The NAM has two great concerns in this debate: helping American firms retain their competitive edge and helping our workers gain the skills they need both to contribute to our economic growth and [to] enjoy a *good* standard of living.[10]

Two economists put the danger of a skills mismatch between youth and ever-changing jobs even more bluntly: "In this world you go to war every day, and short of being a millionaire, a very good education is your best armor." However put by private-sector officials or academics, high school graduates' skill deficits have been indicted for slowing national economic growth, lowering wages, and decreasing workplace productivity. In the hand-wringing language of the *Nation at Risk* report (1983), public schools had become a virtual threat to national security in economic warfare with the rest of the world.[11]

The argument that a skills deficit causes lower wages and higher unemployment among young people has both individual and collective implications, fusing the two human capital arguments into one. In other words, according to this argument, youth unemployment, a widening gap between high-salary and low-wage jobs, low worker productivity, and decreasing global competitiveness all result from the lack of knowledge and skills that high school graduates bring to the modern workplace.

This line of argument appeared first in the late nineteenth century, when industrial leaders became deeply concerned about British and

German manufactured products outselling U.S. ones. The president of the National Association of Manufacturers, for example, told members at its annual conference in 1898: "There is hardly any work we can do or any expenditures we can make that will yield so large a return to our industries as would come from the establishment of educational institutions which would give us skilled hands and trained minds for the conduct of our industries and our commerce."[12]

A broad coalition of civic, business, union, and educational leaders pressed district, state, and federal policymakers to introduce vocational curricula into U.S. schools to prepare students for an industrial economy. Beginning during World War I, federal funds subsidized high school industrial arts and home economics courses while states and districts forged ahead to adopt vocational education and guidance in all of its schools.[13]

Through the Great Depression, World War II, the Cold War, and the years of the war in Vietnam, vocational education received steady political and economic support from business and civic elites. Yet youth unemployment still rose and fell, and remained especially high among minority populations. Wage differentials and inequalities in wealth between high school dropouts and college graduates continued to grow, particularly for women and minorities. Nonetheless, even in flush times employers grumbled that high school graduates were unprepared for the workplace.[14]

Critics of the mismatch theory challenge the claim directly. They say that focusing on skills deficits largely blames the individual worker, shifting attention from institutional structures that maintain gender, race, social class, ethnic, and anti-union biases. Wage gaps, for example, between whites and blacks and between female and male workers in certain industries have been noted again and again. That wages differ in the same industries between unionized and non-unionized companies has been established many times. Thus, according to critics, one has to examine not just skill levels but also institutional mechanisms that determine wages.[15]

Doubters of the mismatch theory similarly point out that the Japanese automakers Honda, Nissan, and Toyota have located plants in low-income parts of the United States with minimally educated inhabitants and yet these workers have produced high-quality automobiles as efficiently as in Japan. Moreover, many U.S. corporations relocate factories to other countries where workers are far less educated, receive lower wages, and seldom have unions. Hewlett-Packard, Sun Microsystems, Ford, General Electric, and many other corporations using high-tech production methods have shifted production to Latin America, Southeast Asia, and other developing areas of the world, not because the workforce in those areas possess the requisite skills but to gain access to workers, as in Mexico, who "are 50 percent under the age of 20, average pay [of] $6 per day, [and have] friendly unions."[16]

One critic of the skills deficit argument concluded:

> The point is not that education and training are unimportant; they have always been good ideas. However, they are not enough. The recent growth in inequality [in the 1990s] does not have its origins in the growth of a gap between worker skills and job skill requirements . . . inequality is unlikely to be reduced by skill development initiatives alone. A decline in inequality requires macro policies to maintain growth and full employment and minimum wage and labor policies that directly support . . . [those] in the lower part of the wage distribution.[17]

Another weakness of the mismatch theory is that "skills" are ambiguously defined. Notions about precisely which skills are important for workers to have and are linked to higher wages have shifted repeatedly. A typical list of the "New Basic Skills" needed "to get a middle-class job," according to the economists Richard Murnane and Frank Levy, are:

- The ability to read at the ninth grade level or higher.
- The ability to do math at the ninth grade level or higher.
- The ability to solve semistructured problems where hypotheses must be formed and tested.
- The ability to work in groups with persons of various backgrounds.
- The ability to communicate effectively, both orally and in writing.
- The ability to use personal computers to carry out simple tasks like word processing.[18]

Skeptics point out several problems with such lists of skills. Seldom do the lists overlap very much with the qualities that, according to many surveys, employers want in their entry-level employees: a strong work ethic, reliability, and positive attitudes. In survey after survey, punctuality, dependable work habits, grooming, and being personable trump academic achievements and computer skills.[19]

A 1997 U.S. Census Bureau survey of employers' needs found that the most important measures companies used to hire new employees were attitude and work habits. One senior manager in a major retail chain described what her corporation looks for: "I tell my . . . personnel managers, 'If they don't smile, don't hire them.' I don't care how well-educated they are, how well-versed they are in retail, if they can't smile, they're not going to make a customer feel welcome. And we don't want them in our store." In short, the qualities that matter to employers are personality, dependability, conscientiousness, and motivation.[20]

Finally, one doesn't have to be a skeptic about the skills mismatch thesis to be aware of the rise in youth unemployment during recessions, when high school dropouts and graduates, even those with college degrees, fail to find jobs. In 2001, for example, when the national unemployment rate ticked upward from 5.6 to 5.8 percent, the teen unemployment rate was 17.7 percent. The recession hit younger workers far harder than older ones; of all jobs lost in the recession, 56 percent were held by individuals between the ages of sixteen and twenty-four.[21]

The answer to the question of whether a skills mismatch between high school graduates and the needs of employers has caused wage inequalities and youth unemployment, then, hardly has the taken-for-granted certainty that policymakers, business leaders, journalists, and opinion-setters have expressed for the past thirty years. Increasing the job-ready skills of high school students would hardly erase youth unemployment when millions of jobs go overseas in search of lower wages, not higher skill levels. Yet state and federal policies calling for standards-based reform, testing, and accountability are deeply rooted in the assumption that inadequate skills of youth entering the job market cause unemployment and wage differentials. Although I do not question the contribution that schooling and training can make to reducing skills gaps, critics have raised substantial reservations to make the answer doubtful enough to give policymakers pause.

Education and Productivity

Does more education make workers more productive? The question arises from the sharp drop in worker productivity that occurred in the early 1970s after the burst of economic growth and rising standards of living that the United States enjoyed in the two decades after World War II. Between World War II and 1973, average annual productivity growth was 2.8 percent, sufficient to nearly double living standards in a quarter-century. Since 1973, annual productivity growth has averaged less than 1 percent, a pace that would take over three-quarters of a century to equal the rise in living standards after

World War II. Not until the mid-1990s did labor market productivity again register strong and sustained growth.[22]

Why the sharp drop in the 1970s and 1980s? According to one economist who studied the slowdown, "What happened is, to be blunt, a mystery." In spite of such puzzlement, explaining the reduction in productivity has become a flourishing industry for academics, business leaders, and politicians. And the reason is that explaining decreases in worker productivity—a serious problem related to wages, standards of living, and economic growth—identifies for opinion-setters what the problem is. If policymakers adopt that view of the problem, then certain solutions become attractive.[23]

Economists and social scientists have offered various explanations for the productivity slowdown. Some have pointed out that manufacturing, the engine of economic growth after World War II, had run out of new ideas and techniques by the late 1970s and 1980s, and that new technologies such as robotics, personal computers, fax machines, cell phones, and personal data assistants had not yet achieved critical mass to affect worker productivity. Hence, the slowdown. The solution embedded in this explanation is patience. In time, the new technologies will yield higher productivity.[24]

Other scholars and pundits have turned toward social explanations for slackening productivity. Post–World War II prosperity coincided with a large generational bulge, affectionately called "baby boomers," who were raised in relative affluence compared to their parents' generation, and who were exposed to the new medium of television. Boomers grew up in suburbia during dramatic cultural changes including challenges to all forms of authority, the rise of an urban underclass, and educational mindlessness as evidenced by lower academic standards, falling test scores, and rising drug use in schools. These social and cultural changes, affecting an entire generation, according to some social scientists, explain the productivity slowdown. Shoring up core cultural norms by improving key social institutions (such as schools) will lead to higher productivity.[25]

A third explanation having nothing to do with public schools focuses on government tax and regulatory policies as the source of decreasing productivity. Heavy taxation discouraged consumers from buying products and businesses from investing in new ventures and technologies. Moreover, government regulations added unnecessary costs to businesses, weakening their capacity to compete domestically and in world markets. Public officials, according to this explanation, should cut taxes, especially to help consumers and businesses, and should encourage more competition by freeing up heavily regulated sectors of the economy. In response to tax cuts and deregulation, advocates believe, productivity will rise and economic growth and standards of living will increase.

In the past thirty years, threads of these three explanations appeared in the fabric of adopted policies as Republicans and Democrats moved in and out of the White House, the U.S. Congress, and state offices. The Republican presidents Reagan, George H. W. Bush, and George W. Bush, for example, pursued fiscal policies that cut taxes and deregulated industries while censuring the erosion of cultural values. The Democratic presidents Carter and Clinton also pursued deregulation to foster competition but sought to raise, rather than cut, taxes to provide revenues to alleviate poverty, reduce crime, improve housing, and invest in job training. Business leaders, as usual, lobbied both political parties extensively for favorable fiscal policies.[26]

Most noticeable in these years is that education steadily rose to the top of federal and state political agendas. While Republican presidents fought for lower taxes and deregulation on the theory that individuals would spend more and businesses would invest more thereby triggering more production, job growth, higher wages, and reduced inequalities in wealth, they also fixed upon failing schools as the culprit—among the rival explanations—in slowing down productivity and economic growth. Improving public schools gained both Republican and Democratic support at the federal and state levels, goaded often and persistently by business leaders, allied with civic elites, who endorsed policies that would furnish students with the skills indispensable in high-paying information-based jobs.

The major conceptual problem for economists, social scientists, and policymakers has been to connect schooling to worker productivity. The metrics used by scholars and policymakers are helpful but leave a lot to be desired. For example, focusing on the relationship between annual and lifetime earnings and years of schooling says everything about the amount of schooling and the level of earnings but nothing about the content of schooling or actual performance in the workplace.[27]

What measures are used? Many economists assume that student cohorts' scores on paper-and-pencil tests of general intelligence and math and reading achievement can be linked to wages and supervisors' ratings within and across different private-sector industries. Economists connect test scores to hourly wages by taking gains in scores and computing corresponding increases in dollars earned. They also use supervisors' judgments of worker performance (high, medium, and low) to estimate worker productivity. These measures are, of course, proxies for actual productivity. They do stretch reality.[28]

Using existing standardized achievement tests, for example, assumes that these tests measure the analytical, creative, and practical skills as well as positive attitudes valued by employers. Paper-and-pencil tests become surrogates for the entire quality of a school's faculty, pedagogy, curriculum, ethos, and relationships between and among students and teachers. Few tests can capture these markers of the vital content of schools. Moreover, using hourly wages as a metric assumes that employers and workers have complete information about competitive markets and negotiate the best wages for both parties. As for supervisor ratings, the varied meanings that supervisors across and within industries have of "good," "fair," or "poor" performance (or high, medium, and low) and the high subjectivity of such ratings raise grave doubts about whether such judgments can be used as surrogates for productivity. Finally, these measures require complex manipulation of data and substantial interpretation, and they contain many methodological problems. Experts disagree on the worth of such data in estimating worker productivity. Yet the measures are accepted as factual and real.[29]

Spotlighting improved schools as the solution to the problem of low worker productivity is unsurprising given the long history of public officials and business elites turning to school reform to solve serious national problems. And yet from another point of view it *is* surprising—because economists and other social scientists have offered policymakers three alternative solutions: adopt policies that increase the quantity and quality of business capital (for example, cut taxes, increase investment incentives); encourage public measures (such as funding technology research) that support the private sector; and improve the quality of workers (invest in schooling and job training). Yet "no reasonable economist can claim that we have an accurate accounting of the value of each of these three sources of growth [in productivity]." One economist put it more bluntly: "We can devise policies to raise these markers [test scores in math and reading]. But will those policies have any effect on productive skills or individual or national income? There are almost no studies that attempt to show a causal link from educational policy reforms to test scores to adult outcomes such as earnings." Nonetheless, improving low-performing public schools has long been a primary goal of elected officials, business leaders, and educational policymakers. Although economists have disagreed among themselves as to what extent and in what ways more and better education lifts worker productivity, the dominant popular and scholarly belief in human capital has glossed over these experts' squabbles.[30]

Productivity and Global Competitiveness

Do increases in worker productivity increase the nation's global competitiveness? For the Stanford professor of education Ellwood P.

Cubberley the answer was yes. In 1909 he said: "Whether we like it or not, we are beginning to see that we are pitted against the world in a gigantic battle of brains and skill, with the markets of the world, work for our people, and internal peace and contentment as the prizes at stake." Eighty years later, Xerox CEO David Kearns agreed, voicing the common assumption held by top business leaders: "We can't have a world-class economy without a world-class workforce, from senior scientists to stock clerks. And we cannot have a world-class workforce without world-class schools."[31]

The argument that increased labor force productivity (as measured by students' performance on international and domestic standardized tests) will not only increase standards of living but also strengthen U.S. standing in world markets has been used for decades, by business and civic leaders and journalists, as a reason to reform the public schools. The rock-hard faith in the ties between worker productivity, higher standards of living, and global competitiveness has been invoked time and again to justify tax cuts (and increases), more spending (or less) on defense, and policies to change the schools.[32]

Yet some economists and social scientists contest this taken-for-granted belief. One leading critic, for example, argues that the central issue in the U.S. economy is the need to regain the productivity growth of the post–World War II decades in non-manufacturing sectors—not to enhance global competitiveness—because higher productivity is closely linked to better wages and a rising standard of living. About 20 percent of U.S. workers are engaged in manufacturing (which does produce goods traded on the world market); 80 percent work in services not traded in world markets (although some services are, such as banking, finance, insurance, filmmaking, and higher education). Thus raising productivity in manufacturing would increase overall economic productivity far less than raising productivity in the service sector, which would mean higher wages and enhanced standard of living for the entire country.[33]

That economists duel with one another is common. The claim that low worker productivity has slowed down the U.S. economy and made for a shrinking share of global markets, however, was weakened considerably by nearly a decade of unbroken prosperity in the 1990s amid high foreign trade deficits and increased worker productivity. (In fact, given the increases in productivity during the late 1990s, a reasonable person might have expected schools to be praised for preparing the graduates who contributed so well to this remarkable economic growth. Yet few corporate leaders or U.S. presidents or state governors publicly attributed either the prosperity or the increased productivity to improved U.S. schools.)

Moreover, after the early 1980s, when the media magnified perceptions that Japan and Germany were outperforming the United States in world markets, the mid-1990s found these previously successful foreign competitors in a prolonged slump, precisely when the U.S. economy enjoyed an eight-year stretch of prosperity. Few pundits or business leaders pointed out that the highly productive employees contributing to the U.S. boom were the very same cohorts who supposedly had been poorly schooled in the 1980s. Even when the years after that economic surge brought with the U.S. recession of 2000–2002, growing federal deficits, and increasing costs of occupying Iraq and fighting terrorism around the world, few economists or public officials doubted the predominance of the U.S. economy in the global economy or its international competitiveness.[34]

As we have seen, the causal linkages between students' test scores, worker productivity, and the nation's global competitiveness are rooted in a robust popular conviction but surrounded by factually frail assumptions. Invoking an idea grounded more in mainstream belief than in evidence may be useful to politicians interested in reforming a vulnerable social institution, but this approach hardly meets the standards of evidence that CEOs demand before adopting new policies and putting them into practice in their own organizations. This brings us to the cardinal premise anchoring the entire logic of business-inspired reform: that public schools are like businesses.

Questioning the Basic Assumption

Enough stories have been told of business leaders spending time in schools and coming to realize their sheer complexity. Recall Jamie Vollmer's anecdote about blueberry ice cream. Loaded with advice gained from experience in their companies, many business leaders enter schools confident of their ability to improve them yet come away humbled by their contact with principals, teachers, and students and questioning the apparent similarities between schools and business firms. Still, few business leaders actually study or experience the daily demands of schools; for those who do, their voices seldom reach beyond an occasional news item in a paper or a vignette on a TV program. The overwhelming consensus remains that businesses have much to teach educators and that if school folks would only listen carefully to what company leaders have learned and then apply the lessons, schools would improve.

What Worked and What Failed

In earlier chapters I described the ideological success of beliefs in individual and collective benefits flowing to the nation from cementing schooling to a strong economy. I also pointed out the triumphant grafting of business-inspired designs onto public school goals, governance, organization, and curriculum. In tallying up the reform successes in schools from the late 1800s to the present, I also described the practical failures of merit pay and school-based decisionmaking. Recall also the early twentieth-century progressive business leaders' enthusiasm for learning by doing and the installing of vocational courses in secondary schools. Learning by doing barely reshaped teaching practices in formal schooling beyond the primary grades. As time passed, vocational education became a second-class curriculum that college-bound students largely avoided. In many cities it became a dumping ground for those who were failing academic courses.

Districts and schools did adopt business-designed reforms fairly often, thanks to the stature, organizing capabilities, and resources that the private sector possesses, particularly when corporate leaders forged political alliances with civic elites. At best, then, the historical record of applying business principles to school organizations is mixed.

There is one principle, however, drawn from multiple sources in the history of American education, that market ideologists and business leaders polished up and took as their own: parental choice in schools. Economists, corporate leaders, and the Republican party, astutely building upon a long tradition in public schooling, sought to restore greater family influence in their children's education. This tradition began with the experiences of urban Catholics seeking schools for their parishioners and German parents in the Midwest wanting their local schoolteachers to teach in German in the mid-nineteenth century. A century later, in the 1960s and 1970s, political liberals promoted parental choice through vouchers because of their deep concern about ghetto-bound parents having to send their children to ineffective urban schools. Thus different versions of choice with no ties to market principles have been advocated by reformers. By the 1990s, however, parental choice in schooling had been confiscated by market-oriented reformers, and the issue had been rephrased to read: More consumer choice leads to competition among schools and more innovation, both of which ultimately improve the education children receive.[35]

Vouchers, Charters, and For-Profit Schools

Advocates of school choice, such as the economists and Nobel laureates Milton Friedman and Gary Becker, the Federal Reserve Board chairman, Alan Greenspan, and economic advisers serving the current U.S. president, promote the market axioms that wherever monopolies or cartels reign the public seldom benefits and that competition and consumer choice improve products. Government-run schools (a.k.a. public schools), according to these believers in choice and competition, are a public monopoly, and more parental choice will yield better schooling. Deregulating (or to use the critics' word, privatizing) public schools will lead to improved performance. Yet policies designed to give parents more choice within public education have been fiercely contested for nearly four decades.[36] As part of my analysis of the application of business principles to public schools I want to examine briefly the claim that expanded choice (by means of vouchers, charter schools, inter- and intra-district transfers) yields heightened competition between private and public schools and among public schools, and that this improves the overall quality of teaching and learning.

Although state-subsidized vouchers and charter schools have existed over a decade and affect only a tiny fraction of U.S. public school students, the available evidence is controversial. Even if we put the best spin on that evidence, the causal claims of proponents of choice and competition are transparently weak. Studies of charter schools and voucher experiments in selected cities try to answer the following questions: Do voucher or charter school students perform the same as, better, or worse on standardized reading and math tests than a matched set of students? Have districts where charter schools have been established and where voucher-carrying students leave public schools to attend private schools responded to the competition by reducing inefficiencies and making improvements?

Both advocates and opponents of school choice dispute the research design, sample selection, methodologies, and quality of evidence of these studies. In any case, the findings of these studies hardly bang the drums for either vouchers or charter schools. Frederick Hess concludes his study of vouchers in three cities by saying: "Competition did not rapidly bulldoze away inefficiencies or drive systemic improvement in teaching and learning; nor did it lead school systems to revamp governance, management, or operations . . . These results are properly understood not as simple precursors of dramatic change, but as evidence that the political pressure unleashed by choice programs will yield complex outcomes."[37] For charter schools, Richard Rothstein concludes: "Letting many flowers bloom through chartering may, in the end, be the best thing that could happen to public schools. This will not be because—as charter proponents expect—charters will transform regular education. On the contrary: as charter schools face the same problems regular schools confront, they will find themselves, perhaps to their own astonishment, developing remarkably similar solutions."[38]

In Texas, George W. Bush pushed hard for charter schools when he served as governor, and there were about two hundred such schools in 2003. But at that time almost 15 percent of charters had closed their doors, and nearly two-thirds of the forty-six schools rated by the state as low performing were charters. Still popular in Texas but competing for ever-shrinking state funds, the choice movement in the state that gave the nation No Child Left Behind looked tattered in 2003. States and districts, thus far, have responded minimally, circuitously, or not at all to threats of losing students to other schools— contradicting the grounding premise of those who advocate choice and competition.[39]

Of course, research seldom determines the fate of a reform strategy. Politics and judicial decisions move policymakers far more than the results of researchers' inquiries. The U.S. Supreme Court's *Zelman* decision (2002) declaring that Cleveland's voucher program was constitutional, for example, directly prompted the state of Colorado to establish a voucher program less than a year after the court ruled. The political popularity of charter schools as alternatives for minority students, teachers, and parents seeking customized options makes it highly unlikely that elected officials will rescind legislation authorizing charters.[40]

A more direct way to test the application to schooling of lessons learned in the marketplace is to examine for-profit firms that have contracted with school boards to operate individual public schools.[41] Since 1998, nearly 50 profit-seeking firms—or to use a phrase invented by investment bankers, education management organizations (EMOs)—have contracted with school boards to manage more than 400 public schools (many of which are already charter schools) in 24 states and the District of Columbia. Edison Schools Inc., for example, operates 150 public schools (including some charter schools) enrolling 82,000 students in 23 states and 48 cities. Edison's promotional material announces that of the nearly 15,000 public school systems in the nation, "Edison has grown to become the 36th largest."[42]

But why the boom of privatizing or deregulating public schools in the 1990s? Compelling explanations point to Americans' reduced faith in government coinciding with swelling support for conservative ideas and the crescendo of support for market capitalism that followed the fall of Soviet communism in Eastern Europe and Russia. Not to be ignored is the "businessification" of American life or what other writers have called the pervasive consumer culture that has enveloped the society in recent decades, and that reached a peak in the eight-year stretch of unparalleled prosperity of the 1990s.[43]

Evidence for these trends can be found in Americans' increasing participation in the stock market. In 1983 about 20 percent of American households owned stock directly or through mutual funds; by 1999 nearly 50 percent did. Sports and entertainment have become corporate efforts where "salary caps" and "labor strikes" compete with newspaper box scores on sports and style pages and TV programs. Toddlers and kindergartners have become full-fledged consumers steering parents in stores to brand-name products advertised on television.

While I find these explanations persuasive, the fact that for-profit schools (and, I might add, voucher experiments and most charter schools) are largely located in heavily minority low-income urban districts suggests that an equally credible explanation is sheer desperation on the part of poor parents and elected policymakers over finding cheap ways to improve schools for the poor. No sure-fire solutions have yet appeared to reduce the enormous test score gaps between minorities and whites, or the high dropout rates of urban minority youth as the grim statistics of ghetto life take their toll on schools. In such a dire situation, many parents see choice as their children's ticket out of ghettos and barrios. They welcome schools run by for-profit firms, accept vouchers, and support charters, all of which seem sensible and fair to elected policymakers seeking both votes and social justice for children locked in poverty.[44]

Explaining why the upsurge of for-profits, voucher experiments, and charters occurred since the early 1990s, however, does not answer the larger question of whether the proliferation of for-profits has produced better schools. Because for-profit ventures in the public sector are controversial—consider for-profit prisons and hospitals —studies of effectiveness are highly charged, and one would expect pronouncements of success to be challenged quickly by opponents of corporate ventures in running schools. And that is exactly what has happened to assertions about how successful for-profit schools have been. Putting aside the thorny issue of exactly what success means, the policy elites have generally accepted the use of test scores to measure it. Investors look for rising value in company stock and dividends on their holdings. For parents, a feeling that their children are attending a better school than their previous one is a measure of success. Thus far the results have been, at best, uncertain.

Most for-profit firms publish test score data. Edison Schools Inc., for example, collects test scores and compares each of its schools with similar schools in other districts rather than with other schools in the same district. Using these methods, Edison has claimed that its schools are doing as well as or better than schools elsewhere with similar populations. Critics have challenged each of Edison's reports on test scores.[45]

A 2002 report by the General Accounting Office (GAO) departed from this tennis match of conflicting claims by examining three private for-profit firms (Edison, Mosaica, and Chancellor Beacon) and five studies of their effectiveness using commonly accepted standards for such research. The GAO concluded: "Little rigorous research exists on the effectiveness of the three educational management companies . . . in the schools they manage across the country; as a result, we cannot draw conclusions about the effect that these companies' programs have on student achievement, parental satisfaction, parental involvement, or school climate."[46]

When return on investment is considered, for-profits have had a difficult time in gaining investor confidence. Annual reports have shown far more red than black ink. And the losses may be even greater than the reports indicate, because privately held companies do not have to open their books even when they manage public schools. Publicly held for-profit companies such as Edison Schools do. Apart from privately held Nobel Learning Communities Inc., which manages more than 175 private schools and charter schools and has turned a profit, most for-profit companies have failed the bottom-line test.[47]

Educational Alternatives Inc., Advantage, and other EMOs have gone out of business or merged with other for-profit ventures. Even after Edison Schools Inc. landed a large contract to manage twenty of Philadelphia's lowest-performing public schools, prices for the company's stock fell from a high of $37 per share a few years ago to less than a dollar a share in late 2002, almost resulting in the company being delisted from the NASDC exchange. Edison's CEO, Chris Whittle, who holds more than 14 percent of the company's stock, was "financially soaked" and had to put his Long Island mansion on the market for $45 million. A *Fortune* magazine writer concluded that even with record revenues of $525 million in 2001, Edison rang up losses of $86 million while carrying a debt load of $160 million. The writer determined that after seven years in business "the verdict is clear: it doesn't work." In 2003 Edison Inc. returned to private hands.[48]

The verdict may be clear that Edison Schools Inc. has so far failed to give its investors strong confidence in the company by churning out regular dividends, but I do not believe that the "verdict is clear" on the overall future of for-profit schools. It is simply too early to make that judgment. The No Child Left Behind Act (2002) mandates that districts with schools that fail to make "adequate yearly progress" two years in a row must offer to parents of students in those low-performing schools choices of other, better-performing schools (and pay transportation costs). This is a slightly open door that will beckon advocates for vouchers, charter schools, and for-profit firms to continue to enter the public school marketplace.[49]

At best, then, the principle of choice and competition as applied by business-inspired reformers has yet to show much evidence of academic success, public school transformation, or financial stability— or, for that matter, increased confidence in schools. Although policy decisions concerning education, both past and present, are driven more by political power than by the clarity and volume of compelling evidence, I doubt that the success, transformation, and stability sought by advocates will occur.

Those doubts arise from a simple observation. Choice and competition are inexpensive strategies currently aimed at low-income minority schools in big cities and inner-ring suburbs. Most U.S. schools are located in largely white middle- and upper-middle-income suburban districts and small towns. Few of these districts establish charter schools, form coalitions of citizens asking for vouchers, or seek for-profit companies to come in and run their schools.

As urban phenomena, schools based on strategies of choice and competition seek both higher student performance and colorblind equity—but the populations they serve desperately need the types of support networks that families with middle and upper-middle incomes take for granted. And yet the de facto urban strategy targets the school as the institution that must do everything to raise low-income minority children's performance up to high academic standards and renew trust in public schools. Because the problems of low achievement and the gap in test scores between minorities and white students have been framed as the fault of the schools, the schools, with their teachers, principals, and other staff, are expected to solve these problems. Alone.

"Success" stories—about vouchers, charters, or for-profits that seemingly have raised student performance—are an established genre of writing about urban schools, and appear periodically in newspapers, magazines, and television programs. Yet these stories cover a tiny fraction of the total number of urban schools. Moreover, sustained academic and behavioral success in a school over five or ten years is largely absent from these triumphal accounts. Few journalists return two or three years later to the same school and report what has happened since their earlier visit. The reasons are not hard to find. Cadres of highly motivated principals, teachers, and parents, working hard with limited funds, devote all of their energies for a few years to turning around a failing school; they create a safe, orderly, academically achieving institution; they inspire confidence in parents and neighbors. But then exhaustion sets in, and the fragile success earned by so much hard work slowly unravels.[50]

Far larger numbers of poor families, however, send their children to segregated schools where inexperienced and poorly qualified teachers and principals work, where staff turnover is high, where materials are in short supply—I could go on listing problems but will stop here. These are the families and schools whose stories seldom turn up on TV programs or in newspapers, except when violence occurs. The causal assumption that high academic standards, tests, and accountability harnessed to choice and competition can provide colorblind equal opportunities for poor and minority students in largely segregated schools is quietly betrayed by the daily realities of urban life and business-inspired reformers' strong preferences for restraining school spending and tax rates.[51]

Current reforms are school-centric, focused on individuals' academic performance, and relatively inexpensive. They largely ignore the economic and political structures of urban life that maintain racial, ethnic, and class-driven inequalities in housing, employment, and social services. By urging already underfunded urban schools single-handedly to eliminate gaps in academic performance, the current business-inspired reform agenda paradoxically helps to maintain wide disparities in income and segregated communities—both of which deeply influence families and their children in schools. Worse yet, the reformers' belief that improved school performance will yield higher levels of public trust, in the face of policies that isolate the school from its community and virtually guarantee that most schools in poor urban neighborhoods will fail to meet the mandated academic standards, perversely ends up perpetuating the cycle of school bashing that has marked the past century.[52]

Recognizing that what happens outside schools matters a great deal to children would require elite opinion-setters, including business leaders, to reframe the problem of failing urban schools beyond blaming individual students and their low-performing schools. The new definition of the problem would have to include insufficient resources and the absence of a national coordinated policy for children and families that covers both schools and other institutions. Such a reframing would demand far higher investment of federal and state funds than is currently being spent on schools and cities.[53]

So, not only is "choice and competition" part of the larger strategy of standards, testing, and accountability, it is also an urban strategy that projects an image of an equity-seeking, colorblind approach to the transformation of U.S. schools. Yet the strategy is faulty in its assumptions. Advocates of choice and competition assume that determined teachers and administrators alone could erase low achievement, eliminate skill deficits, and turn poor children into high-salaried employees and civically engaged homeowners. The strategy assumes that teachers and administrators are withholding their best efforts and will release their energies once market forces are brought to bear on them. The strategy also assumes that once teachers and administrators transform schools, these high-performing schools will be able to stand on their own feet without help, year in and year out, as if sustaining change is merely a matter of resoluteness. It assumes that earnest staff members can overcome decades of institutional racism embedded in employment, housing, and the criminal justice system. Finally, as noted earlier, civic, business, and educational policy elites have assumed that the market-driven principles of choice and competition, like other time-tested principles of business success, can be successfully applied to schools because the two types of organizations have common features. It is to this fundamental assumption that I now turn.

Significant Differences

Since the dissolution of the Soviet Union, the triumph of market capitalism has strengthened corporate leaders' conviction that public institutions—health care, criminal justice, radio and television—should become more businesslike. Reformers across the institutional spectrum have repeatedly stressed the ability of business firms to raise capital, freely reorganize their practices without answering to public authorities, and gain from economies of scale. Consider, for example, that for the past seventy years the Federal Communications Commission (FCC) has controlled the radio frequency spectrum (airwaves), has issued licenses to radio and TV broadcasters, and has regulated those and, later, other media under the concept that reporting the news to the public is different from selling products for a profit. Since the early 1980s, a gradual process of corporate mergers, loosening of FCC rules, and the rise of "infotainment" have begun to blur the distinctions between federally regulated public institutions and profit-seeking companies. One FCC chairman described the softening of boundaries between the public and private sectors when he said that television was "only a toaster with pictures." The 1996 Telecommunications Act and FCC rule changes in 2003 permitting greater concentration in ownership of radio, television, and news outlets moved a public institution much closer to an unregulated market than ever before.[54]

Within such a market-favorable climate, where media, medical care, health insurance, and other public institutions have adopted market prescriptions for success, the idea of making schools businesslike strikes many observers as too obvious to question. Business leaders have long recognized, particularly since the early twentieth century, that schools produce both their workforce and their customers. U.S. schools buy nearly $35 billion a year in goods and services—about 10 percent of the total amount spent for K–12 schools —from businesses.[55]

In addition, schools and businesses do have many common characteristics. Both have leaders, headquarters staff who coordinate and control people, plan for the future, provide services, budget and expend funds, and develop staff capacities. So I do not question the historical advantages that businesses have in working in the public sector, or the similarity of organizational tasks between private and public organizations. I do question the underlying premise, however, that schools are just like businesses and any differences between the two are trivial.

I find major and consequential differences between schools and businesses. Business, educational, and civic elites have either worked hard at erasing these crucial distinctions between the public and private or pushed them to the margins of policy debates on school reform in the past few decades.[56] These major differences include the multiple purposes of tax-supported public schools (and public responsibility for achieving those purposes), democratic deliberations in deciding policies, and criteria for determining school success.[57]

Multiple Purposes

The current attention to academic achievement as a proxy for future performance in the workplace fails to capture the historical and continuing popular wish for public schools to do more than raise test scores or prepare future workers. The requirements that everyone, with or without children, pay taxes to support schools, and that families send their sons and daughters to school, indicate that schools serve larger public purposes. Immature and unwilling children need to be socialized to accept community standards, especially at a time when most parents of young children have full-time jobs. Schools are expected to strengthen common moral values, promote civic engagement, and offer students social, economic, and political opportunities on an equal basis. The results of a recent poll illustrate the rich array of collective and individual purposes that parents and taxpayers expect public schools to fulfill. In order of importance, the top five were:

- to prepare people to become responsible citizens,
- to help people become economically self-sufficient,
- to ensure a basic level of quality among schools,
- to promote cultural unity among all Americans,
- to improve social conditions for people.

Tied for sixth and seventh were "to enhance people's happiness and enrich their lives" and "to dispel inequities in education among certain schools and certain groups."[58]

To market-minded proponents of deregulation of schools, parents and children resemble customers. Educators need to appeal to and satisfy them just as companies selling cars or cereals need to please those who buy their products. With an invisible hand at work, choice and market competition will magically produce a better product.

Yet, the "customer" analogy breaks down quickly when the above public purposes are noted. Historically, civic leaders, business executives, and taxpayers have wanted schools to do more than satisfy students and parents. They want children to be literate, law-abiding, engaged citizens who are informed about issues, economically independent, and respectful of differences among Americans. Few voucher plans, charter schools, or EMOs either acknowledge these multiple and often contradictory purposes or are held responsible for achieving them. This is a profound difference between the purposes of public schools and private-sector firms, a difference that advocates of privatization seldom note in public debates.[59]

Granted, school boards and superintendents, reflecting the social geography of location and particular socioeconomic groups, accent some purposes more than others—assuring, for example, that inner-city children are fed breakfast before starting school. Nonetheless, parents and taxpayers count on elected officials to give heed to these diverse aims in their schools. If some of these purposes are ignored —say, promoting acceptance of diverse cultures among students— civic leaders will call upon the board and superintendent publicly to pay attention because it is their responsibility to do so.

While business firms, too, surely entertain multiple goals, more often than not, private rather than public purposes dominate their agendas: increasing total revenues, net profits, dividends to investors, and other "bottom line" outcomes. Surely, for many companies, customer and employee satisfaction, developing staff capabilities, and community relations are important—yet these and similar outcomes are means toward the end of higher net profits.

Cultivating civic engagement, heightening cultural awareness, enhancing individual well-being, and reducing economic and social inequalities are seldom mentioned as purposes of private-sector companies. And the reason is simple enough: these are public purposes that are meant to enhance the collective good, not private interests. These multiple public purposes place decidedly different demands on the elected and appointed public officials responsible for schools than the demands faced by CEOs or their non-elected boards of trustees who lead private-sector firms.[60]

Democratic Deliberations

Beginning in 2000, stories emerged from corporate offices that CEOs fiddled with earnings reports in order to keep investors happy and stock prices high. The importance of earnings statements (and forecasts) as signs of corporate success—15 percent growth per year, for example—had pressured corporate officers to claim as earnings funds that had little to do with actual transactions with customers in a given year. For example, CEOs of Computer Associates and Xerox claimed revenues in one year that their customers were actually paying them over three years. Revelations of such corporate trickery often forced firms to issue "restatements" (more than 150 in 2000 compared with fewer than 50 between 1990 and 1997) or chagrined confessions that the original reports had been deceptive. In some cases, the chicanery was so blatant that firms went bankrupt or CEOs and their minions were indicted, tried by juries, and sent to prison. The bending of flexible accounting rules went too far, as Kenneth Kozlowski of Tyco, Ken Lay and Jeff Skilling of Enron, John Rigas of Adelphi, and the accounting firm of Arthur Andersen discovered. The collapse of these corporations destroyed investments, jobs, and the lives of employees and investors.[61]

Decisions about CEOs' pay, earnings reports, sweetheart loans to friends, and bending auditing rules that occurred in corporate boardrooms were private transactions and unavailable for public deliberation or inspection until after the damage was done. In effect, corporate leaders were not accountable to their investors, their employees, or the larger public. Without doubt, shareholder activism increased in the wake of the scandals and revelations. Apple shareholders endorsed a resolution requiring that the company treat stock options as expenses in their financial reporting. A few months after the vote, the board of directors announced that it "appreciates and takes seriously the views expressed by . . . shareholders" but would disregard the shareholders' resolution. Many investors forget that shareholder votes are not binding on corporate boards of directors. As one reporter put it, "Shareholder democracy is an oxymoron." Federal legislation in 2002 aimed to solve the problems of failed corporate governance and misconduct by injecting limited public oversight.[62]

I offer examples of corporate malfeasance to illustrate a major difference between businesses and schools. School boards are obliged by law to consider, debate, and make decisions in public; elected officials are held accountable for those public actions. Corrupt practices do occur in schools, especially as pressures increase for higher test scores. Incidents have been reported of administrators being caught changing students' scores and "losing" the tests of low-performing students in order to raise the school's average score. But these offenses pale in magnitude and frequency in comparison with the dishonesty in the private sector. Far more important, school board decisions are subject to media and public scrutiny. Not so in the private sector, where corporate leaders are often appointed by self-perpetuating boards of directors who then deliberate and make decisions behind closed doors without public hearings or journalists in attendance.[63]

With corporate misconduct in the news, the injection of limited public oversight is a tiny step in the direction of more open decision-making. Were corporate governance to be opened to investors and the larger public, some of the basic differences between public and private might diminish. One veteran activist shareholder observed that boards of directors are like "subatomic particles: they behave differently when they are being observed." How serious legislators are about moving in this direction, only time will tell.[64]

That school boards have entered and exited from contracts with Edison Schools Inc., added and dropped charter schools, and accepted or refused to join voucher experiments illustrates a decision-making process that is open to public inspection and sensitive to input from the community. This public deliberation (including scrutiny) is a profound difference between schools and businesses.[65]

Criteria for Determining Success

With the multiple purposes that tax-supported public schools are expected to serve and the variety of "customers" they are expected to satisfy, one would expect multiple criteria to be used for judging whether schools are successful. In the last chapter I analyzed the complexity of the task of determining success and failure and pointed out that in the past quarter-century one particular criterion has come to dominate any discussion of school success: scores on standardized tests.[66]

That dominance, in my judgment, is a result of business-inspired efforts to improve schools, efforts that tap into the popular belief that numbers reveal quality and the assumption that schools are just like businesses. Companies that turn handsome profits year after year inspire confidence. Firms that perform poorly disappear. Or as one federal official put it, in the U.S. economy we "get rid of non-performing assets." Schools could regain public trust, reformers believed, if they improved their performance on tests and consistent low performers were closed.[67]

Earlier in this chapter I described the widespread belief that measures of economic productivity can be linked to school test scores. Reinforcing this notion of correspondence between businesses and schools is the outcome-driven psychology of reformers who see corporate earnings reports and published test scores as equivalent signs of school efficiency and productivity. But they are not equivalent.

Consider Honda, Ford, or any other automaker. To earn profits and investor confidence, the company has to produce cars at low cost that appeal to customers. When net profits are substantial, investors are satisfied. Value, then, is created by car sales that translate into eventual profits. For schools, there are clearly costs to educating children—buildings, staff, supplies, and so on. But money for schools does not come from satisfied customers; it comes from taxes. Elected government authorities allocate tax revenues not to attract "customers" but to achieve social and economic goals set through a public deliberative process. Moreover, seldom are the total costs of schooling covered by tax revenues. If public school "customers" don't cover the full cost of schooling, how is the pricing of these services to be calculated?

Take the very same private-sector automaker and place him in the situation facing public school administrators—that is, letting him know nothing about revenues earned from car sales—and he would experience great difficulty. The savvy business insider and management expert Mark Moore imagines such a scenario:

> He would probably try to work his way out of the trouble by doing many of the things that government managers try to do. He would conduct surveys to determine how much his customers liked the cars they bought. He would ask different kinds of engineers to set standards for what constituted a "good car" and see how closely his cars matched those standards . . . The point is this: he would face serious challenges in determining the value of the cars he produced if he were denied information about how much customers had paid for his product.[68]

So, given the major differences between the public and private sectors in the way they calculate revenues and costs, the use of test scores to measure the product of schooling misleads parents and tax-payers into believing that there is a common "bottom line" when none exists. Consider the serious problems of assessing the worth of current reforms that face business and civic leaders, parents, media editors, and practitioners who continue to believe that students' test scores are, indeed, "bottom line" measures. First, they need to determine whether the widely praised business strategies and practices actually produce the higher test scores, and second, they need to determine that the scores are accurate measures of school success and predict future achievements.

The causal chain of logic runs as follows. Were state-mandated curriculum standards implemented as intended, and if so, did the standards influence teaching practices, and if so, did those practices shape what students learned as measured by the state tests? The first causal linkage requires evidence that state policies were fully put into practice and thereby steered classroom practices. The second requires that changed instructional practices resulted in desired outcomes. Even here, test score gains require scrutiny of the contribution that classroom experiences made to student achievement over a specific period of time, with prior test performance and socioeconomic status of students held constant.[69]

Another issue is whether test scores do indeed measure current and predict future success. I have already raised questions about test scores as proxy measures of school productivity. The many purposes of public schools, their orientation toward service, the values that draw educators to teach and administer, and the varied cultures that inhabit schools make single, quantifiable measures of success dubious.

The difficulties of measuring success are not confined to schools. When a mental hospital's effectiveness is measured by how many beds are occupied, as Peter Drucker put it, "this yardstick leads to mental patients being kept in the hospital—which, therapeutically, is about the worst thing that can be done to them." Drucker raises the same issue in determining whether universities are successful. He asks which of these are measures of "doing a good job": The salaries of students twenty years after graduation? The reputation of the faculty? The number of Ph.D.'s? Scientific prizes earned by alumni? "Each yardstick," Drucker points out, "bespeaks a value judgment regarding the purpose of the university—and a very narrow one at that. Even if these were the right objectives, such yardsticks measure performance just as dubiously as the count of bed utilization measures performance in mental hospitals."[70]

For business-inspired school reformers who are dead-set on using test scores, these three points—Were standards fully implemented? Did implemented standards change teaching and learning? And did the changes yield desired student outcomes?—are essential in demonstrating the effects of policy changes and the impact of those changes upon instruction and, ultimately, upon student achievement. Thus far, business and civic elites have failed to take up these issues in public and the causal logic remains hidden or relegated to academic journals and gadflies.

The profound differences between businesses and schools in purposes, in deliberative decisionmaking, and in accountability for outcomes mean that the core assumption of business-inspired reformers is deeply flawed. The defects in this and other assumptions about the problems of schools raise serious questions about the merits of business-inspired school reform, including coercive accountability measures in state and federal mandates. But in showing the flaws in the causal chain of logic behind business-minded school reform, as earlier in delineating the limits of business influence, I do not assert that all business-inspired efforts to improve schools have been futile or harmful. Indeed, as we will see in the next chapter, they have not.

6

HAS BUSINESS INFLUENCE
IMPROVED SCHOOLS?

Not long ago, careful yogurt shoppers noticed a change. Dannon yogurt containers went from 8 ounces (or 16 spoonfuls) to six ounces
(12 spoonfuls), a decrease of 25 percent, yet the price remained the
same. Called "weight-out," this practice is federally approved as long
as the label on the container says accurately what the contents weigh.
With $2.6 billion in total yogurt sales and a lunchtime and snack
market that had grown by 60 percent between 1995 and 2002, Dannon took this step because, after fifty-eight years of dominating the
business, it had lost ground to Yoplait, which now held a larger market share. After the downsizing of Dannon's containers, sales slowly
increased, and the company now made a larger profit out of each
sale. Less is more.[1]

The clever tactic of shrinking yogurt servings is one of many lessons arising from the basic market principle of competitiveness. Vigorous competition fuels a market economy. It also accounts, in part,
for business leaders' tendency to turn to school reform not only to
enhance the position of the United States in global markets but also
because they believed that sluggish, low-performing public schools
detracted from national competitiveness.

Tallying Successes and Failures

At the end of the nineteenth century, desires to beat Germany and Britain in gaining world markets and to remedy the ills of urban life stirred U.S. business leaders to join civic-minded progressives to improve both city governance and public schools. To eliminate the mismatch between the skills of American high school graduates and those needed in the workplace—a mismatch that, in their judgment, reduced labor productivity and weakened competitiveness in world markets, reformers introduced vocational education in U.S. schools. Business and civic leaders also streamlined city and school governance and operations to make them more efficient, less politically entangled, and more like those of corporations.

Nearly a century later, business leaders, jolted by global competition with Japan and Germany, mobilized civic and policy elites in another school reform movement. Once more, an alleged mismatch of skills between entry-level workers, especially those in cities, and the economy became reformers' rationale for changing the schools. This time the business-inspired reforms included giving parents more choice about which schools their children attended, installing a standardized curriculum in all schools, measuring students' achievement by a panoply of tests, and enforcing steel-tempered rules making schools accountable for their students' performance.

Like the historical markers seen along highways, milestones of business-inspired reform are highly visible when one considers public schools. Since 1900 preparing students for the workplace has become a taken-for-granted goal of public schooling. Since the late 1970s, when manufacturing and service workplaces were becoming increasingly computerized, high school students have marched through a more and more standardized academic curriculum aimed at preparing them for college and decent-paying entry-level jobs. A swiftly changing economy provided few job opportunities for graduates lacking adequate cognitive and social skills. Choice and competition, core principles of market success, have been converted into the popular policy options of vouchers, charters, and for-profit schools. Efficient and high-performing schools are routinely listed in magazines. Add also the transformation of educators' vocabulary (students as "customers," "strategic planning," "benchmarks," renaming superintendents CEOs). In short, public schooling in the past three decades has become more and more like business.[2]

Some of the changes that accompanied these historical markers of business involvement in school reform are viewed by many educators and scholars as distinct benefits. From Andrew Carnegie to Walter Annenberg, corporate leaders have donated large sums of money to improve schools. Business firms have lent their high status and their access to the media to place public schools and related issues (such as the health and welfare of young children, the school-to-work transition, the quality of teachers) on policymakers' agendas. Many corporate partnerships with schools have provided jobs for youth while making it possible for company employees to tutor and provide technical support to school staffs.

In mobilizing community elites to change schools, business and civic leaders, using the media to spread their message, built social trust by bringing together parents, taxpayers, and neighbors to improve a critical social institution. In a process that scholars call building "civic capacity" and "social capital," business-inspired school reform in many—but not all—places glued together disparate segments of a city to act for the common good. Educators also welcomed the resources and public attention for the added luster they offered a low-status occupation and the help they gave to hardworking staff. They, like business elites, blended altruistic and interest-driven impulses.[3]

Business-endorsed systemic reform also contributed the idea of colorblind equity. Popular slogans such as "all children can learn," "everyone can go to college," and "leave no child behind" have been bandied about in the media, at political rallies, and in parent-teacher meetings. Implied in the slogans is the belief that striking inequalities in the distribution of income in the United States could be eventually reduced through better schooling. Often used as clubs by avid reformers to beat urban teachers and principals into raising their expectations for low-performing children, the catchphrases represent a seismic shift in the political rhetoric of school reform. Republicans endorsing business-led school reform popularized the meritocratic belief in colorblind equity, albeit one carrying little additional funding.

Counting roadside markers does not complete the story of school reform. No markers exist for the business-inspired reforms that arrived with hullabaloo and yet, in time, quietly disappeared. Relegated to the back roads and covered by brush are traces of school reforms that were adopted but, after trials in schools, turned out to be pale versions of the original concepts or simply failed. Merit pay, school-site decisionmaking, classrooms revolutionized by computers, and Total Quality Management, to mention only a few, stand out as instances of business-inspired reforms with feeble applications to schooling. The notable failure of progressive-minded business and educational leaders to spread the learning-by-doing approach to teaching in the early twentieth century beyond the early grades in elementary school, and the slow demise of secondary school vocational education, also bear stark witness to the difficulty of altering daily classroom practices.

Fast-forward to the early twenty-first century and the top-down systemic reform of standards-based testing and coercive accountability. Federal and state policymakers have pressed teachers to teach prescribed content and skills sufficiently well for all students to show test score gains on mandatory tests. Although satisfactory test scores occur as a matter of course in mostly white middle- and upper-middle-income schools with stable, experienced staffs, in mostly minority and poor urban schools with high student mobility and large percentages of inexperienced teachers the traditional version of teaching and learning has had some success but, overall, has failed to produce sustained high performance.

Standardizing content and teaching into uniform practices enforced by tests and penalties for low-performing students, teachers, and administrators plays well in public opinion polls, among minority parents, and in the media but narrows considerably what teachers are expected to do in classrooms. Most teachers do their best with the tools and resources they have. Many steer their classrooms to conform to academic standards that will be tested. Others use literacy programs that require them to use scripted lessons. Some teachers who have used progressive and untraditional approaches and experienced success with students continue teaching as they have, and collaborate with other like-minded colleagues to maintain their sanity. Here, again, substantial alteration of what happens in most classrooms seems to be beyond the reach of business-inspired school reformers.[4]

Any account of policy victories and defeats in school and classroom practices returns to the assumptions that business leaders made about the ties between schooling and the economy. Those assumptions and the logic of action that reform coalitions advanced, particularly about the fundamental similarities between schools and businesses, were conceptually flawed and factually contested. Neither the defects nor the disputed evidence ever entered public deliberations.

The sheer complexity of the task of transforming schools, particularly classroom practices, in dramatically different settings was lost in the rush to extract strong student performance on tests. Pointing out the conceptual and factual flaws in core assumptions, as some critics did, hardly gave pause to righteous-minded promoters wielding political muscle and eager to apply business and market principles to public schools. Let me reassert the obvious: well-organized, politically powerful groups holding defective theories of action aimed at effecting school reforms trump facts time and again.

One example of many will suffice. Because Florida law requires students who fail the state test to be left behind in their grade, Lake Silver Elementary in Orlando did not promote 23 out of 101 third graders. Twenty of the 23 were poor and 18 of the 23 were black. The school's teachers and principal had no say in the matter. State department of education officials consulted more than a half-century of educational research and warned legislators that holding back children who had failed the test for another year in the third grade had no long-term benefits, and that, furthermore, students who flunked more than once were more likely to drop out of high school. Legislators went ahead and made the test law. Again, as in other states where standards-based accountability reigns, test results overwhelm both facts and practitioners' judgment.[5]

Educational policy, of course, is not alone in this regard. From global warming to missile defense systems, from domestic oil consumption to reproductive cloning, policies lacking substantial evidence pushed by solidly financed, well-organized, and powerful groups get adopted.[6]

The century-long record of attempts by business, civic, and policy elites to reform schools includes victories and defeats. My description, however, is a micro-view that falls far short of capturing the larger picture of what it means in a democracy when policymakers make public schools like business and a virtual arm of the economy. Of equal importance is to go beyond analyzing triumphs and failures and answer the larger question of whether public schools have, indeed, improved overall as a result of this extensive business involvement since the late 1800s.

The Wide-Angle View

In earlier chapters I pointed out that when the country faced serious social, political, and economic problems business and civic leaders, policymakers, and assorted allies often sought indirect solutions in school reform. Deeply entrenched social beliefs that education could solve collective and individual problems provided fertile ground on which to sow the seeds of reform.

The impulse to turn to the schools to solve problems is virtually an automatic reflex. For example, to stamp out predatory lending practices in Philadelphia's ghettos, in 2003 the city's director of consumer affairs proposed a financial literacy course that all high school students would have to take. "One of the basic building blocks for such a fight is education," he said. "We want to teach children how to manage their paychecks, the real cost of high interest loans . . . and check cashing institutions so they can keep as much of their paychecks as possible." John Dewey noted in 1916 this penchant for using public schools to remedy national ills. "The public school is the willing pack horse of our social system," he said, "it is the true hero of the refrain: Let George do it."[7]

From reducing crime, unemployment, and poverty, to defending the nation against domestic and foreign enemies, and, yes, to preparing future workers for a changing labor market—reformers resorted to school-based solutions. They seldom tried altering socioeconomic and political structures or reducing inequalities (direct public and private intervention to narrow the income gap between the rich and poor or to reduce residential segregation) when politically vulnerable public schools were available.

Also, political rhetoric pledging equality in public schools resonated with Americans' hopes for their children. Equality of educational opportunity easily fit into the historic American creed, promising the right of all children not only to go to school but to exceed, through personal merit and competition, the fondest dreams of their parents.[8]

Surely, the history of the United States documents how spiteful treatment and severe income inequalities have warped the words again and again. Nonetheless, the soaring hope of colorblind equal opportunity and individual merit has persevered and the struggle to open doors and sustain fair treatment has continued, in spite of the obvious and persistent race, class, and gender inequities. In the early twenty-first century, however, after three decades of making schools more like businesses, the larger struggle to reduce inequalities, particularly in the distribution of income, has ebbed.[9]

If competitive spirit is the fuel of a market economy, the engine is the individual entrepreneur, free of governmental restraints, creating new, efficient, and better products that will yield success in the marketplace and personal wealth. Constant change and inequalities in income distribution are both central and inexorable to capitalism. Depending on which of the giants among economists one admires —Adam Smith, Karl Marx, John Maynard Keynes, or Joseph Schumpeter—these outcomes may be positive or negative. But all these giants agree on the inevitability of constant change and income inequalities in market economies.[10] It is to the increasingly unequal distribution of income in the United States and the damage to a democracy that accompanies such inequality that I now turn.

I do so because reformers intent on making schools resemble businesses have used the politically compelling argument of colorblind access to college-preparatory schooling, with its promise of personal advancement through individual merit and hard work (all students reach high standards, go to college, and get high-paying entry-level jobs). In doing so, they have claimed that such access to a better education would eventually reduce the yawning income gaps between those living in gated communities and those living in ghettos. Betraying that promise of colorblind meritocratic equity, however, has been the enduring inequality between the richest and poorest Americans.

In 1910 the top 1 percent of the population in the United States received one-third of all personal income while the bottom 20 percent earned only 8.3 percent. The high-water mark of disparities in income in the twentieth century was in 1929, when the top 1 percent received 44 percent of all personal income. The gap narrowed during the Great Depression and World War II and was at its smallest in the mid-1970s, when that same 1 percent of the population earned less than 20 percent of all personal income. Since then, the high-income 1 percent has steadily increased its share to reach 40 percent, even higher than in 1910 and almost reaching the level of 1929.[11]

Making the point about enormous disparities is easy, given the facts. Making sense of the statistics is harder and requires interpretation. Ideologies often frame interpretations. Those who believe that unequal distribution of income is a natural outcome of capital accumulation in a competitive, market-driven society—or, more crassly, that in a market economy winners win big and losers lose badly— can hardly be expected to question the obvious. But to those who see the same concentration of income as undermining democracy, a question comes to mind: What are the social, political, economic, and personal costs to these glaring and persistent economic inequities?

Kevin Phillips stresses the high price a nation pays when so much money is held by so few. Increased concentration of wealth in the 1890s, 1920s, and the 1990s, he concludes, corrupted the nation. Financially, he says, "ethics loses to greed and the sleazy results come out of the dirty linen closet and go into the history books. We all know the current list—Enron, Tyco, WorldCom, Global Crossing, Vivendi, Merck, and counting." Political corruption also occurs when rich campaigners buy elections and shape policy decisions. A third form of corruption, according to Phillips, is ideological, a polishing up of ideas that flatter the wealthy such as "survival of the fittest, laissez faire, [and] idolatry of markets."[12]

Other prices the nation pays for glaring inequalities in income go unmentioned by Phillips. One is the quiet crushing of hope and the erosion of Americans' trust in one another. A sizable portion of working Americans dream of a financially secure future but hold minimum-wage jobs. Called the "working poor," they find it hard to pay for an adequate roof over their heads, nourishing food for their families, or medical bills when their children are sick. Moreover, although there is a tiny fraction of minorities among the richest 1 percent and more among middle-income groups, most minority families are located in the bottom half of the national distribution of income. When median family income figures during the twentieth century are parsed by race and ethnicity, black and Hispanic incomes dip well below those of whites and far greater percentages of minorities than of whites are mired in poverty. Although the gaps have narrowed in the past quarter-century, sizable discrepancies remain, producing what one scholar called the "estranged poor."[13]

Maldistribution of income, of course, mirrors other inequalities between minorities and whites in unemployment, receipt of public assistance, infant mortality rates, incidence of crime, and other social indicators. I have already mentioned the test score gap and major differences in college attendance. In short, income distribution inequities are accompanied by disparities in access to a better life. Erosion of dreams and of trust in the wider community resulting from these inequities is a social and individual cost that often goes uncounted by business leaders and public officials in periods such as the prosperous 1990s when ideologies of entrepreneurial independence dominate policy talk. This point on ideologies needs elaboration.[14]

Among academics, policymakers, and civic and business-minded reformers, interpretation of statistics registering inequalities between whites and racial and ethnic groups often follows one of two directions. One line of explanation concentrates on the individual's attributes and efforts to overcome obstacles to account for achievements and failures. A poor California Latino youngster, for example, who is the first in a family of migrant laborers to go to college and become an engineer, is a poster child for this ideology. Individual pluck trumps circumstances. Talent and guts, not history, families, geography, or the federal government, determine who succeeds and who fails.

Solutions to inequities, then, in this view, entail removing barriers to individual effort and ensuring unfettered access to opportunities. The ideology of individualism, meritocracy, and survival of the fittest, enhanced considerably by the political slogan of colorblind equity, accompanies this explanation for inequalities, suggesting ever so implicitly that once access is gained any subsequent failure is clearly the fault of the individual. No excuses permitted. Although this explanation has been advanced by policymakers and leaders in both political parties, in the twentieth century it was Republicans who found this explanation most congenial.[15]

Vocational education early in the twentieth century and standards-based testing and accountability reforms at the end of same century, inspired and supported by business leaders, were driven by an ideology of individuals climbing the ladder of success with little help from government save for guaranteeing equal access. Closing the test score gap and getting all students into college while telling teachers and principals to pull up their socks and stop whining is a bipartisan formula for producing more winners consistent with the individualistic, competitive, and market-driven explanation of inequalities.[16]

Another explanation for inequities focuses on the social and economic structures beneath the surface that determine individual outcomes. Historical discrimination against minorities in employment, housing, schools, health care, and other facets of life accounts for inequalities. Institutional racism appears in circumstances as different as hiring a white rather than a qualified minority bookkeeper, counseling a poor black high school student to try sales work rather than go to college, and finding a home mortgage in a high-risk area redlined by banks. Context, then, trumps individual grit.[17]

This explanation blames the system for inequities and seeks remedies in revamping institutional structures. President Harry Truman's executive order desegregating the armed forces, the U.S. Supreme Court's *Brown* decision, the Civil Rights Act, and the Americans with Disabilities Act altered deeply entrenched and hidden structures and processes to modify individual behavior. Again, while business leaders and members of both political parties hold these views, since the Great Depression it has been Democrats who have articulated this ideology and have assigned government a larger role than the private sector in reducing structural inequalities. Proposals for federal and state programs that fund job training, college scholarships, Individual Development Accounts that provide scarce assets for families, loans for small businesses, and universal health insurance seek direct action to improve the life chances of poor and middle-class families.[18]

A less favored explanation blends the two accounts, acknowledging that social and economic structures pattern individual behavior but do not determine it solely. Just such a hybrid explanation helps me understand both the trajectory of business-inspired reforms in the twentieth century and their effects.[19]

But trying to blend the explanations is hard work. For example, Rona Wilensky, a Colorado high school principal, questions the popular belief, held by policymakers and most parents, that high schools should prepare all students for college. "Given that most jobs do not require a college education, that most people don't actually go to college, that fewer than 60 percent of all freshmen at four year schools finish college, and that most people really don't like the type of work that is involved in earning a college degree . . . reformers should stop focusing on 'college readiness' as the goal of high school reform." Wilensky is correct in her facts. In the year 2000 less than 30 percent of jobs were filled by employees who had schooling beyond high school. Recent estimates of jobs that will require more than twelve years of schooling in 2010 are just over 30 percent. Clearly, the popular solution to economic and social inequities is out of synch with the realities of the labor market.[20]

Angry critics dismiss such arguments as excuses for freeing educators from responsibility for raising student academic performance or even as straightforward bigotry. "It's a new century," says Kati Haycock, director of the Education Trust, an organization promoting college preparatory curriculum for all students. "It's time to set aside our Industrial Age curriculum and agree on a common core curriculum for the Information Age . . . To do anything else is nothing short of educational malpractice." In minority and poor urban high schools, where in the past few students took college preparatory courses, a core academic curriculum is evidence of strong beliefs in equal access and students' potential to open employers' doors. Individual grit will triumph. Yet requiring everyone to take a core curriculum to enter college means high schools have to sort out winners from losers—that is, those who pass the required tests from those who do not—reinforcing the individual competition that mirrors a market economy.[21]

Competing explanations of inequalities between minorities and whites end up as gift-wrappings for different reform packages. Although these explanations identify the ideological basis for school reforms, neither answers the question of whether business-inspired reforms have improved public schools.

Answering the Question

The question of whether the influence of business has been good for the public schools asks for a judgment, an evaluation of the total worth of business-inspired reforms that have been adopted and put into practice in schools. To answer the question I have to ask two prior ones.

- What does one have to know to answer the question?
- Can the question be answered decisively to the satisfaction of anyone who would ask it?

To answer the first of these prior questions, it is helpful to know the details of what policies have been adopted and implemented and to know how the implementation has been connected to the over-all goals of business-inspired reformers (such as reducing the skills deficits of graduates facing a changed workplace or tying the schools more closely to the economy). Moreover, it is helpful to know the other historical and important goals for U.S. public schools that these twentieth-century reformers acknowledged but largely ignored (such as engaged citizenship, enjoyment of learning, connections be-tween school life and the community). Both knowledge of these var-ied goals and clarity about what actually occurred in schools are es-sential to coming to a conclusion about the worth of these business-inspired reforms. I have provided enough knowledge about these goals and their implementation to render a judgment.

I am much less confident about answering the second prior ques-tion decisively and to the satisfaction of most readers. The reasons have to do with the different values that readers bring to this book and the multiple goals they hold for the nation's public schools.

In attempting to answer the question it is important to keep in mind the distinction between change and improvement. Even though our culture prizes change and innovation as valued achieve-ments in and of themselves, saying that a reform has permanently changed the topography of schooling—say curriculum or gover-nance—is far from declaring that those changes are, indeed, im-provements. When a married couple divorces, one spouse may see the change as joyful emancipation and the other as a tragedy. Change is not necessarily improvement; improvement, a value judgment, is in the head and heart of the beholder.

Beyond this conceptual distinction, what complicates matters con-siderably is the fact that public schools have multiple and sometimes conflicting goals. Creating literate adults, engaging children in their communities, building students' character, getting students ready for college and jobs—these are among the chief goals voters and opin-ion-setting elites have sought for public schools. Each goal singly and in combination with others has had (and continues to have) its champions. Historically, reformers of all stripes have capitalized on disagreement over which goals should take priority in schooling America's children. Thus, constant conflict over public school goals among well-intentioned parents and citizens makes it especially hard to determine whether particular changes were improvements.

Tensions over competing goals extend to disagreements over which criteria to use in judging improvement. Recall that the various criteria for determining schools' success described in Chapter 1—effectiveness, fidelity, popularity, and adaptiveness—derived from different theories and different core values. Teachers saw success in their tailoring a new policy or innovation to fit their students and the goals they sought to achieve in the classroom. Business leaders, school boards, and superintendents heeded data, particularly test scores, as indicating whether they achieved their specific objectives. Political leaders listened carefully to what their constituents desired even if supporting evidence was slim. Researchers wanted the programs they designed to be faithfully implemented to achieve their selected outcomes. Self-interest and political aims contended with impartial analysis among groups supporting one or more standards in making judgments. Of course, these value-laden criteria for improvement and judgments of success are seldom mutually exclusive. Some overlap (effectiveness and fidelity, for example); some are contradictory (popularity versus effectiveness, fidelity versus adaptiveness). Reformers and critics may hold more than one in mind without recognizing the internal strains as they consider the question of whether schools have improved.

So I cannot expect my own judgments of the worth of business-inspired school reforms to find agreement from all readers. Nonetheless, offering judgments is merited, particularly because so few reform advocates, pundits, or academics have acknowledged the value conflicts that are entangled in what appears as a straightforward question. So, if improvement is a value judgment located in the head and heart of the beholder and multiple value-laden criteria can be applied, where do I stand? Has business influence improved schools?

Drawing on my experience as a practitioner, my research, and my personal values, I use a mix of criteria to determine improvement. Because schools are complex institutions nested in many layers (nation, state, district, school, classroom) with strong differences between regions and among urban, suburban, and rural settings, policies must often be tailored to fit different contexts. So I prize adaptiveness and flexibility. I also prize coherent policy logic of action, informed by evidence that is connected to anticipated outcomes but still responsive to different contexts. Moreover, parts of both effectiveness and fidelity criteria are present in my judgment. Finally, I reject a logic inspired by the politically attractive moment, ignoring available evidence, or seeking widespread appeal. On the basis of these personal yardsticks of adaptiveness, effectiveness, and fidelity, I judge that business-inspired reformers have changed schools both for the better and for the worse.

Progressive reformers early in the twentieth century sought to adapt traditional schooling to an urbanized, industrialized society. I consider their explicit aim of having schools prepare students for the workplace an improvement insofar as the aim inculcates an appreciation for the dignity and productiveness of labor. I also consider the adding of vocational education to the curriculum as a wise recognition of the diversity in children who are required to attend school and whose varied interests and motivations go well beyond academics. Finally, I count the increase of civic capacity resulting from business leaders' mobilization of community support for school reform a decided gain for both communities and the nation.

But business-minded reformers and their allies have also destroyed portions of these contributions. In urban high schools, vocational education turned into an inflexible, low-status track for the non-academic student (often minority and poor), and since the 1980s reformers have slowly eliminated such courses in favor of college preparation. This change does a disservice to those students who learn best through active work on real-life projects. The press of state-imposed standards-based testing and coercive accountability, now expanded by federal NCLB legislation, has narrowed the idea of good schooling to only required academic courses. Furthermore, business-inspired reformers have elevated preparation for the workplace, and later preparation for college, to the virtual exclusion of traditional goals of building citizens and enhancing moral growth.[22]

Moreover, although business-inspired reformers' success in mobilizing communities to seek school improvement has been a decided gain, it too has been undercut by a fixation on test scores and accountability and a lack of attention to structural inequalities in the larger society. I consider the narrowing of the purposes of tax-supported public schools to a primary focus on job and college preparation, the intensification of an individualist ideology, and the erosion of goodwill caused by persistent criticism serious losses.

In turning again and again to public schools for solutions to national problems, reformers picked a profoundly traditional institution—surely the type of institution least capable of correcting social, political, and economic woes. And because they expected the schools to be able to provide solutions, they criticized practitioners constantly for failing. The attempts to solve society's problems by changing the schools also allowed reformers to avoid direct action, thereby postponing solutions to the next generation. This familiar political strategy is designed to distort the full range of facts about schooling in order to convince voters that a serious social, political, or economic issue has to be solved by educators. This strategy has been used many times over the decades, not only by business leaders but also by U.S. presidents, state governors, and opinion elites. Public expectations that schools will conserve traditional values while at the same time providing solutions to broad national problems remains a painful contradiction facing those who support public schools and those who work in them.

In that contradiction, and in the inexorable scolding that accompanied reformers' emphasis on schools' shortcomings, public trust in the schools often became the first casualty. As we have seen, the logic of reform action used by policy elites is flawed; for example, some economists contest human capital assumptions linking education, productivity, and global competition. Yet elected policymakers neglect to point out experts' disagreements about these assumptions and, instead, present them to the public as unqualified promises of personal success in the workplace. The rise in unemployment of graduates during economic recessions and the hemorrhaging of jobs to other countries contribute to a further grinding away of public trust in schools. In my judgment, another loss for schooling.

Moreover, in the two periods of business-inspired reform described in this book, the reformers and their allies seldom examined the internal coherence of their own logic of action. Missing links, disjointed connections, and a startling lack of evidence dogged their efforts at every step. Recall the causal chain of logic: state-mandated curriculum standards will be implemented, will steer teaching practices, which in turn will shape what students learn, as measured by the state tests—and then will lead to success in college and the marketplace. The first two causal links require evidence that state policy has, indeed, been implemented and has guided classroom practices. Beyond correlational studies, which cannot establish causality, that evidence remains to be found. The third lapse in logic is the assumption that changed instructional practices will result in higher student test scores, and the fourth is that higher test scores predict future success in college and in the workplace. Little evidence is available to demonstrate that scores on standardized tests translate to getting a college degree or a well-paid job. The linked assumptions remain unfounded. Even new autos get tested for safety before they go into full production. No standards-based testing and accountability policies have been yet field-tested and found effective.

Finally, I question the core assumption that schools are like businesses. That assumption has led reformers to graft onto schools inapplicable principles of success and to accept as truth the market metaphor (that, for example, shopping for sneakers is just like shopping for a high school).[23]

I should add that most educators gritted their teeth in public and seldom denounced critiques of schools or the flawed assumptions guiding reformers' strategies, because they feared that disputing the charges in a climate of distrust of educators' expertise would be seen by parents and voters as sheer defensiveness and camouflage for self-interest. Further, many educational policymakers and administrators privately endorsed many of the reforms promoted by critics. More computers, preschools, and qualified teachers were, for example, changes that most educators approved. In this sense, external criticism has been useful to these policymakers, superintendents, and principals, helping them to advance their organizational agendas. Moreover, veteran educators have learned that, in the inexorable cycle of criticism of schools, after public scoldings more dollars than before flow into schools as surely as B follows A in the alphabet.[24]

Even when schools improved in performance (as measured by test scores), however, public trust in these institutions seldom rose. The reason is straightforward: there is always something else to condemn in schools. Critics rail at poor discipline, insufficient prayer or patriotism, too little grammar and spelling, or too much drinking, drug use, and sex. Like the child who can never please demanding parents because they keep setting another target, just out of the child's reach, the schools can never satisfy all their critics. The result is a loss both of practitioners' confidence in their own expertise and of public trust in a core social institution.

Another cost comes from the highly charged rhetoric of color-blind equity: the assertion, for example, that all children can learn and everyone can go to college. Although the connection between more schooling and higher lifetime earnings is strong over time, well over two-thirds of minority students in college do not complete their bachelor's degree and are disadvantaged in a competitive job market. When minority students do achieve college degrees, decent-paying jobs may still be out of their reach when the economy sours. Between January 2001 and August 2003, for example, the U.S. economy had flat-line growth with unemployment claims rising every week; over

2.5 million jobs disappeared, and high school and college graduates had to scrounge for jobs. Trust in the reform agenda to provide secure employment ebbed at such moments.[25]

All in all, the evidence adds up to a mixed picture of pluses and minuses. Business-inspired reformers have indeed changed schools —in some instances for the better and in other instances for the worse.

Proposals for the Future

After all of this analysis and weighing of pros and cons, let me make a few suggestions for the future of business-inspired school reform— for I am sure that the business community will continue to influence public education. My suggestions draw from my experiences in schools, my research-based knowledge, and my values, as well as from my conclusions about what business-motivated reformers have achieved and what they have stumbled over. Here are my six proposals:

- Tone down the rhetoric about the failure of U.S. schools and show more humility in advising changes.
- Target the urban and rural schools that most need direct help.
- Give practitioners ownership of the reforms.
- Restore civic engagement as the primary goal of tax-supported public schools.
- Revive the ethic of community service within businesses.
- Educate and train employees within businesses.

Tone Down the Rhetoric

Time and again, critics have assailed the public schools for causing national problems and have exaggerated the schools' shortcomings while offering simplistic solutions in order to muster political support for reform. The cycle of overheated speechifying needs to be broken. Who better to break it than well-organized associations of business leaders with both resources and access to opinion-setting elites? None of this is to argue that school problems do not exist or that reformers are peddling myths. Big-city schools and those mired in rural poverty across the nation have been and still are in serious trouble. That is where business-minded reformers would do well to concentrate, not on generic solutions applied uniformly to all schools.

Consider the following advice from an unlikely source: "Policy-makers should be risk-averse when it comes to changing public school systems. To alter the institutional structure of U.S. schools radically without sufficient evidence that the 'reforms' would be successful is to put our children at risk . . . careful experimentation and evaluation should proceed on a limited basis before wide-scale institutional changes are introduced." No policymaker, corporate leader, governor, or U.S. president offered this opinion. Nor is it from the business leader-turned-school reformer Jamie Vollmer. The advice comes from a member of a group highly favored by elected officials and CEOs when they seek guidance on public policy: an economist. Alan B. Krueger, who has analyzed massive databases on U.S. schooling, responded to both technical economic and educational policy questions with this sober and humble opinion.[26]

I can imagine the rebuttal to these points. Look at the rankings of U.S. students on international tests. Look at the tough times employers have finding entry-level workers with appropriate skills and the problems college professors have getting students to put a coherent paragraph together. Look at how worker productivity and economic growth require hardworking and skilled graduates. And on and on. These problems do exist.

Yet I question whether the problems are of such a magnitude and pressing urgency in middle- and upper-income suburbs that a uniform national solution should be applied to all schools. I have argued that business-inspired reformers, using the highly charged rhetoric of equal opportunity and individual merit, have framed the problem only in national terms, and as a consequence have produced a defective logic of action.

The current reform agenda constricts the definition of a "good" school to a factory for churning out students prepared for college. With the current two-thirds dropout rate for minority and poor students who do go to college, reconsidering the agenda is a necessity. Not every student should go to college: most jobs do not require education beyond high school. Not every student can afford to go to college. Not every student wants to go to college. Business-inspired reformers have harmed many youth from rich, middle-class, and poor families who find a steady regimen of academic coursework, preparation for tests, and fears of being denied diplomas stultifying and hostile to either thinking or lifelong learning. Suppose business leaders were to support fusing high school and community college programs—to appeal to young people of ages fourteen through twenty-one who want college preparation as well as to those who seek vocational-technical careers in crafts, health fields, sales, management, or the arts. This type of change would realign a severe imbalance in school opportunities. Such a major realignment and reorganization, uniting high school and community college curriculum and pedagogy, would recognize students' diversity of interests, motivation, and academic performance, a recognition that is sadly missing from the current reform agenda.

Target Schools That Most Need Help

Schools that enroll largely poor children do need help, but not just because of low test scores. The quality of schooling and the access to community services they offer are inferior to what most middle- and upper-middle-income students routinely receive. No colorblind rhetoric about equal access to high academic standards can make up for the uncomfortable fact that urban schools, in their funding and staffing, end up duplicating the nation's social and economic inequalities—except for the few students who become grist for the media mill as "success" stories. The democratic promise of schools as institutions that offer personal success, social stability, and economic growth to all Americans is eroded by the corrosive effects of economic and social structures that sustain poverty and racism.

Some business leaders have recognized that school interventions in preschool and in elementary grades have achieved positive results, with their students doing better in their teen years than others who lacked such interventions. They have urged federal funding of preschools for all three-year-olds. Others have pushed states and cities to expand preschool to all day and to make it available to children even younger than three. Not only do such expenditures become investments, but also, in the words of a report by the Committee for Economic Development, preschools for urban children help make a "just society."[27]

Yet even these measures are insufficient to overcome the caustic effects of poverty on families or those of underfunded schools staffed with inexperienced and uncertified teachers who enter and leave schools as if schoolhouse doors were turnstiles. School interventions are important, but they are not polio vaccines.[28]

Other efforts to help poor urban and rural children have shown repeatedly that current funding, class size, and staffing are simply insufficient to flatten a hilly playing field. It is a lesson that many poor and middle-income parents already know when they aggressively seek out opportunities for their children in their district or neighboring ones. A glimpse of actual dollar costs can be seen in the Maya Angelou Charter School in Washington, D.C., founded by two young entrepreneurs who designed a college-preparatory program with an array of support services for District youth who had done poorly in regular high schools. Called "School for Success," it costs $28,000 per student per year, part of which comes from the D.C. schools with the rest raised by the charter school's directors. The District public schools spend just over $10,000 per student.[29]

Or consider the 2003 opening of Columbia University's private elementary school on the Upper West Side of New York City for children of faculty. University officials let half of the seats in the school go to neighborhood children by lottery. Teacher salaries go as high as $100,000. Twenty percent of the teachers have doctorates, and the student-teacher ratio is five to one. Total costs per student (undisclosed by university officials) probably run higher than the $22,000 charge for annual tuition (the university pays 80 percent of the tuition for students who come from the local community). New York City public schools spent $10,500 per student in 2001.[30]

The underfunding of urban schools and support services is also a lesson learned for private foundations that have promised a college education to poor students if they graduate from high school drug-free and not pregnant. The Ewing Kauffman Foundation found that their pledge to all ninth-graders at Westport High School in Kansas City, Missouri, to pay the costs of attending college yielded only 16 percent who gained bachelor's degrees. To raise that percentage the foundation hired a staff to provide services to students during high school; it will spend more than $20,000 per student just for support services in addition to what the district spends to educate each student. "We are going to build a safety net around these kids," says the foundation's president.[31]

An entire generation of low-income children, white, Hispanic, Native American, and black, needs sustained attention, smaller classes, an array of support services in and out of school, and well-qualified teachers and principals to help them graduate and attend college. Purveyors of colorblind access to high academic standards and race-neutral accountability seldom mention these important details. Ewing Kauffman, who made his fortune in pharmaceuticals, and other business leaders (past and present) have learned that "colorblind equity" means little in the absence of additional resources targeted at urban and rural poor children who need individual attention and help beyond what schools routinely do. Class action suits pursuing equity in funding urban children's education have been filed in New Jersey (*Abbott v. Burke,* 1988), New York (*Campaign for Fiscal Equity v. New York State,* 2003), and other states—but seldom with support from business associations. Business and civic leaders lobbying policymakers for education policies need to heed the truth about underfunding of low-income schools, or the historical inequalities in services to urban children will be perpetuated for another generation.[32]

Let Practitioners Own the Reforms

Most business leaders recognize the importance of recruiting, training, and developing better teachers. Business organizations and individual executives have often called for getting qualified and experienced teachers in all classrooms, especially in poor urban and rural schools, because of their conviction that high-quality teaching, improved student academic performance, and global economic competitiveness are linked. Louis Gerstner, a former IBM chairman and an advocate for standards-based reform, has headed a commission making recommendations to raise teacher salaries and entice more qualified individuals into classrooms. "For the cost of 15 B-2 bombers, we can give three million teachers real incentives to raise student achievement and stay in the classroom," the press release for Gerstner's commission said. The ex-CEO added: "For long-term national security, well-educated workers—and not just weapons and bombers—are crucial." Such support for the core principle of learning—the relationship between a teacher and students—albeit for "national security" goals, has become increasingly evident, especially in the wake of meager returns in achievement from massive investments in new technologies.[33]

With rising support for improving the quality of teaching, the paradox that often arises in movements for school reform—that educators are blamed for the problem and yet those very same educators are expected to provide the solution—became apparent again. Yet a growing number of savvy business leaders, wise in the ways of organizational change, have learned that designing and adopting policies without significant involvement by teachers is a recipe for failure. Putting the policies into practice, developing the capacities of teachers and administrators to use the policies as they were intended to be used, and recognizing the worth of adaptations that practitioners make are also crucial for the reforms to be sustained.

Sustainability of reform, that is, the long-term and widespread incorporation of reforms into district operations, is hard to achieve because of competing and changing demands of reformers, unstable resources, turnover of teachers and administrators, and districts' uneven capacity to consolidate reforms. Without substantial participation by practitioners in the design and adoption of reforms, most plans for improvements in teaching and learning—and the effects of those plans on what occurs in classrooms—will fall apart. Because the debris of discarded reforms litters schoolhouses across the nation, sustainability—"moving beyond numbers to deep and lasting change"—is essential for the success of any new reforms.[34]

This sustainability depends greatly upon business leaders moving beyond their longtime allergy against teachers' unions and deciding to trust teachers' expertise, giving them a broad array of opportunities to take leadership in and out of the classroom in designing, adopting, and adapting reforms. Without practitioners' ownership of the reforms, without policymakers' endorsement of the adaptations that teachers and principals make to these policies, the odds of reforms evolving, sticking, and lasting are sharply reduced.

Make Civic Engagement the Primary Goal

The political scientist Benjamin Barber put it clearly: "We may be natural consumers and born narcissists, but citizens have to be made." Citizens are made in the home, in the community, and, historically, in schools. Nineteenth-century civic and business elites knew this and sought the inculcation of civic values as the primary goal of public schools, especially in times of social tumult.[35]

In the twentieth century, however, the single-minded focus on preparing students for the workplace shoved aside civic responsibilities, relegating them to throwaway lines in commencement addresses or perfunctory items on business leaders' lists of worthy educational outcomes. Schools can certainly teach students to appreciate productive labor, but they cannot generate jobs, alleviate unemployment, or reduce poverty. The national economic problem that elites and policymakers have identified as a school-based issue, that is, the apparent mismatch of skills between what companies needed in an ever-changing economy and what graduates have to offer, has narrowed the perceived purpose of schooling to preparing students for work and college—in effect, offering more of an actual vocational education than an earlier generation of progressives promoted.

This narrow view of schooling has crowded out competing views of an appropriate education. Historically, community-based schools, various versions of progressive schools, and democratically driven schools existed side by side with traditional schools. Hybrid versions of the above types of schools also evolved over the decades. Even amid the clamor for testing and accountability of recent decades, such public schools exist in scattered locations. In the past, business leaders and philanthropists promoted and nurtured such visions of schooling as best for the nation and appropriate for all children. Few do so today.[36]

Here are a few reasons why civic and business elites should promote such diversity in schooling. First, public schools whose primary purpose is to prepare students for work and college will disappoint many graduates and their parents. As federal and private funds for supporting minority high school graduates' entering college decrease, expectations get crushed. Nearly half of all students who do go on to college (and two-thirds of minority students) will fail to get a bachelor's degree. Those who go directly from high school into entry-level jobs depend on whether economic prosperity or recession is in season. When jobs are in short supply, college graduates driving taxis or working at Starbucks become clichés. And they take jobs away from younger students just leaving high school. When recessions ease and jobs are again created, employment rises, and graduates with bachelors' and advanced degrees soon learn that they are overcredentialed for the jobs they accept. A harvest of disillusionment lies in wait for graduates and their parents when the primary goal of schooling is getting a job. Diverse schools can provide a range of high-quality public school options that match students' varied interests, motivations, and academic inclinations and not create graduates angry at being denied jobs they were promised.

The second reason for broadening the range of good schools is that we live in a multicultural society where working with people of various cultures, religions, and values is a fact of life. Respect for those differences is essential in a democratic society where the workplace, voting precinct, shops, PTA, church, and community meetings throw people together to deliberate trivial to serious questions. Respect for differences—not simply toleration—needs to be cultivated in schools because no other institution, including the family, is better suited to inculcate values of civic responsibility for the public good and to nurture those crucial social values in the young. Respect is the foundation of civic engagement, that is, caring for one's own community and working to make it better than it is. And civic engagement, if not instead of workplace preparation then surely in combination with it, may well be more promising in dealing with the social isolation, gated communities, and abiding income inequalities that undermine democratic institutions. Current policymakers have assumed (with crossed fingers behind their backs) that testing- and accountability-driven traditional school goals can advance the values of respect and civic engagement. There is, however, another social institution, in addition to schools, that can nurture respect and civic engagement—the business community.

Revive Community Service within Companies

A tradition of businesses serving the community evolved initially in the 1920s in the wake of World War I, when many corporations identified with the war effort and tied their economic interests to national purposes. Part of the tradition also came from the introduction of public relations and the desire to curry public favor as political protection from muckrakers. Thus the president of Metropolitan Life Insurance Company could say in 1922: "Metropolitan desires that it shall not be considered by the public a money-making institution, which is doing work for profit . . . What we are trying to do is use that business as a public institution for the purpose of serving the American people."[37]

Throughout the 1930s and the World War II years, corporate leaders sought civic responsibilities. In 1946 an advertisement for a division of General Motors in Muncie, Indiana, declared: "We are genuinely interested in the civic welfare and in the activities we share with our neighbors. We try to be good citizens. We contribute what we can to the city's interests, and we like to think that the employment we provide and the taxes we pay are important to the community . . . Our main concern is with the hope that folks here are also glad to have us as neighbors." Similar corporate language today amid scandals and the dominance of global corporations in U.S. life would be met with ridicule, but back then the strong impulse to be good corporate citizens mirrored the business community's desire to become, in Peter Drucker's phrase, "America's representative social institution."[38]

The tradition of civic responsibility is still alive in the advertising copy and images of many businesses. Scholars have documented efforts by CEOs during the late 1970s and throughout the 1980s to be "good citizens" by joining elected officials and parents in improving schools. The political scientist Clarence Stone called these efforts in various cities building "civic capacity" and judged the success of school improvement by the degree to which businesses had been involved. Business partnerships with local schools and districts, from Boeing to the Boston Compact, fall within this service tradition of working to build stronger communities.[39]

Much would have to be done to revive this tradition fully, particularly since the exuberant greed of CEOs, investment bankers, and corporate directors gripped public attention in the 1990s. Corporate nonpayment of taxes and excessive tax abatements would have to be corrected. Commercial penetration of schools to sell products and use public space to advertise, and similar ventures that large segments of the public find offensive, would need to be curbed. A new business agenda for schools would include more preschool education; recruiting, training, and developing new and experienced teachers; and strong support for career-tech education as an alternative to preparing every high school student for four-year college.

Most important, business leaders would need to commit themselves to the idea—absent thus far in the ideological focus on attaining the one best version of a "good" school—that there are (and have been) many kinds of "good" schools that can maintain high standards, academic achievement, and core values. Jamie Vollmer, the former business executive whose epiphany about the differences between schools and businesses I quoted in the Introduction, has often declared in speeches that the narrowness of age-graded schools with their uniform curriculum is not in the best interest of either children or the country:

Schools should not be in the business of selecting and sorting, but should be in the business of unfolding potential and helping every child meet his or her full potential . . . All children are going to school the same number of hours and days. As soon as you hold time constant, you are selecting and sorting, because some people take longer to learn what they need to know. But, if you don't give them more time, you're judging on the basis of the speed at which people learn.

Were other business leaders to advance such expanded views of "good" schooling and push to restore the tradition of being engaged citizens in a multicultural community, schools would begin to move toward addressing social and economic inequalities that have long marred the nation.[40]

Educate and Train Employees

Finally, were businesses themselves to work actively to educate their employees, the effects could ripple outward to encompass schools. CEOs and their lieutenants say again and again that education is crucial to the success of business, but only a few companies invest substantial funds in worker training. Of the hundreds of thousands of employers in the United States, fewer than two hundred companies (IBM, Xerox, Motorola are familiar names) spend more than 2 percent of their payroll on educating their workers. About two-thirds of their corporate training dollar is spent on formal programs for college-educated men and women in professional, managerial, and technical jobs. Machine operators, maintenance and repair workers, and clerical personnel receive few corporate dollars. Training is tied closely to managerial innovations (such as team building or quality-control procedures), new machinery, and safety regulations. The irony is that the workers most likely to need on-the-job training are the least likely to get it—the youngest, those whose native language is not English, and the oldest.[41]

Some firms have charted a different course. At IBM's circuit-board factory in Austin, Texas, in the mid-1980s, for example, $60 million in costs had to be cut. Managers reorganized the plant into teams and redefined the factory's jobs so that every worker had much broader responsibilities and a potential career within the company. Five percent of the plant's payroll went into education of workers. Some had to learn to read and do basic arithmetic; all workers learned how to maintain the machines, use computers, trouble-shoot problems that arose, and plan production schedules. What happened? By 1990, productivity had increased 200 percent and circuit-board quality was five times better.[42]

Consider Vera, who had worked at IBM since 1969 and fed circuit boards one by one into a machine that put in transistors and capacitors. She removed a board from the machine about twelve hundred times a day, inspected it, and put it into either a "pass" bin or a "reject" bin. After the reorganization, Vera still loaded circuit boards into the machine but for only one-quarter of her workday. She belonged to a team that met each morning to discuss the work for the day, decide what materials needed to be ordered, kept records of "pass" and "reject" boards, and called suppliers and customers. What did Vera think about the change? "I've been working a lot harder . . . but it's worth it . . . I can make decisions. I am also learning things that will be useful to me in all kinds of jobs."[43]

Vera's work after reorganization put a high premium on her (and her frontline colleagues) learning many more tasks and skills in working with team members. Here were concrete lessons on the connection between academic and social skills and daily work. She stretched her capacities with IBM staff pushing while also supporting her as she learned. Self-direction on the job increased. It is worth considering what effects Vera's greater autonomy on the job might have on the attitudes she communicates to her young children—how changes in their mom's work and her opportunities for education at IBM might influence their aspirations, what they expect from school, and how they perform in school. These are crucial links that go well beyond the questions researchers ask today. These ties between parents' occupational self-direction and children's aspirations spilling over to their work in school carry the promise of breaking the iron-clad grip of parents' social class on children's academic performance. Suppose business leaders, instead of blaming the public schools for sending poorly prepared graduates into the job market, decided to take more responsibility for educating and training their employees. Such a change would benefit the firms themselves, and might yield strong benefits to the schools as well. Educating employees is not a job to be wholly assigned to tax-supported schools; it should be the business of business.[44]

I am pessimistic about whether business leaders and policy elites will seriously consider the modest suggestions I have offered. I say "modest" because I have not gone so far as to suggest changes in tax laws to channel more funds to schools, racial and ethnic integration of sub-urban neighborhoods, government incentive grants to poor families for buying homes and sending their children to college, health insurance for the poor, or similar measures that would challenge deep-seated economic and social structures that sustain poverty and racial discrimination.

Many opinion setters, I suspect, will view even my modest suggestions as politically naive. After all, being an "education president" or an "education governor" who endorses standards-based reform, testing, and tough accountability sells well in the voting booth these days. The prospect of investing more money in schools and attracting experienced, well-qualified practitioners into largely minority classrooms, much less asking CEOs to spend more on employee education and grant employees more autonomy, may seem as remote as the likelihood of winning a multimillion-dollar lottery.

Yet the mix of altruism and self-interest that propelled earlier generations of business leaders to join civic officials, elected policymakers, educators, and others to improve schools is still alive and well today. Corporate leaders who look for ways businesses can rehabilitate their scandal-tarnished reputation for self-serving greed, commercial exploitation of the young, and neglect of the common good may well opt for building civic capacity and serving the community. Many of these leaders already give employees opportunities to learn on the job and to take on increased responsibility. If business leaders decided that the best ways for them to improve public schools and increase public trust in schools were to better educate their own employees and to encourage schools to stress civic engagement, practitioners' ownership of reforms, and service to the common good, the entire nation would owe such men and women a deep debt of gratitude.

NOTES

ACKNOWLEDGMENTS

INDEX

NOTES

Introduction: Business and School Reform

1. Addams quoted in Merle Curti, *The Social Ideas of American Educators* (Totowa, N.J.: Littlefield, Adams, 1966), p. 203.

2. Ellwood P. Cubberley, *Public School Administration* (Boston: Houghton Mifflin, 1916), p. 338.

3. Rod Paige, letter to the editor, *New Yorker*, October 6, 2003, p. 12.

4. Business interest in school reform has involved private individuals and groups drawn from a variety of large, mid-sized, and small businesses. There is no monolithic business community such as "Big Business" that has shaped and steered U.S. public schools. Of course there are corporate elites in the United States. Private-sector firms are highly organized and possess resources that many other types of groups lack. But the businesses involved in school activities are diverse, from multinational Fortune 500 companies to regional and national business associations to local Chambers of Commerce.

5. "Reality Check 2000," *Education Week*, February 16, 2000, pp. S1–S8; Richard Ingersoll, *Who Controls Teachers' Work?* (Cambridge, Mass.: Harvard University Press, 2003), pp. 219–228.

6. Jamie Robert Vollmer, "The Blueberry Story," *Education Week*, March 6, 2002, p. 42. I have encountered this story on the Internet a number of

times and it has been sent to me by colleagues and students. Vollmer is an entrepreneur helping school districts engage their communities in system-wide improvements. His web page displays products that his firm sells: *www.jamievollmer.com/*.

7. The Reverend William Rainsford of New York City quoted in Lawrence Cremin, *Transformation of the School* (New York: Vintage, 1961), p. 85. I will use the word "reformer" to encompass policymakers such as local, state, and federal legislators, persons with authority (such as superintendents) who make decisions about schools, business leaders participating in school improvement, civic leaders who hold no formal positions in government, and informed citizens, including parents, who seek school improvement. While educators, individually and as members of unions and professional associations, often join reform coalitions, they seldom assemble political groups. Reformers often perceive them as reluctant allies. There have been exceptions, of course. Educational reform in the late nineteenth and early twentieth centuries included numerous academics and some superintendents who called themselves progressives, and in the late twentieth century a number of academics took the lead in school reform: James Comer, Henry Levin, Robert Slavin, Theodore Sizer, and others (see Chapter 1).

8. Quotation from Marvin Lazerson, *Origins of the Urban School: Public Education in Massachusetts, 1870–1915* (Cambridge, Mass.: Harvard University Press, 1971), p. 202. Historians and social scientists have noted the frequency of reformers turning to schools to solve national problems. See Michael Katz, *Reconstructing American Education* (Cambridge, Mass.: Harvard University Press, 1987), pp. 111–135; Lawrence Cremin, *Popular Education and Its Discontents* (New York: Harper and Row, 1990), pp. 85–127; Carl Kaestle, "The Public Schools and the Public Mood," *American Heritage* 41 (February 1990): 61–81; David Tyack and Larry Cuban, *Tinkering toward Utopia* (Cambridge, Mass.: Harvard University Press, 1995), pp. 40–59. Also see John Chubb and Terry Moe, *Politics, Markets, and America's Schools* (Washington: Brookings Institution Press, 1990), pp. 53–55, for a discussion of how interest groups in a democracy foist goals upon public schools.

9. The historian Robert Wiebe concluded: "The social theory of the business community resembled in a general way the view of comfortable

Americans everywhere. Its major tenets—a restricted definition of the people, a belief in a leadership elite, a denial of [social] classes, and a faith in individualism—all belonged to the standard philosophy of the early twentieth century." Wiebe, *Businessmen and Reform: A Study of the Progressive Movement* (Cambridge, Mass.: Harvard University Press, 1962), p. 204. The political scientist Mark A. Smith captures the ideology, political structures, institutions, and public response to business leadership in the last third of the twentieth century in *American Business and Political Power: Public Opinions, Elections, and Democracy* (Chicago: University of Chicago Press, 2000), chs. 7–8. For opinion polls on "big business" in the mid-twentieth century, see Burton Fisher and Stephen Withey, *Big Business as the People See It* (Ann Arbor: Institute for Social Research, University of Michigan, 1951), p. xi.

10. A business leader heavily involved in school reform would undoubtedly write a very different book—and some have done so. See, for example, David Kearns and Denis Doyle, *Winning the Brain Race* (San Francisco: ICS Press, 1989); and Louis Gerstner, Roger Semerad, and Denis Doyle, *Reinventing Education: Entrepreneurship in Today's Schools* (New York: Dutton, 1994).

1. The Logic of the Reforms

1. A. Caswell Ellis, *The Money Value of Education,* Department of Interior, Bureau of Education, Bulletin no. 22 (Washington: U.S. Government Printing Office, 1917), p. 30.

2. For nineteenth-century beliefs about education, see Rush Welter, *Popular Education and Democratic Thought in America* (New York: Columbia University Press, 1962), chs. 11 and 13.

3. Ibid., p. 6.

4. Quoted in Harvey Kantor, "Choosing a Vocation: The Origins and Transformation of Vocational Guidance in California, 1910–1930," *History of Education Quarterly* 26, no. 3 (1986): 354.

5. In a report from the National Association of Manufacturers in 1912, a section was entitled "Our Human Capital": "There are two kinds of capital in the world. The one we call property. It consists of lands and machinery, of stocks and bonds, etc. . . . The other kind is human capital—the character,

brains, and muscle of the people." Quoted in Marvin Lazerson and Norton Grubb, *American Education and Vocationalism: A Documentary History, 1870–1970* (New York: Teachers College Press, 1974), p. 92.

6. Joe Baird and Kirsten Stewart, "Education Pays, Census Says," *Salt Lake Tribune,* July 18, 2002, p. A1; D'Vera Cohn, "Census Report Says Education Pays, Even More So Now," *Washington Post,* July 18, 2002, p. A20.

7. An example of unflagging support for the No Child Left Behind legislation can be seen on the Business Roundtable's website. See the "Toolkit" at *www.businessroundtable.org/taskforces/taskforce/issue.aspx?qs=6BF5BF159F8 49514481138A74FA1851159169FEB56C38B3* and a commissioned poll of attitudes toward the legislation at *www.brtable.org/press.cfm/966.*

8. For an early version of theories of action, see Arthur Wise, *Legislated Learning* (Berkeley: University of California Press, 1979), pp. 54–58. Wise describes and criticizes the "hyper-rational" policies of the 1960s and 1970s, including state and federal efforts to legislate accountability and tests (see ch. 2). He also critiques business leaders' and economists' assumptions about schools (see pp. 71–72). For more recent discussions of theories of action, see Chris Argyris and Donald Schon, *Theory in Practice* (San Francisco: Jossey-Bass, 1982); Carol Weiss, "Nothing as Practical as Good Theory" in J. P. Connell, A. Kubisch, L. Schorr, and C. Weiss, eds., *New Approaches to Evaluating Community Initiatives* (Washington: Aspen Institute, 1995), pp. 65–92. Applications of theories of action to particular policies and reforms can be found in Thomas Hatch, "The Differences in Theory That Matter in the Practice of School Improvement," *American Educational Research Journal* 35, no. 1 (1998): 3–31; Betty Malen, Robert Croninger, Donna Muncey, and Donna Redmond-Jones, "Reconstituting Schools: 'Testing' the 'Theory of Action,'" *Educational Evaluation and Policy Analysis* 24, no. 2 (2002): 113–132.

9. A fine example of competing school reform coalitions in Chicago, one of which was business-driven, is analyzed in Dorothy Shipps, "Pulling Together: Civic Capacity and Urban School Reform," *American Education Research Journal* (forthcoming).

10. For more on the topic of this section, see Larry Cuban, *Oversold and Underused: Computers in Classrooms* (Cambridge, Mass.: Harvard University Press, 2001).

11. Larry Cuban, *Teachers and Machines* (New York: Teachers College Press, 1986); Business Roundtable, "Essential Components of a Successful Education System," *www.brtable.org/document.cfm/467*.

12. Steve Case, interview, *Business Week,* September 25, 2000, *www.business week.com/2000/00_39/b3700119.htm*.

13. Jeff Archer and Mark Walsh, "Summit Garners Mixed Reviews from Pundits, Practitioners," *Education Week,* April 3, 1996, pp. 12, 15. Policy statement is on p. 13.

14. See Cuban, *Oversold and Underused,* pp. 177–179; Leslie Brooks Suzukamo, "Lawson Will Cut 82 More Jobs," *Pioneer Press,* September 23, 2003, *www.twincities.com/mld/pioneerpress/6836104.htm*.

15. Cuban, *Oversold and Underused,* ch. 3.

16. Data on the economy in the 1970s from David Vogel, *Fluctuating Fortunes: Political Power of Business in America* (New York: Basic Books, 1989), pp. 113–114, 136, 230, 256.

17. Ibid., p. 256.

18. Henry Aaron, *Politics and the Professors* (Washington: Brookings Institution, 1978).

19. Quotations from Carol Ray and Roslyn Mickelson, "Business Leaders and the Politics of School Reform," *Politics of Education Association Yearbook, 1989,* p. 123.

20. One of the better summaries of this view can be found in Chester E. Finn Jr., *We Must Take Charge: Our Schools and Our Future* (New York: Free Press, 1991); also see Diane Ravitch, "The Test of Time," *Education Next, www.educationnext.org/20032/32.html,* and, in the same issue, a reprint of Albert Shanker's retrospective (May 9, 1993) on the *Nation at Risk* report. Quotation from "Joint Statement by Norman Augustine, Ed Lupberger, and James Orr, July 2, 1996," *www.brtable.org/taskforces/taskforce/document.aspx? qs=6A25BF159F849514481138A74EB1851159169FEB56236*.

21. For an analysis of changes in the economy that raised major points beyond blaming schools, see Barry Bluestone and Bennett Harrison, *The Deindustrialization of America* (New York: Basic Books, 1982).

22. Vollmer quoted at *www.graves.k12.ky.us/news/district/rethinking_ed .htm*.

23. I have drawn these assumptions from a voluminous collection of

newspaper and journal articles, trade books, research studies, and national commission reports over the past three decades. For example, economists and widely respected analysts produced bestsellers that judged schools as failures in teaching students to think and solve problems: see Ray Marshall and Marc Tucker, *Thinking for a Living: Education and the Wealth of Nations* (New York: Basic Books, 1992); Robert Reich, *The Work of Nations* (New York: Knopf, 1991); and Lester Thurow, *Head to Head: The Coming Economic Battle among Japan, Europe, and America* (New York: Morrow, 1992). Many of the assumptions are stated explicitly by national business organizations, individual corporate leaders, and ad hoc groups of public officials and corporate leaders: see Thomas Toch, *In the Name of Excellence* (Philadelphia: American Philological Association, 1991). In ch. 2 Toch summarizes various business and governmental reports following *A Nation at Risk* that draw connections between education and a stronger economy. Also see David Kearns and Denis Doyle, *Winning the Brain Race: A Bold Plan to Make Our Schools Competitive* (Oakland, Calif.: ICS Press, 1988). Articles from the *Wall Street Journal* and the *National Review* offer views from the conservative side of the political spectrum. On the progressive side, articles from the *Nation* and the *American Prospect* offer views that, by and large, accept these assumptions, although far more challenges appear in these journals.

24. Low public confidence in schools has long been one of the reasons given for pursuing reform. And yet opinion polls throughout the 1980s and 1990s showed that public confidence in schools was split. Respondents giving the nation's public schools an A or B ranged from 20 to 30 percent. But when respondents were asked about their neighborhood school, the percentage designating A and B rose to 30 to 45 percent. In 1999 an Educational Testing Service poll of parents found that "between 70 and 95 percent of households with children were satisfied with their public elementary schools." Suburban parents registered confidence in the mid-90 percentages. Poll data reveal both deterioration of support and increasing confidence, a confusing picture. Yet, as one scholar pointed out, "This decline starkly contrasts with the behavior of some of education's most important actors—students, parents, and governments. They act in significant ways as if they are dealing with an institution in exquisite health. Historically large percentages

of students are staying in school, parents in increasing numbers choose public schools over private schools, and governments allocate scarce public revenues to schools far in excess of inflationary pressures." Tom Loveless, "The Structure of Public Confidence in Education," *American Journal of Education* 105 (February 1997): 140–141, 150. Also see Anthony Carnevale and Donna Desrochers, *School Satisfaction: A Statistical Profile of Cities and Suburbs* (Princeton: Educational Testing Service, 1999), p. 7.

25. Carl Kaestle and Michael Smith, "The Federal Role in Elementary and Secondary Education, 1940–1980," *Harvard Educational Review* 52 (November 1982): 384–408.

26. On the Saturn Corporation, see *www.saturn.com/saturn/aboutus/our story/index.jsp?nav=1100*. Jeanne Allen, ed., *Can Business Save Education?* (Washington: Heritage Foundation, 1989), p. 1.

27. Carol Ray and Roslyn Mickelson, "Business Leaders and the Politics of School Reform," in *Politics of Education Association Yearbook* (London: Taylor and Francis, 1990), pp. 119–135; Dorothy Shipps, "Echoes of Corporate Influence: Managing Away Urban School Troubles," in L. Cuban and D. Shipps, *Reconstructing the Common Good in Education: Coping with Intractable American Dilemmas* (Stanford, Calif.: Stanford University Press, 2000), pp. 82–106. David Kearns and Denis Doyle, *Winning the Brain Race: A Bold Plan to Make Our Schools Competitive* (Oakland, Calif.: ICS Press, 1988). Nancy Perry, "Saving the Schools: How Business Can Help," *Fortune Magazine,* November 7, 1988, pp. 42–46, 50–56. Quotation from Marsha Levine and Roberta Trachtman, eds., *American Business and the Public School* (New York: Teachers College Press, 1988), p. xxiii.

28. Here I draw on case studies of business involvement in district school systems. See, for example, an in-depth study of a corporate elite heavily involved in one city's school politics and reform by Dorothy Shipps, "The Invisible Hand: Big Business and Chicago School Reform," *Teachers College Record* 99, no. 1 (1997): 73–116; also Roslyn A. Mickelson, "Corporations and Classrooms: A Critical Examination of the Business Agenda for Urban School Reform," in Karen McClafferty, Carlos Torres, and Theodore Mitchell, eds., *Challenges of Urban Education: Sociological Perspectives for the Next Century* (Albany, N.Y.: State University of New York Press, 2000), pp. 127–173.

29. Influential educational policymakers evolved a similar strategy that derived from the approach used by California's state superintendent, Bill Honig, between 1983 and 1990. By the early 1990s this strategy, which had come to be called systemic reform, nicely converged with the market-driven prescriptions for improving schools. For the 1980s, see Paul Berman's chapter on California in Marsha Levine and Roberta Trachtman, eds., *Corporate Involvement in Education* (New York: Teachers College Press, 1988). See Marshall Smith and Jennifer O'Day, "Systemic School Reform," in Susan Fuhrman and Betty Malen, eds., *The Politics of Curriculum and Testing: The 1990 Yearbook of the Politics of Education* (Philadelphia: Falmer, 1991); also see Maris Vinovskis, *History and Educational Policymaking* (New Haven: Yale University Press, 1999), pp. 171–202. For descriptions of standards and accountability policies adopted by states and the federal government, see "Quality Counts 2003: The Teacher Gap," *Education Week,* January 9, 2003, pp. 75–76, 78. Jodi Wilgoren, "For 2000, the G.O.P. Sees Education in a New Light," New York Times, August 2, 2000, p. A15; David Sanger, "Bush Pushes Ambitious Education Plan," *New York Times,* January 24, 2001, pp. A1, A14; "Quality Counts '99," *Education Week,* January 11, 1999.

30. See, for example, the U.S. Chamber of Commerce's policy position on education at *www.uschamber.com/government/issues/education/education .htm.*

31. The following discussion has been adapted from Larry Cuban, "How Schools Change Reform: Redefining Reform Success and Failure," *Teachers College Record,* 99, no. 3 (1998): 453–477.

32. See Wise, *Legislated Learning.*

33. Statistics on fourth graders come from George Farkas and Shane Hall, "Can Title I Attain Its Goal?" in D. Ravitch, ed., *Brookings Papers on Educational Policy* (Washington: Brookings Institution Press, 2000), p. 90. And see Milbrey McLaughlin, "Implementation of ESEA Title I: A Problem of Compliance," *Teachers College Record* 77 (1976): 397–415; Geoffrey Borman, "Title I: The Evolution and Effectiveness of Compensatory Education," in Sam Stringfield and Deborah Land, eds., *Educating At-Risk Students,* Yearbook of National Society for the Study of Education, part 2 (Chicago: University of Chicago Press, 2002), pp. 231–247; Timothy Hacsi, *Children as Pawns* (Cambridge, Mass.: Harvard University Press, 2002), pp. 21–61.

34. Mark Zbaracki, "The Rhetoric and Reality of Total Quality Management," *Administrative Science Quarterly* 43 (1998): 602–636.

35. Stephen Kramer, "Letter to a State Test Scorer," *Education Week,* September 3, 2003, p. 43.

36. For a recent study that nicely considers the role of adaptiveness of policies in schools, see Amanda Datnow, Lea Hubbard, and Hugh Mehan, *Extending Educational Reform from One School to Many* (New York: Routledge Falmer, 2002).

37. See Amanda Datnow, "Power and Politics in the Adoption of School Reform Models," *Educational Evaluation and Policy Analysis* 22, no. 4 (2000): 357–374.

38. Charles Rabin, "Leaders Threaten Boycott on FCAT," *Miami Herald,* May 12, 2003, *www.miami.com/mld/miamiherald/news/local/5839954.htm;* David Hoff, "As Stakes Rise, Definition of Cheating Blurs," *Education Week,* June 21, 2000, pp. 1, 14–16. Larry Slonaker, "State Cancels Exit Exam," *San Jose Mercury News,* June 14, 2003, p. 1A; Peter Schrag, "'High Stakes Are for Tomatoes,'" *Atlantic Monthly,* August 2000, pp. 19–21; Michael Winerup, "A 70 Percent Failure Rate? Try Testing the Testers," *New York Times,* June 25, 2003, p. B9; Robert Linn, *Assessment-Based Reform: Challenges to Educational Measurement,* First Annual Angoff Lecture, November 7, 1994 (Princeton: Educational Testing Service, 1995).

2. How the Reforms Have Changed Schools

1. Kevin Phillips, *Wealth and Democracy* (New York: Broadway Books, 2002), 43; David Tyack and Elisabeth Hansot, *Managers of Virtue* (New York: Basic Books, 1982), 109.

2. On the fundamental changes in business organization, see Alfred D. Chandler Jr., *The Visible Hand: The Managerial Revolution in American Business* (Cambridge, Mass.: Harvard University Press, 1977); Louis Galambos, *The Public Image of Big Business in America, 1880–1940* (Baltimore: Johns Hopkins University Press, 1975), ch. 1. The point about corporations focusing on public relations and service comes from Roland Marchand, *Creating the Corporate Soul: The Rise of Public Relations and Corporate Imagery in American Big Business* (Berkeley: University of California

Press, 1998). Swope quoted in Marchand, *Creating the Corporate Soul,* p. 166.

3. Quotation from Marvin Lazerson and W. Norton Grubb, *American Education and Vocationalism, A Documentary History, 1870–1970* (New York: Teachers College Press, 1974), p. 90.

4. David Hogan, *Class and Reform: School and Society in Chicago, 1880–1930* (Philadelphia: University of Pennsylvania Press, 1985), pp. 162–163.

5. Robinson, speech to National Education Association (1910), quoted in Julia Wrigley, *Class Politics and Public Schools: Chicago, 1900–1950* (New Brunswick, N.J.: Rutgers University Press, 1982), p. 69. Chicago is a prime example of a city where business leaders explicitly sought school and civic reforms in the late nineteenth century and throughout most of the twentieth.

6. Gompers, speech to American Federation of Labor convention, 1909, quoted in Herbert Kliebard, *Schooled to Work: Vocationalism and the American Curriculum, 1876–1946* (New York: Teachers College Press, 1999), p. 37. Riis quoted in Lawrence Cremin, *The Transformation of the School* (New York: Vintage, 1961), p. 85.

7. David Tyack, *One Best System* (Cambridge, Mass.: Harvard University Press, 1974), p. 189. Miles quoted in Wrigley, *Class Politics and Public Schools,* p. 74. Robert J. Taggart, *Private Philanthropy and Public Education: Pierre S. Du Pont and the Delaware Schools, 1890–1940* (Newark: University of Delaware Press, 1988).

8. Quotations from Edward Kirkland, *Dream and Thought in the Business Community, 1860–1900* (Chicago: Quadrangle, 1964), pp. 69–70.

9. Joseph M. Rice, *The Public-School System of the United States* (New York: Arno Press and the New York Times, 1969), pp. 151, 98.

10. Ayres quoted in Kliebard, *Schooled to Work,* pp. 50–51.

11. Thomas Cochran quoted in Tyack and Hansot, *Managers of Virtue,* p. 110.

12. In the classic intellectual history of the progressive education movement, *Transformation of the School,* Lawrence Cremin divided progressive education into three wings: the scientific, the child-centered, and the reformist. I use the typology that David Tyack worked out in *The One Best System,* the exemplary study of urban schools that remains both useful and

relevant three decades later. In *Managers of Virtue*, Tyack and Hansot elaborate further about who administrative progressives were and what they did (pp. 105–179). Also see Ellen Lagemann, *An Elusive Science: The Troubling History of Education Research* (Chicago: University of Chicago Press, 2000), chs. 2–3. On the importance of tests to administrative progressives, see Daniel Resnick, "History of Educational Testing," in Alexandra Wigdor and Wendell Garner, eds., *Ability Testing: Uses, Consequences, and Controversies* (Washington: National Academy Press, 1982), pp. 173–194; Jerome D'Agostino, "Achievement Testing in American Schools," in Thomas Good, ed., *American Education: Yesterday, Today, and Tomorrow*, 99th Yearbook of the National Society for the Study of Education, part 2 (Chicago: National Society for the Study of Education, 2000), pp. 313–337. For the rhetorical and policy impact of scientific management that administrative progressives sought to apply to public schools, see Raymond Callahan, *Education and the Cult of Efficiency* (Chicago: University of Chicago Press, 1962).

13. Larry Cuban, *How Teachers Taught* (New York: Teachers College, 1993). Diane Ravitch, in *Left Back: A Century of Failed School Reforms* (New York: Simon and Schuster, 2000), and E. D. Hirsch, in *The Schools We Need and Why We Don't Have Them* (New York: Doubleday, 1996), argue that these progressives exerted great influence on teachers and principals and shaped what happened to children. Other educational progressives were libertarians and social reconstructionists. Libertarian progressives saw individual solutions to the problem of traditional schools. They sought to develop the emotional side of each child. Heavily influenced by the work of Sigmund Freud, these progressives often founded private schools where psychoanalytically inclined teachers devoted themselves to unwrapping the emotional, intellectual, and artistic talents of each child by using such Freudian concepts as the unconscious and transference. Margaret Naumberg's Children School, later the Walden School, is one example of such schools, where educators focused intensely on the inner lives of individual children and cared less about their schools solving social, economic, or political problems in the larger community. Another group of progressives were the social reconstructionists like George S. Counts, Harold Rugg, and John Childs of Teachers College, Columbia—occasionally joined by John Dewey. They believed that schools should be in the vanguard of reforming society. Writing

and speaking during the Great Depression and as European fascism spread, these progressives saw schools as "advancing the welfare and interests of the great masses of people who do the work of society—those who labor on farms and ships and in the mines, shops, and factories of the world." Beyond publishing books and the magazine *Social Frontier,* they had little influence on most teachers and administrators, much less on policy. See Cremin, *Transformation of the School,* pp. 209–215, 225–234. For women leaders among progressive educators, see Alan Sadovnik and Susan Semel, eds., *Founding Mothers and Others: Women Educational Leaders during the Progressive Era* (New York: Palgrave, 2002).

14. I omit the manual education movement that began in the 1880s because within a decade the vocational education movement overwhelmed those who saw manual arts courses (such as drawing and woodworking) as ways of enhancing academic learning. The manual arts movement is summarized in Marvin Lazerson and W. Norton Grubb, eds., *American Education and Vocationalism: A Documentary History, 1870–1970* (New York: Teachers College Press, 1974), pp. 2–17. Also see Cremin, *The Transformation of The School,* pp. 24–34. For union involvement in vocational education reform, see Ira Katznelson and Margaret Weir, *Schooling for All* (New York: Basic Books, 1985), ch. 6.

15. For the history of the National Society for the Promotion of Industrial Education, the evolution of the Smith-Hughes Act, and the growth of vocational education in schools, see Lazerson and Grubb, *American Education and Vocationalism,* introduction; Kliebard, *Schooled to Work,* pp. 39–44; and Harvey Kantor, *Learning to Earn: School, Work, and Vocational Reform in California, 1880–1930* (Madison: University of Wisconsin Press, 1988). For vocational education and blacks, see James Anderson, "The Historical Development of Black Vocational Education" in H. Kantor and D. Tyack, eds., *Work, Youth, and Schooling: Historical Perspectives on Vocationalism in American Education* (Stanford: Stanford University Press, 1982), pp. 180–222; for women and vocational education, see Geraldine J. Clifford, "'Marry, Stitch, Die, or Do Worse': Educating Women for Work," ibid., pp. 223–268; Jane Powers, *The "Girl Question" in Education: Vocational Education for Young Women in the Progressive Era* (London: Falmer, 1992); and John Rury, *Education and Women's Work* (Albany: State University of New York Press, 1991).

16. The percentage of young males aged fourteen to eighteen who were working rather than attending school declined from 43 in 1900 to 12 in 1930. For females at work in the same category, the percentage dipped from 18 in 1900 to 5 in 1930. Enrollments in high school went from 4 percent of those aged fourteen to seventeen in 1890 to 28 percent in 1920. By 1930 almost half of those who could attend school were enrolled. In 1900 just over 6 percent of all seventeen-year-olds graduated from high school; by 1930 it was 29 percent. Norton Grubb and Marvin Lazerson, "Education and the Labor Market," in Kantor and Tyack, eds., *Work, Youth, and Schooling*, p. 117. Enrollment figures are from Lazerson and Grubb, *American Education and Vocationalism*, pp. 21–22. For the differentiated high school curriculum, see Arthur Powell, Eleanor Farrar, and David Cohen, *The Shopping Mall High School* (Boston: Houghton Mifflin, 1985), ch. 5; for one city, see Jeffrey Mirel, *The Rise and Fall of an Urban School System, Detroit, 1907–1981* (Ann Arbor: University of Michigan Press, 1993), pp. 66–79.

17. Harvey Kantor, "Vocationalism in American Education: The Economic and Political Context, 1880–1930," in Kantor and Tyack, eds., *Work, Youth, and Schooling*, pp. 14–44; Kantor, *Learning to Earn*, ch. 7. Larry Cuban, "Enduring Resiliency: Enacting and Implementing Federal Vocational Legislation," in Kantor and Tyack, eds., *Work, Youth, and Schooling*, pp. 45–78.

18. Kantor, *Learning to Earn;* Cuban, "Enduring Resiliency."

19. Larry Cuban, *How Teachers Taught,* 2d ed. (New York: Teachers College Press, 1993); Arthur Zilversmit, "The Failure of Progressive Education, 1920–1940," in L. Stone, ed., *Schooling and Society* (Baltimore: Johns Hopkins University Press, 1976); Arthur Zilversmit, *Changing Schools: Progressive Education Theory and Practice, 1930–1960* (Chicago: University of Chicago Press, 1993). David Tyack, Robert Lowe, and Elisabeth Hansot, *Public Schools in Hard Times: The Great Depression and Recent Years* (Cambridge, Mass.: Harvard University Press, 1984).

20. Tyack, Lowe, and Hansot, *Public Schools in Hard Times.*

21. By "policy elites" I mean loose networks of corporate leaders, public officials, foundation officers, and academics who use both public and private funds to run projects and circulate ideas consistent with their versions of school reforms. They have ready access to media and the capacity to frame problems and set a public agenda for discussion. Political party labels

do not define them, although there are clearly Republican and Democratic members who carry their affiliation on their sleeves and, when administrations change, move in and out of office. I do not use the phrase to suggest conspiratorial groups secretly meeting and designing action plans. I suggest only that these overlapping networks of like-minded individuals share values and tastes and seek school improvements aligned to those values and tastes. They convene frequently in various forums, speak the same policy talk, and are connected closely to sources of influence in governments, media, businesses, academia, and foundations. They help create a climate of opinion that hovers around no more than a few hundred influentials in policymaking. Familiar with the ways of the media, they extend and shape that climate of opinion by working with journalists. Few members of these policy elites have had direct or sustained experience either as or with school principals or teachers, much less teaching children. Yet their recommendations touch the daily lives of both educators and children. See John Kingdon, *Agendas, Alternatives, and Public Policies* (Boston: Little, Brown, 1984); James Fallows, *Breaking the News* (New York: Random House, 1996); William Safire, "Elite Establishment Egghead Eupatrids," *New York Times Magazine*, May 18, 1997, p. 16.

22. Johnson quoted prior to preface in Henry Perkinson, *The Imperfect Panacea: American Faith in Education, 1865–1965* (New York: Random House, 1968).

23. Herbert Kohl, *36 Children* (New York: New American Library, 1968); David Rogers, *110 Livingston Street* (New York: Random House, 1968); Peter Schrag, *Village School Downtown: Boston Schools, Boston Politics* (Boston: Beacon Press, 1967). The words "mindlessness" and "joy of learning" come from Charles Silberman, *Crisis in the Classroom* (New York: Random House, 1970), pp. 10–11.

24. Ben Brodinsky, "Back to the Basics: The Movement and Its Meaning," *Phi Delta Kappan* 57 (March 1977): 522–527.

25. In the late 1960s a number of retrenching defense-related firms and eager entrepreneurs aware of newly authorized federal funds saw an emerging market for educational products and services to help school districts improve schooling of poor minority children. See David Tyack and Larry Cuban, *Tinkering toward Utopia* (Cambridge, Mass.: Harvard University Press,

1995), pp. 114–120. By the mid-1970s these programs had disappeared. Different versions of these education-connected business firms reappeared in the late 1980s; the bargain negotiated by business leaders, policymakers, and educators in many states in the 1980s is captured in Marsha Levine and Roberta Trachtman, *American Business and the Public School: Case Studies of Corporate Involvement in Public Education* (New York: Teachers College Press, 1988), chapters on California and Minnesota; also see Thomas Toch, *In the Name of Excellence* (New York: Oxford University Press, 1991), pp. 20–22.

26. Committee for Economic Development, *Investing in Our Children: Business and the Public Schools* (New York: Committee for Economic Development, 1985), pp. 5, 39.

27. Shanker quoted in Nancy Perry, "Saving Schools: How Business Can Help," *Fortune,* November 7, 1988, p. 44. Price quoted in Jeanne Allen and Michael J. McLaughlin, "A Businessman's Guide to the Education Reform Debate," Backgrounder 801 (Washington: Heritage Foundation, December 21, 1990).

28. See Brodinsky, "Back to the Basics"; Toch, *In The Name of Excellence,* p. 21; Dorothy Shipps, "The Invisible Hand: Big Business and Chicago School Reform," *Teachers College Record* 99, no. 1 (1997): 73–116; Joseph Cronin, "Corporations and Urban School Reform: Lessons from Boston," Occasional Paper no. 12 (Washington: Institute for Educational Leadership, 1991); Richard M. Jaeger and Carol Tittle, *Minimum Competency Achievement Testing: Motives, Models, Measures, and Consequences* (Berkeley: McCutchan, 1980).

29. U.S. Commission on Excellence in Education, *A Nation at Risk* (1983). Quotations from Jeffrey Henig, *Rethinking School Choice: The Limits of the Market Metaphor* (Princeton: Princeton University Press, 1994), p. 47. For an insightful and highly critical analysis of *A Nation at Risk* and similar publications in the early 1980s, see Marshall Smith, "Educational Improvement Which Makes a Difference: Thoughts about the Recent National Reports on Education," Science and Public Policy Seminar, February 24, 1984 (Washington: Federation of Behavioral, Psychological, and Cognitive Sciences, 1984). Smith, who had written the seminal piece (with Jennifer O'Day) on systemic reform when he served as dean of the School of Education, Stan-

ford University, became deputy secretary of education during the Clinton administration (1993–2001). He helped write the Goals 2000 legislation and similar initiatives that pressed for standards-based reform. For a critique of the sequence of events in the same quarter-century when employers focused on workers' lack of skills and the need for more training and education to equip employees for the future workplace, see Gordon Lafer, *The Job Training Charade* (Ithaca, N.Y.: Cornell University Press, 2002).

30. National Education Goals Panel, *The National Education Goals Report: Building a Nation of Learners, 1995* (Washington: U.S. Government Printing Office, 1995), pp. 4, 15.

31. Alexander quote cited in Keith Hammonds, "The Mission: David Kearns's Crusade to Fix America's Schools," *Business Week Online,* March 22, 1999, *www.businessweek.com/1999/99_12/b3621153.htm.* John Akers, Chairman of IBM, advertisement in the *New York Times Magazine,* April 28, 1991, p. 21.

32. Toch, *In The Name of Excellence,* pp. 13–71; *National Education Goals Report;* Jane David and Paul Goren, *Transforming Education: Overcoming Barriers* (Washington: National Governors Association, 1993); Cathie Jo Martin, *Stuck in Neutral: Business and the Politics of Human Capital Investment Policy* (Princeton: Princeton University Press, 1999), pp. 192–207.

33. Quotations from Robert Behn, "Government Performance and the Conundrum of Public Trust," in John Donahue and Joseph Nye, eds., *Market-Based Governance* (Washington: Brookings Institution Press, 2002), p. 334. For an extended analysis of the mid-1960s, when a similar movement emerged, see Arthur Wise, *Legislated Learning* (Berkeley: University of California Press, 1979).

34. Larry Cuban, "How Schools Change Reforms: Redefining Reform Success and Failure," *Teachers College Record* 99, no. 3 (1998): 453–477.

35. Ron Edmonds, "Effective Schools for the Urban Poor," *Educational Leadership* 37, no. 10 (1979): 18–24; Pamela Bullard and Barbara Taylor, *Making School Reform Happen* (Boston: Allyn and Bacon, 1993); Stewart Purkey and Marshall Smith, "Effective Schools: A Review," *Elementary School Journal* 83, no. 4 (1983): 427–452; Cuban, "How Schools Change Reforms."

36. See *www.NoChildLeftBehind.gov/* and the Business Roundtable's pub-

lication devoted to spreading the particulars of NCLB, *www.businessround table.org/taskforces/taskforce/issue.aspx?qs=6BF5BF159F849514481138A74F A1851159169FEB56C38B3.*

37. Louis V. Gerstner Jr., "Staying on Course," remarks to Achieve, Inc., November 13, 2002, *www.achieve.org/achieve.nsf/StayingOnCourse_ Speeches-Gerstner.*

38. I thank Dorothy Shipps for pointing out the widespread support of large and small businesses for making schools businesslike. Cathie Jo Martin makes a similar point about small, medium, and large businesses concurring on human resource and training issue. See Martin, *Stuck in Neutral*, pp. 194–197.

39. David Tyack, *Seeking Common Ground* (Cambridge, Mass.: Harvard University Press, 2003), pp. 158–180; Marie Gryphon and Emily Meyer, "Our History of Educational Freedom," *Policy Analysis*, no. 492, October 8, 2003 (Washington: Cato Institute).

40. I have used Alan Brinkley's analysis of three strands of modern American conservatism, one of which places high value on personal liberty and choice minimally constrained by governmental regulation. See Brinkley, *Liberalism and Its Discontents* (Cambridge, Mass.: Harvard University Press, 1998), pp. 277–297. For a passionate analysis and argument that favors choice and competition, see John Chubb and Terry Moe, *Politics, Markets, and America's Schools* (Washington: Brookings Institution Press, 1990). Frederick Hess, in *Revolution at the Margins: The Impact of Competition on Urban School Systems* (Washington: Brookings Institution Press, 2002), examines voucher experiments in the late 1990s; for a critical examination of the market metaphor and its flaws as applied to choice, see Henig, *Rethinking School Choice*, chs. 3–7; for policy statements with no mention of vouchers, see Business Roundtable, *www.businessroundtable.org/taskforces/ taskforce/issue.aspx?qs=6535BF159F849514481138A6DBE7A7A19BB6487BF 6B3B*, and U.S. Chamber of Commerce, *www.uschamber.com/government/ issues/education.htm.*

41. Peter Cookson and Sonali Shroff, "School Choice and Urban School Reform," ERIC Clearinghouse on Urban Education, Urban Diversity Series no. 100, 1997; Peter Schrag, "The Voucher Seduction," *American Prospect*, November 23, 1999, pp. 46–52. One organization that has supported vouch-

ers unreservedly has been the Cato Institute. In commenting on the U.S. Supreme Court decision on Cleveland's voucher plan, the Institute said that the court "paid homage to America's important tradition of educational freedom." The Institute has published four policy analysis papers on vouchers since 1996; see *www.cato.org/research/education/vouchers.html#commentary.*

42. Patrick McEwan, "The Potential Impact of Large-Scale Voucher Programs," *Review of Educational Research* 70, no. 2 (2002): 103–149; James Ryan and Michael Heise, "Taking School Choice to the Suburbs," *Washington Post,* July 3, 2002, p. A23.

43. Del Jones, "Business Not Feeling So Charitable toward Schools," *USA Today,* September 17, 2002; David Sanger, "Bush Defends Financing of Schools," *New York Times,* September 9, 2003, p. A26.

44. National business associations such as the Business Roundtable and the U.S. Chamber of Commerce (both cited above) have promoted these strategies to improve schools since the mid-1990s. Achieve, Inc., founded by CEOs and state governors after the 1996 national summit on education, is another organization concentrating on improving schools using many of the same strategies. See *www.achieve.org.*

45. Quotation from Joseph Tucci, CEO of EMC Corporation, in Business Roundtable, "Press Release," July 2, 2003. For more citations on the topic of this paragraph see the notes to Chapter 1.

46. *www.NoChildLeftBehind.gov/.*

47. "Quality Counts 2001," *Education Week,* January 23, 2001; Alex Molnar, *Giving Kids the Business: The Commercialization of America's Schools* (Boulder: Westview Press, 1996); Amy Wells, *Time to Choose: America at the Crossroads of School Choice Policy* (New York: Hill and Wang, 1993); Carrie Lips, "'Edupreneurs': A Survey of For-Profit Education," *Policy Analysis* 386 (Washington: Cato Institute, 2000); Alex Molnar and Joseph Reaves, *Buy Me! Buy Me! Fourth Annual Report on Trends in Schoolhouse Commercialism, 2000–2001* (Tempe: Education Policy Studies Laboratory, Arizona State University, 2001).

48. National Center for Education Statistics, "Vocational Education in the United States: Toward the Year 2000," NCES 2000-029 (Washington: U.S.

Department of Education, Office of Educational Research and Improvement, 2000).

49. Ben Feller, "Bush Eyes Changes to Vocational Schools," *Boston Globe,* March 31, 2003, p. A4; Michael Winerup, "When the Learning Is the Hands-on Kind," *New York Times,* April 9, 2003, p. A14; also see Alex Lyda, "Putting the Brakes on Auto Shop," *San Diego Union-Tribune,* July 14, 2003, *www.signonsandiego.com/news/education/20030714-9999_1n14shop.html.* *National Center for Education Statistics,* "Stats in Brief: Changes in High School Vocational Coursetaking in a Larger Perspective," NCES 2001-026 (Washington: U.S. Department of Education, Office of Educational Research and Improvement, 2001).

50. Anne Bradley, "The Business of Reforming Cincinnati's Schools," *Education Week,* May 19, 1993, pp. 1, 16; Jay Mathews, "Chief Academic Officers," *www.aasa.org/publications/sa/2001_06/mathews_cao.htm.* National Institute of Standards and Technology, "Fact Sheet on 2001 Malcolm Baldrige National Quality Award Education Category," *www.nist.gov/public_affairs/factsheet/education.htm.*

51. For the military-business-school evolution of computers and other technologies, see Douglas Noble, *The Classroom Arsenal: Military Research, Information Technology, and Public Education* (London: Falmer, 1991).

52. Henry Becker, Jason Ravitz, and Yan Tien Wong, "Teaching, Learning, and Computing: 1998 National Survey" (Center for Research on Information Technology and Organizations, University of California, Irvine, and University of Minnesota, 1999); Mark Walsh, "Ka-Ching! Business Cashing in on Learning," *Education Week,* November 24, 1999, pp. 1, 14–16; Constance Hays, "Today's Lesson: Soda Rights," *New York Times,* May 21, 1999, pp. C1, C19; Molnar and Reaves, *Buy Me! Buy Me!*

53. Larry Cuban, *Oversold and Underused: Computers in the Classroom* (Cambridge, Mass.: Harvard University Press, 2001). For tensions over traditional and progressive approaches to teaching and learning that have surfaced as standards-based reforms took hold in U.S. schools, see Alfie Kohn, "Tests That Cheat Students," *New York Times,* December 9, 1999, p. A31; Maureen O'Donnell, "Test Prep Book for 3rd-graders Causes Stir," *Chicago Sun Times,* September 12, 2000; Carol Barnes, *Standards Reform in High-*

Poverty Schools: Managing Conflict and Building Capacity (New York: Teachers College Press, 2002); Cynthia Coburn, "Collective Sensemaking about Reading: How Teachers Mediate Reading Policy in Their Professional Communities," *Educational Evaluation and Policy Analysis* 23, no. 2 (2001): 145–170.

54. For social, political, and cultural histories of the 1960s and 1970s, see William Chafe, *The Unfinished Journey: America since World War II* (New York: Oxford University Press, 1986); Milton Viorst, *Fire in the Streets* (New York: Simon and Schuster, 1979); Clayborne Carson, *In Struggle: SNCC and the Black Awakening of the 1960s* (Cambridge, Mass.: Harvard University Press, 1981); James Sundquist, *Politics and Policy: The Eisenhower, Kennedy, and Johnson Years* (Washington: Brookings Institution, 1968); Kenneth Jackson, *Crabgrass Frontier: The Suburbanization of America* (New York: Oxford University Press, 1985); William Wilson, *The Declining Significance of Race: Blacks and Changing American Institutions* (Chicago: University of Chicago Press, 1978).

55. Frank Levy and Richard Murnane, *Teaching the New Basic Skills* (New York: Free Press, 1996).

56. *www.businessroundtable.org/taskforces/taskforce/issue.aspx?qs=6535BF 159F849514481138A6DBE7A7A19BB6487BF6B3B.*

57. See Wise, *Legislated Learning,* esp. ch. 4, for an analysis of the 1960s and 1970s when the rationalizing of government operations and the use of business-inspired approaches spilled over into schools and classrooms.

58. One typical example of this durable business support for standards-based reform can be seen in the Business Roundtable's continuous production of information on No Child Left Behind legislation since 2002 such as a "Toolkit" at *www.businessroundtable.org/taskforces/taskforce/issue.aspx?qs= 6BF5BF159F849514481138A74FA1851159169FEB56C38B3* and a commissioned poll of attitudes toward the legislation at *www.brtable.org/press.cfm/ 966.*

3. Why Schools Have Adopted the Reforms

1. I thank David Tyack for pointing out to me that during the Great Depression, media and popular opinion were highly critical of business leaders,

many of whom were blamed for economic hard times. See David Tyack, Robert Lowe, and Elisabeth Hansot, *Public Schools in Hard Times: The Great Depression and Recent Years* (Cambridge, Mass.: Harvard University Press, 1984), pp. 85–91, for the role of business elites in Chicago and Detroit and how each district endured the worst years of the Depression. Also see Robert Wiebe, *Businessmen and Reform: A Study of the Progressive Movement* (Cambridge, Mass.: Harvard University Press, 1962). Educational policymakers such as district superintendents and state and national school officials, according to Merle Curti, historically had "accepted, in general, the business man's outlook and consciously or unconsciously molded the school system to accord with the canons of a profit-making system." Curti, *The Social Ideas of American Educators* (Totowa, N.J.: Littlefield, Adams, 1966), p. 230.

2. President G. W. Bush, State of The Union address, *New York Times,* January 30, 2002, p. A22. Lowell Rose and Alec Gallup, "The 32nd Annual Phi Delta/Gallup Poll of the Public's Attitudes toward the Public Schools," *Phi Delta Kappan,* September 2000, p. 48.

3. On the history of America and technologies, see Howard Segal, *Technological Utopianism in American Culture* (Chicago: University of Chicago Press, 1985); Douglas Noble, *The Classroom Arsenal: Military Research, Information Technology, and Public Education* (New York: Falmer, 1991).

4. Thomas Landauer, *The Trouble with Computers: Usefulness, Usability, and Productivity* (Cambridge, Mass.: MIT Press, 1995), pp. 14–16, 47–72; Sue Berryman and Thomas Bailey, *The Double Helix of Education and the Economy* (New York: Teachers College/Columbia Institute on Education and the Economy, 1992), pp. 10–23; Robert Reich, *The Work of Nations* (New York: Vintage Books, 1991), pp. 177–180.

5. Alan Krueger, "How Computers Have Changed the Wage Structure: Evidence from Microdata, 1984–1989," *Quarterly Journal of Economics* 108 (February 1993): 33–60; Leslie Helm, "High Tech Sales Fuel Reach into Schools," *Los Angeles Times,* June 9, 1997, p. A1.

6. James Kulik, "Meta-Analytic Studies of Findings on Computer-based Instruction," in E. Baker and H. O'Neill, eds., *Technology Assessment in Education and Training* (Hillsdale, N.J.: Lawrence Erlbaum Associates, 1994), pp. 9–33; David Tyack and Larry Cuban, *Tinkering toward Utopia* (Cambridge, Mass.: Harvard University Press, 1995), pp. 117–120; Todd Oppen-

heimer, *The Flickering Mind* (New York: Random House, 2003), pp. 31–32, 116–117. Oppenheimer has a vignette on an ILS in use in a Harlem school computer lab, pp. 79–82.

7. CEO Forum on Education and Technology, "Education Technology Must Be Included in Comprehensive Education Legislation," Policy Paper, March 2001, p. 3.

8. Charlie Euchner, "Passage of 'Apple Bill' Sought by E.D. and Computer Firm," *Education Week*, November 24, 1982; *Business Week Online*, "Apple's Steve Jobs: 'Our Vision Is That We Have Just Begun,'" September 25, 2000, *www.businessweek.com/2000/00_39/b3700122.htm*.

9. "Technology Counts 1998," *Education Week*, October 1, 1998, pp. 7, 8; quotation from high school principal in Oppenheimer, *Flickering Mind*, p. 10.

10. Oppenheimer, *Flickering Mind*, pp. 143, 162, 167.

11. *http://clinton4.nara.gov/WH/New/other/sotu.html*.

12. "Technology Counts," *Education Week*, November 10, 1997, p. 8; "Pencils Sown: Technology's Answer to Testing," *Education Week*, May 8, 2003, p. 45. For use of computers in homes with children, see *sacramento.bizjournals.com/sacramento/stories/2001/09/03/daily21.html*.

13. "Technology Counts 2002," *Education Week*, May 9, 2002, p. 54; "Survey Shows Widespread Enthusiasm for High Technology," *NPR Online*, March 2, 2000, *www.npr.org/programs/specials/poll/technology/*.

14. The fear of a "digital divide" that swept across the media and stirred policymakers and business leaders in the early 1990s dissolved within a few years as access to computers climbed among low-income families and access to computers in schools became widespread. That fear joined a concern for the poor with a faith in the power of computers to "solve" the problem of poverty, another excursion into using schools to cope with larger economic problems. See Andrew Trotter, "Study Shows a Thinner 'Digital Divide,'" *Education Week*, March 26, 2003, p. 9; Robert J. Samuelson, "Debunking the Digital Divide," *Washington Post*, March 20, 2002, *www.washingtonpost.com/ac2/wp-dyn/A53118-2002Mar19?language=printer*.

15. Pepper at National Education Summit, quoted at *www.bcer.org/newsletters/nl-97-2.cfm*; Millicent Lawson, "Summit Accord Calls for Focus on Standards," *Education Week*, April 3, 1996, p. 1.

16. Interest group analyst quoted in John Kingdon, *Agendas, Alternatives, and Public Policies* (New York: HarperCollins College, 1995), p. 165. For an earlier effort to make conceptual sense of recurring school reforms, see Larry Cuban, "Reforming Again, Again, and Again," *Educational Researcher* 19, no. 1 (1990): 3–13. The institutional theory that I cite in that work and similar conceptual work done since then I use as the spine of the argument in this chapter. See my *Oversold and Underused: Computers in the Classroom* (Cambridge, Mass.: Harvard University Press, 2001), pp. 156–170.

17. Jeff Faux, "Can Liberals Tell a Credible Story?" *American Prospect,* November/December 1997, pp. 28–33.

18. Report of the California Education Technology Task Force, "Connect, Compute, and Compete," July 8, 1996, p. 5.

19. California state superintendent, Delaine Eastin, quoted in news release for her task force report, "Connect, Compute, and Compete," July 10, 1996. Gerstner quoted in *Business Week Online,* September 25, 2000, *www.businessweek.com/2000/00_39/b3700120.htm.*

20. Cuban, *Oversold and Underused,* ch. 5; Oppenheimer, *Flickering Mind,* ch. 3 and pp. 391–393.

21. Kathryn Henderson, *On Line and On Paper: Visual Representations, Visual Cultures, and Computer Graphics in Design Engineering* (Cambridge, Mass.: MIT Press, 1999), p. 189; John Meyer and Brian Rowan, "Institutional Organizations: Formal Structure as Myth and Ceremony," *American Journal of Sociology* 83 (1977): 340–363; Mary Metz, "Real School," in D. Mitchell and M. Goertz, eds., *Education Politics for the New Century: The Twentieth Anniversary Yearbook of the Politics of Education Association* (Philadelphia: Falmer, 1990), pp. 75–91.

22. A similar phenomenon of rhetoric and reality and the importance of symbolic language can be seen in the "total quality management" innovation that swept through the business sector in the 1980s. See Mark J. Zbaracki, "The Rhetoric and Reality of Total Quality Management," *Administrative Science Quarterly* 43 (1998): 602–636.

23. For an early history of school boards, see E. P. Cubberley, *Public School Administration* (Boston: Houghton Mifflin, 1916); for changes in district control of schools since the Civil War, see David Tyack, *Seeking Common Ground: Public Schools in a Diverse Society* (Cambridge, Mass.: Harvard Uni-

versity Press, 2003), ch. 5. A survey of both historical and contemporary research on school boards can be found in Deborah Land, "Local School Boards under Review: Their Role and Effectiveness in Relation to Students' Academic Achievement," *Review of Educational Research* 72, no. 2 (2002): 229–278.

24. Scott Nearing survey cited in Raymond Callahan, *Education and the Cult of Efficiency* (Chicago: University of Chicago Press, 1962), p. 150; for George Counts, see *The Social Composition of Boards of Education: A Study in the Social Control of Public Education,* Supplementary Educational Monographs no. 33, University of Chicago, 1927.

25. Land, "Local School Boards under Review," pp. 232–233.

26. Don McAdams, *Fighting to Save Our Urban Schools . . . And Winning! Lessons from Houston* (New York: Teachers College Press, 2000), p. 221. For examples of business elites strongly influencing school district governance and organizational policies, see Dorothy Shipps, "Corporate Influence on Chicago School Reform," in C. Stone, ed., *Changing Urban Education* (Lawrence: University Press of Kansas, 1998), pp. 161–183; Thomas Longoria, "School Politics in Houston: The Impact of Business Involvement," in Stone, ed., *Changing Urban Education,* pp. 184–198; Joseph Cronin, "Corporations and Urban School Reform: Lessons from Boston," Occasional Paper no. 12 (Washington: Institute for Educational Leadership, 1991).

27. For the role of local school boards in the decentralized system of U.S. public education, see Frederick Wirt and Michael Kirst, *The Political Dynamics of American Education* (Berkeley: McCutchan, 1997), ch. 6; for an example of business interests mobilized to support a superintendent by trying to reshape a school board and failing, see Stephen S. Smith, "Education and Regime Change," in Stone, ed., *Changing Urban Education,* pp. 204–206; and see Larry Cuban and Michael Usdan, "Fast and Top-down: Systemic Reform and Student Achievement in San Diego Schools," in L. Cuban and M. Usdan, eds., *Powerful Reforms with Shallow Roots* (New York: Teachers College Press, 2003), pp. 83–84.

28. For a sampling of the arguments see Clarence Karier, "Business Values and the Educational State," in Clarence Karier, Paul Violas, and Joel Spring, eds., *Roots of Crisis: American Education in the Twentieth Century* (Chicago: Rand McNally, 1973), pp. 6–29; Joel Spring, *Education and the Rise of the*

Corporate State (Boston: Beacon Press, 1972); Samuel Bowles and Herbert Gintis, *Schooling in Capitalist America: Educational Reform and the Contradictions of Economic Life* (New York: Basic Books, 1976), esp. pp. 187–191.

29. Vallas quoted in Marjorie Coeyman, "A Turnaround Plan for Philly Schools," *Christian Science Monitor,* January 14, 2003. Official quoted in Dean Mensah, "District, Microsoft Partners in New $46M High School," *Philadelphia Daily News,* September 5, 2003, p. 3.

30. Ballowe quoted in Philip J. Bossert, "Lessons Learned: An Inside Look at Four of the Top Technology School Districts in the Nation," *THE Journal Online,* November 2001, *www.thejournal.com/magazine/vault/articleprint version.cfm?aid=3748.*

31. Business Week and McGraw-Hill Educational and Publishing Group, *Smart Links: Schools That Use Technology for Learning,* Tenth Annual Business Week Awards for Instructional Innovation (New York: McGraw-Hill, 1999), pp. 2–3.

32. Barbara Means, William Penuel, and Christine Padilla, *The Connected School: Technology and Learning in High School* (San Francisco: Jossey-Bass, 2001), p. 217. I have not yet found any studies or reports that challenge Means and her colleagues' conclusions. Also see Janet Schofield, *Computers and Classroom Culture* (New York: Cambridge University Press, 1995).

4. Limits to Business Influence

1. Herbst quoted in Lamar Alexander and Richard Riley, "A Compass in the Storm," *Education Week,* October 9, 2002, pp. 48, 36, 37.

2. Council for Corporate and School Partnerships, "Guiding Principles for Business and School Partnerships," 2002, *www.corpschoolpartners.org/ guiding_principles.shtml.*

3. Semerad quoted in Meg Sommerfeld, "RJR Nabisco Lays $30 Million Bet on 'Bottom Up' Reform Strategy," *Education Week,* June 10, 1992, pp. 1, 10.

4. Ibid., p. 10.

5. Jones quoted in *NASDC Update,* the newsletter of the New American Schools Development Corporation, spring 1992, p. 5. For a history of NASDC and its later incarnation, New American Schools, see Jeffrey Mirel,

"Unrequited Promise," *Education Next,* 2002, *www.educationnext.org/20022/64.html.*

6. Wilson quoted in Roberta Trachtman, "The Policy Arena," in Marsha Levine and Roberta Trachtman, eds., *American Business and the Public School: Case Studies of Corporate Involvement in Public Education* (New York: Teachers College Press, 1988), p. 208.

7. Ibid., pp. 210–213; Council for Aid to Education Award to Boeing in 2001, *www.publiceducation.org/connections/connections-Fall2002-Condit. htm.* For an account of another state business roundtable, see Julie Mc-Daniel and Cecil Miskel, "Stakeholder Salience: Business and Educational Policy," *Teachers College Record* 104, no. 2 (2002): 325–356.

8. Boeing News Release, October 24, 2002, *www.boeing.com/news/releases/2002/q4/nr_021024a.html.*

9. Philip Condit, "Achieving Excellence," Public Education Network, *www.publiceducation.org/connections/connections-fall2002-Condit.htm.*

10. See *www.ed.gov/programs/compreform/2pager.html.*

11. Roslyn Mickelson, "Corporations and Classrooms: A Critical Examination of the Business Agenda for Urban School Reform," in K. McClafferty, C. Torres, and T. Mitchell, eds., *Challenges of Urban Education: Sociological Perspectives for the Next Century* (Albany: State University of New York Press, 2000), pp. 140–144.

12. How business agendas for public schools were curtailed by labor unions in Chicago can be seen in Julia Wrigley, *Class Politics and Public Schools: Chicago, 1900–1950* (New Brunswick, N.J.: Rutgers University Press, 1982). Also see Ira Katznelson and Margaret Weir, *Schooling for All* (New York: Basic Books, 1985), ch. 6.

13. See Richard Murnane and David Cohen, "Merit Pay and the Evaluation Problem: Why Most Merit Pay Plans Fail and a Few Survive," *Harvard Educational Review* 56, no. 1 (1986): 14–30. For contracting-for-performance see David Tyack and Larry Cuban, *Tinkering toward Utopia* (Cambridge, Mass.: Harvard University Press, 1995), pp. 116–119; for site-based management see Jane David, "Synthesis of Research on School-based Management," *Educational Leadership* 46, no. 8 (1989): 45–53, and Rodney Ogawa, "The Institutional Sources of Educational Reform: The Case of

School-Based Management," *American Educational Research Journal* 31, no. 3 (1994): 519–548.

14. Mirel, "Unrequited Promise."

15. Mark A. Smith, *American Business and Political Power* (Chicago: University of Chicago Press, 2000); Patrick Akard, "Corporate Mobilization and Political Power: The Transformation of U.S. Economic Policy in the 1970s," *American Sociological Review* 57, no. 5 (1992): 597–615; Robert Wiebe, *Businessmen and Reform: A Study of the Progressive Movement* (Cambridge, Mass.: Harvard University Press, 1962); Harvey Molotch and John Logan, *Urban Fortunes: The Political Economy of Place* (Berkeley: University of California Press, 1987); Cathie Jo Martin, *Stuck in Neutral: Business and the Politics of Human Capital Investment Policy* (Princeton: Princeton University Press, 1999), pp. 192–207.

16. Harvey Kantor, *Learning to Earn: School, Work, and Vocational Reform in California, 1880–1930* (Madison: University of Wisconsin Press, 1988); Herbert Kliebard, *Schooled to Work: Vocationalism and the American Curriculum, 1876–1946* (New York: Teachers College Press, 1999); Jane Powers, *The "Girl Question" in Education: Vocational Education in the Progressive Era* (Philadelphia: Falmer, 1992); John Rury, *Education and Women's Work: Female Schooling and the Division of Labor in Urban America, 1870–1930* (Albany: State University of New York Press, 1991); David Tyack and Elisabeth Hansot, *Learning Together* (New Haven: Yale University Press, 1990).

17. Kliebard, *Schooled to Work*, pp. 91–95.

18. Powers, *The "Girl Question" in Education*, pp. 104–105.

19. Robert Lynd and Helen Lynd, *Middletown: A Study in Contemporary American Culture* (New York: Harcourt, Brace, 1929), pp. 194–195.

20. Lawrence Cremin, *The Transformation of the School* (New York: Vintage, 1961); Diane Ravitch, *The Troubled Crusade: American Education, 1945–1980* (New York: Basic Books, 1985); Diane Ravitch, *Left Back: A Century of Failed School Reforms* (New York: Simon and Schuster, 2000).

21. Larry Cuban, *How Teachers Taught*, rev. ed. (New York: Teachers College Press, 1993); Arthur Zilversmit, *Changing Schools: Progressive Education Theory and Practice, 1930–1960* (Chicago: University of Chicago Press, 1993).

22. Cuban, *How Teachers Taught*, pp. 126–127.

23. Ibid., p. 71.

24. Ibid., p. 116.

25. Sara Rimer, "Now, Standardized Achievement Testing in Head Start," *New York Times,* October 29, 2003, p. A23.

26. "Text of Levy's Remarks on Overhauling Staff," *New York Times,* August 8, 2001.

27. Jeannie Oakes, Karen Quartz, Steve Ryan, and Martin Lipton, *Becoming Good American Schools: The Struggle for Civic Virtue in Education Reform* (San Francisco: Jossey-Bass, 2000); Denise Gelberg, *The "Business" of Reforming American Schools* (New York: Teachers College Press, 1997). Norton Grubb, "Dick and Jane at Work: The New Vocationalism and Occupational Literacy Programs," in G. Hall, ed., *Changing Work, Changing Workers* (Albany: State University of New York Press, 1997), pp. 159–188. Principal quoted in Linda Jacobson, "Once Popular 'Multiage Grouping' Loses Steam," *Education Week,* September 10, 2003, p. 1.

28. David Tyack and I make these distinctions the central framework of our book *Tinkering toward Utopia.*

29. Milbrey McLaughlin, *Evaluation and Reform: The Elementary and Secondary Education Act of 1965* (Cambridge, Mass.: Ballinger, 1975); Paul Berman and Milbrey McLaughlin, *Federal Programs Supporting Educational Change: The Findings in Review* (Santa Monica, Calif.: RAND, 1978); Richard Elmore and Milbrey McLaughlin, *Steady Work* (Santa Monica, Calif.: RAND, 1988); Aaron Wildavsky and Jeffrey Pressman, *Implementation* (Berkeley: University of California Press, 1984); Hugh Davis Graham, *The Uncertain Triumph: Federal Education Policy in the Kennedy and Johnson Years* (Chapel Hill: University of North Carolina Press, 1984); Paul Hill, "The Federal Role in Education," in Diane Ravitch, ed., *Brookings Papers on Education Policy* (Washington: Brookings Institution Press, 2000), pp. 11–57; Andrew Porter and John Smithson, "Are Content Standards Being Implemented in the Classroom? A Methodology and Some Tentative Answers," in Susan H. Fuhrman, ed., *From the Capitol to the Classroom: Standard Based Reform in the States,* 100th Yearbook of the National Society for the Study of Education, part 2 (Chicago: University of Chicago Press, 2001), pp. 60–80; James Spillane, "Challenging Instruction for 'All Students': Policy, Practitio-

ners, and Practice," in Fuhrman, ibid., pp. 217–241; Suzanne Wilson and Robert Floden, "Hedging Bets: Standards-based Reform in Classrooms," in Fuhrman, ibid., pp. 193–216; David Cohen and Heather Hill, *Learning Policy: When State Education Reform Works* (New Haven: Yale University Press, 2001). For teachers adapting instructional policies, see Cynthia Coburn, "Collective Sensemaking about Reading: How Teachers Mediate Reading Policy in Their Professional Communities," *Educational Evaluation and Policy Analysis* 23, no. 2 (2001): 145–170; Tyack and Cuban, *Tinkering toward Utopia;* Michael Lipsky, *Street Level Bureaucracy* (New York: Russell Sage Foundation, 1983).

30. See Business Roundtable, "Using the 'No Child Left Behind Act' to Improve Schools in Your State," *www.businessroundtable.org/taskforces/index.aspx;* U.S. Chamber of Commerce statement on education, *www.uschamber.com/government/issues/education/education.htm.*

31. The Title I example comes from Graham, *Uncertain Triumph;* also see McLaughlin, *Evaluation and Reform.*

32. See Milbrey McLaughlin, "Learning from Experience: Lessons from Policy Implementation," in Alan Odden, ed., *Education Policy Implementation* (Albany: State University of New York Press, 1991), pp. 143–155; David Cohen and James Spillane, "Policy and Practice: The Relations between Governance and Instruction," in Susan Fuhrman, ed., *Designing Coherent Education Policy: Improving the System* (San Francisco: Jossey-Bass, 1993), pp. 35–88; Cohen and Hill, *Learning Policy;* James Spillane, Brian Reiser, and Todd Reimer, "Policy Implementation and Cognition: Reframing and Refocusing Implementation Research," *Review of Educational Research* 72, no. 3 (2002): 387–431.

33. Amanda Datnow, "Power and Politics in the Adoption of School Reform Models," *Educational Evaluation and Policy Analysis* 22, no. 4 (2000): 357–374; Spillane, Reiser, and Reimer, "Policy Implementation and Cognition"; Elmore and McLaughlin, *Steady Work;* Lorraine McDonnell and Milbrey McLaughlin, *Education Policy and the Role of the States* (Santa Monica, Calif.: RAND, 1982); Jerome Murphy, "Progress and Problems: The Paradox of State Reform," in Ann Lieberman and Milbrey McLaughlin, *Policy Making in Education* (Chicago: NSSE, 1982), pp. 195–214; David Cohen, "Standards-Based School Reform: Policy, Practice, and Performance," in

Helen Ladd, ed., *Holding Schools Accountable* (Washington: Brookings Institution, 1996), pp. 99–127.

34. Amanda Datnow, Lea Hubbard, and Hugh Mehan, *Extending Educational Reform from One School to Many* (New York: Routledge Falmer, 2002); Janet Fairman and William Firestone, "The District Role in State Assessment Policy," in Fuhrman, ed., *From the Capitol to the Classroom,* part 2, pp. 124–147; Elizabeth deBray, Gail Parson, and Katrina Woodworth, "Patterns of Response in Four High Schools under State Accountability Policies in Vermont and New York," ibid., pp. 170–192; Wilson and Floden, "Hedging Bets."

35. Cynthia Coburn, "Making Sense of Reading: Logics of Reading in the Institutional Environment and the Classroom" (Doctoral diss., Stanford University, 2001).

36. See James Spillane and Nancy Jennings, "Aligned Instructional Policy and Ambitious Pedagogy: Exploring Instructional Reform from the Classroom Perspective," *Teachers College Record* 98, no. 3 (1997): 449–481; Richard L. Allington, "Does State and Federal Reading Policymaking Matter?" in T. Loveless, ed., *The Great Curriculum Debate: How Should We Teach Reading and Math?* (Washington: Brookings Institution, 2001), pp. 268–298.

37. Andrew Porter, Robert Floden, Donald Freeman, William Schmidt, and John Schwille, "Content Determinants in Elementary School Mathematics," in Douglas Grouws and Thomas Cooney, eds., *Perspectives in Research on Effective Mathematics Teaching* (Hillsdale, N.J.: Erlbaum, 1988), pp. 96–113. See Wilson and Floden, "Hedging Bets"; Cuban, *How Teachers Taught;* Spillane, Reiser, and Reimer, "Policy Implementation and Cognition"; Michael Lipsky nicely captures the role of gatekeeper and policy broker played by police officers, social workers, and teachers in *Street Level Bureaucracy.*

38. Policy statement of American Education Research Association, *www.aera.net/about/policy/stakes.htm.*

39. Carol Barnes, *Standards Reform in High-Poverty Schools: Managing Conflict and Building Capacity* (New York: Teachers College Press, 2002); Cohen and Hill, *Learning Policy;* Michael Knapp, "Between Systemic Reform and the Mathematics and Science Classroom," *Review of Educational Research* 67, no. 2 (1997): 227–266.

40. Christopher Shea, "It's Come to This," *Teacher Magazine* 11, no. 8 (2000): 33–34, 36, 38, 40; Lynn Olson, "Researchers Identify the Impact of N.J. Testing on Teaching," *Education Week,* April 18, 2001, p. 6; Richard Rothstein, "The Growing Revolt against the Testers," *New York Times,* May 30, 2001, p. A19; Wilson and Floden, "Hedging Bets."

41. Laura Hamilton, Daniel F. McCaffrey, Brian Stecher, Stephen Klein, Abby Robyn, and Delia Bugliari, "Studying Large-Scale Reforms of Instructional Practice: An Example from Mathematics and Science," *Educational Evaluation and Policy Analysis* 25, no. 1 (2003): 1–29.

42. Larry Cuban, "The Media and Polls on Education—Over the Years," in Gene Maeroff, ed., *Imaging Education: The Media and Schools in America* (New York: Teachers College Press, 1998), pp. 69–82.

43. The concept of "real schools" comes from the application of John Meyer's work on the power of social beliefs in education and Mary Metz's use of his work. See John Meyer and Brian Rowan, "Institutionalized Organizations: Formal Structure as Myth and Ceremony," *American Journal of Sociology* 83 (1977): 340–363; Mary Metz, "Real School: A Universal Drama amid Disparate Experience," in *Education Politics for the New Century,* ed. D. Mitchell and M. Goertz (New York: Falmer, 1990), pp. 75–91.

44. Richard Elmore and Milbrey McLaughlin, "Strategic Choice in Federal Education Policy: The Compliance-Assistance Trade-off," in M. McLaughlin and A. Lieberman, eds., *Policymaking in Education,* 81st Yearbook of the National Society for the Study of Education (Chicago: University of Chicago Press, 1982), pp. 159–194.

45. David Crandall, ed., *People, Policies, and Practices: Examining the Chain of School Improvement* (Andover, Mass.: The Network, 1983); Michael Huberman, "School Improvement Strategies That Work: Some Scenarios," *Education Leadership* 41, no. 3 (1983): 23–27.

46. Stewart Purkey and Marshall Smith, "Effective Schools: A Review," *Elementary School Journal* 4 (1983): 427–452. On the adopting of effective schools research and application to Title I of ESEA throughout the 1980s and 1990s, see Barbara Taylor and Pamela Bullard, *Keepers of the Dream: The Triumph of Effective Schools* (Chicago: Excelsior, 1994). Much of the effective schools research has broadened and been folded into the Comprehensive School Reform Demonstration Program. See Northwest Regional Educa-

tional Laboratory, *The Catalog of School Reform: Helping You Find the Right Model for Your School,* October 2003.

47. See Datnow, Hubbard, and Mehan, *Extending Educational Reform.*

48. Connie Bridge, *The Implementation of Kentucky's Primary Program 1995: A Progress Report* (Lexington: Institute on Education Reform, University of Kentucky, 1995); Betty Lou Whitford and Ken Jones, eds., *Accountability, Assessment, and Teacher Commitment: Lessons from Kentucky's Reform Efforts* (Albany: State University of New York Press, 2000); Patricia Kannapel, Lola Aagaard, Pamelia Coe, and Cynthia Reeves, "The Impact of Standards and Accountability on Teaching and Learning in Kentucky," in Fuhrman, ed., *From the Capitol to the Classroom,* pp. 242–262.

49. David Cohen and Heather Hill, *Learning Policy: When State Education Reform Works* (New Haven: Yale University Press, 2001), p. 6; also see Michael Knapp, "Between Systemic Reforms and the Mathematics and Science Classroom," *Review of Educational Research* 67, no. 2 (1997): 227–266. Other states noted for developing teachers' knowledge and skills in implementing standards-based reform are North Carolina and Connecticut. See Linda Darling-Hammond, "Standards and Assessment: Where We Are and What We Need," *www.tcrecord.org/Content.asp?ContentID=11109.* For an insightful synthesis of the issues researchers have to resolve in determining whether state standards do indeed lead to improved teaching and learning, see Porter and Smithson, "Are Content Standards Being Implemented in the Classroom?"

50. Larry Cuban and Michael Usdan, eds., *Powerful Reforms with Shallow Roots* (New York: Teachers College Press, 2003) on Boston and San Diego; Amy Hightower, Michael Knapp, Julie Marsh, and Milbrey McLaughlin, eds., *School Districts and Instructional Renewal* (New York: Teachers College Press, 2002).

51. For Houston, see Paul Hill, "Digging Deeper," *Education Next,* Fall 2001, pp. 18–23; Don McAdams, *Fighting to Save Our Urban Schools . . . and Winning: Lessons from Houston* (New York: Teachers College Press, 2000); Jane Hannaway and Shannon McKay, "Taking Measure," *Education Next,* September 2001, pp. 9–17. Learning First Alliance reports on five districts that have raised test scores in "Beyond Islands of Excellence," *www.learningfirst.org/lfa-web/rp?pa=doc&docId=62.*

52. David K. Cohen, "Governance and Instruction: The Promise of De-

centralization and Choice," in William H. Clune and John F. Witte, eds., *Choice and Control in American Education: The Theory of Choice and Control in Education* (Philadelphia: Falmer, 1990), pp. 337–386; John W. Meyer, W. Richard Scott, David Strang, and Andrew Creighton, *Bureaucratization without Centralization: Changes in the Organizational System of American Public Education, 1940–1980,* Project Report no. 85-A11, Institute for Finance and Governance, Stanford University, 1985.

5. Are Public Schools like Businesses?

1. The classic work on the nature of teaching and the occupational rewards that teachers seek is Dan Lortie, *Schoolteacher* (Chicago: University of Chicago Press, 1975). Also see David Hansen, *The Call to Teach* (New York: Teachers College Press, 1995). For a sample of European teachers' motivations, see Michael Huberman, *The Lives of Teachers* (New York: Teachers College Press, 1989), ch. 4.

2. This section is adapted from Larry Cuban, "Corporate Involvement in Public Schools: A Practitioner-Academic's Perspective," *Teachers College Record* 85, no. 2 (1983): 183–203.

3. I wish I had understood at the time that employers in urban areas know that most high school graduates will take jobs across school district lines, so that the benefits of local tax monies coming from businesses will go to companies outside the local district. This fact has much to do with the tendency toward underinvestment in education. See Burton Weisbrod, *External Benefits of Public Education: An Economic Analysis* (Princeton: Princeton University Press, 1964). I thank Henry Levin for pointing this out to me.

4. Sharon Feiman-Nemser and Robert Floden, "The Cultures of Teaching," in Merle Wittrock, ed., *The Third Handbook of Research on Teaching* (New York: Macmillan, 1986), pp. 505–526.

5. Anne Newman, a Stanford University doctoral student, told me of seeing the advertisement in New York on January 13, 2004. Choate quoted in Melinda Ligos, "It's Back to School to Become a Teacher," *New York Times,* August 31, 2003, p. C10.

6. Quotation from President G. W. Bush's State of The Union address, *New York Times,* January 30, 2002, p. A22.

7. Richard Murnane, John Willett, Yves Duhaldeborde, and John Tyler,

"How Important Are the Cognitive Skills of Teenagers in Predicting Subsequent Earnings?" *Journal of Policy Analysis and Management* 19, no. 4 (2000): 561–562.

8. A typical example of the literature that connects educational quality as measured by test scores to individual lifetime earnings and national economic productivity and growth is Eric Hanushek, "Lost Opportunities," *Hoover Institution Weekly Essays,* July 21, 2003, *www-hoover.stanford.edu/pubaffairs/we/2003/hanushek07.html.*

9. Henry Levin and Carolyn Kelley, "Can Education Do It Alone?" *Economics of Education Review* 13, no. 2 (1994): 97–108. For the argument that there is a strong relation between higher test scores and income inequalities among black men and white men, see Christopher Jencks and Meredith Phillips, eds., *The Black-White Test Score Gap* (Washington: Brookings Institution Press, 1998), ch. 14.

10. Jerry Jasincowski, statement at the National Skills Summit sponsored by the U.S. Department of Labor, April 11, 2000, *www.dol.gov/_sec/skills_summit/p1s5a.htm.*

11. Quotation from Richard J. Murnane and Frank Levy, *Teaching the New Basic Skills* (New York: Free Press, 1996), p. 4.

12. Quoted in Herbert Kliebard, *Schooled to Work: Vocationalism and the American Curriculum, 1876–1946* (1999), p. 29.

13. Harvey Kantor, *Learning to Earn: School, Work, and Vocational Reform in California, 1880–1930* (Madison: University of Wisconsin Press, 1999); Marvin Lazerson and Norton Grubb, *American Education and Vocationalism: A Documentary History, 1870–1970* (New York: Teachers College Press, 1974); Kliebard, *Schooled to Work.*

14. Kliebard, *Schooled to Work;* Kantor, *Learning to Earn.*

15. For a clear statement of the skills-deficit position, see the Commission on the Skills of the American Workforce, *America's Choice: High Skills or Low Wages!* (Rochester, N.Y.: National Center on Education and the Economy, 1990). An excellent summary of the human capital argument and its emphasis on skills and the rebuttals to it during the 1960s and 1970s can be found in Henry Aaron, *Politics and the Professors* (Washington: Brookings Institution, 1978), ch. 3; later critiques can be found in Richard Rothstein, "The Myth of Public School Failure," *American Prospect,* March 21, 1993, *www.prospect.org/print/V4/13/rothstein-r.html;* Gordon Lafer, *The Job Train-*

ing Charade (Ithaca, N.Y.: Cornell University Press, 2002), ch. 2; Martin Carnoy and Henry Levin, *Schooling and Work in the Democratic State* (Stanford: Stanford University Press, 1985), pp. 161–176.

16. Henry Levin, "High Stakes Tests and Economic Productivity," in Gary Orfield and Mindy Kornhaber, eds., *Raising Standards or Raising Barriers? Inequality and High-Stakes Testing in Public Education* (New York: Century Foundation Press, 2001), p. 48; Lafer, *Job Training Charade,* p. 133.

17. Michael Handel, "Is There a Skills Crisis?" Public Policy Brief no. 62 (Annandale-on-Hudson, N.Y.: Levy Institute of Bard College, 2000), p. 36.

18. Murnane and Levy, *Teaching the New Basic Skills,* p. 32. Many such lists exist. See, e.g., National Academy of Sciences, National Academy of Engineering, and the Institute of Medicine, *High Schools and the Changing Workplace: The Employers' View* (Washington: National Academy Press, 1984), ch. 2. Just after the 1983 *Nation at Risk* report appeared, a survey of personnel officers stated unequivocally that dependability, not academic performance, was the key factor they looked for in hiring high school graduates. See Robert Crain, "The Quality of American High School Graduates: What Personnel Officers Say and Do about It," Report no. 354, Center for Social Organization of Schools, Johns Hopkins University, May 1984.

19. Murnane and Levy, *Teaching the New Basic Skills,* p. 32.

20. Quoted in Lafer, *Job training Charade,* p. 136. Lafer discusses a series of employer surveys in various states and the nation during the 1990s.

21. Andrew Sum and Sheila Palma, "The National Economic Recession and Its Impacts on Employment among the Nation's Young Adults (16–24 Years Old)," Center for Market Studies, Northeastern University, January 2002.

22. David Vogel, *Fluctuating Fortunes: Political Power of Business in America* (New York: Basic Books, 1989), p. 113; Sylvia Nasar, "Higher Worker Productivity Is Good Sign for the Economy," *New York Times,* November 27, 1992, p. 1; Louis Uchitelle, "Big Increase in Productivity by Workers," *New York Times,* November 13, 1999, p. B1.

23. Edward Denison quoted in Edwin Dean, ed., *Education and Economic Productivity* (Cambridge, Mass.: Ballinger, 1984), p. 4.

24. This section draws from Paul Krugman, *Peddling Prosperity* (New York: Norton, 1994), pp. 59–81.

25. See Dean, ed., *Education and Economic Productivity,* esp. Jacob Mincer,

"Overeducation or Undereducation?" pp. 205–212. John Bishop, "Is the Test Score Decline Responsible for the Productivity Growth Decline?" *American Economic Review* 79, no. 1 (1989): 178–197. For impact of the 1960s and cultural changes upon schooling, see Thomas Sowell, *Inside American Education: The Decline, The Deceptions, The Dogmas* (New York: Free Press, 1993).

26. James Patterson, *Brown v. Board of Education* (New York: Oxford University Press, 2001), chs. 7–9; Alan Brinkley, *Liberalism and Its Discontents* (Cambridge, Mass.: Harvard University Press, 1998), ch. 16.

27. Eric Hanushek, "The Seeds of Growth," *Education Next, www.educationnext.org/20023/10.html;* David Card and Alan Krueger, "Does School Quality Matter? Returns to Education and the Characteristics of Public Schools in the United States," *Journal of Political Economy* 100, no. 7 (1992): 1–40.

28. Bishop, "Is the Test Score Decline Responsible"; Levin, "High-Stakes Testing and Economic Productivity."

29. Levin, "High-Stakes Testing and Economic Productivity"; Robert Balfanz, "Local Knowledge, Academic Skills, and Individual Productivity: An Alternative View," *Educational Policy* 5, no. 4 (1991): 343–370; Henry Levin, "Educational Performance Standards and the Economy," *Educational Researcher* 27, no. 4 (1998): 4–10; John P. Smith III, "Tracking the Mathematics of Automobile Production: Are Schools Failing to Prepare Students for Work?" American Educational Research Journal 36, no. 4 (1999): 835–878. Also see Lafer, *Job Training Charade,* chs. 2–3, for a comprehensive summary of evidence revealing how workplace demands are inconsistent with the theory and beliefs of those who argue for better-trained graduates from high school and college. Audrey Amrein and David Berliner, "High Stakes Testing, Uncertainty, and Student Learning," Education Policy Studies Laboratory, Arizona State University, December 2002, *http://edpolicylab.org.* Critics of using standardized test scores as the only or best indicator of improved teaching and learning have often referred to racial bias and other important measures that are either ignored or missing because of measurement difficulties. For racial bias, see Christopher Jencks, "Racial Bias in Testing," in Jencks and Phillips, eds., *Black-White Test Score Gap,* 55–85. For handling measurement difficulties, the work of Lorrie Shepard is best. See "The Role of Assessment in a Learning Culture," *Educational Researcher* 29, no. 7 (2000): 4–14.

30. Quotations from Krugman, *Peddling Prosperity,* pp. 125–126; and David Card, "Education Matters," *Milken Institute Review,* 4th quarter 2002, p. 77.

31. Cubberley quoted in David Tyack and Larry Cuban, *Tinkering toward Utopia* (Cambridge, Mass.: Harvard University Press, 1995), p. 141. David Kearns and Denis Doyle, Winning the Brain Race (San Francisco: ICS Press, 1989), p. 4.

32. Typical examples of the literature connecting worker productivity to schooling are Lester Thurow, *Head to Head: The Coming Economic Battle among Japan, Europe, and America* (New York: Morrow, 1992); Robert Reich, *The Work of Nations* (New York: Knopf, 1991); and Michael Dertouzos, ed., *Made in America: Regaining the Productivity Edge* (New York: HarperCollins, 1990).

33. Krugman, *Peddling Prosperity,* pp. 268–280.

34. For a sampling of writers who have questioned the connection between economic productivity and educational performance, see Lawrence Cremin, *Popular Education and Its Discontents* (New York: Harper and Row, 1990), pp. 102–103; Larry Cuban, "The Corporate Myth of Reforming Public Schools," *Phi Delta Kappan* 74, no. 2 (1992): 157–159; Harold Howe, *Thinking about Our Kids* (New York: Free Press, 1993), pp. 182–185; Levin, "Educational Performance Standards and the Economy"; Richard Rothstein, "Out of Balance: Our Understanding of How Schools Affect Society and How Society Affects Schools," paper presented at Spencer Foundation's 30th Anniversary Conference, January 2002; Michael Porter, Jeffrey Sachs, and John McArthur, *Global Competitiveness Report 2001–2002* (New York: World Economic Forum, 2002).

35. Jeffrey Henig, *Rethinking School Choice: Limits of the Market Metaphor* (Princeton: Princeton University Press, 1994); David Tyack, *Seeking Common Ground* (Cambridge, Mass.: Harvard University Press, 2004); an anonymous reviewer of this manuscript helped me considerably on this point of parental choice.

36. Milton Friedman, "The Role of Government in Education," in R. Solo, ed., *Economics and the Public Interest* (New Brunswick, N.J.: Rutgers University Press, 1955); John Chubb and Terry Moe, *Politics, Markets, and America's Schools* (Washington: Brookings Institution Press, 1990); for a synthesis and scathing analysis of the research in various disciplines' appraisal of

choice both public and private, see Joseph Viterittio, "Schoolyard Revolutions: How Research on Urban School Reform Undermines Reform," *Political Science Quarterly* 118, no. 2 (2003): 233–257.

37. Frederick Hess, *Revolution at the Margins: The Impact of Competition on Urban School Systems* (Washington: Brookings Institution Press, 2002), pp. 219–220. Also see Patrick McEwan, "The Potential Impact of Large-Scale Voucher Programs," *Review of Educational Research* 70, no. 2 (2000): 103–149; Clive Belfield and Henry Levin, "The Effects of Competition between Schools in Educational Outcomes," *Review of Educational Research* 72, no. 2 (2002): 279–341. Paul Peterson's study of a New York City voucher experiment in 2000 trumpeted gains for black students. A reanalysis of the data by the economist Alan Krueger revealed that no statistically significant gains for black students occurred. Michael Winerup, "What a Voucher Study Truly Showed and Why," *New York Times*, May 7, 2003, p. A27.

38. Richard Rothstein, "Charter Conundrum," *American Prospect*, July–August 1998, p. 60. Also see Christopher Lubienski, "Innovation in Education Markets: Theory and Evidence on the Impact of Competition and Choice in Charter Schools," *American Education Research Journal* 40, no. 2 (2003): 395–443.

39. Hess, *Revolution at the Margins*; Luis Benveniste, Martin Carnoy, and Richard Rothstein, *All Else Equal: Are Public and Private Schools Different?* (New York: Routledge Falmer, 2003); William Howell and Paul Petersen, *The Education Gap: Vouchers and Urban Schools* (Washington: Brookings Institution Press, 2002); "A Decade of Charter Schools: From Theory to Practice," *CPRE Policy Briefs*, RB-35 (Consortium for Policy Research in Education, University of Pennsylvania, 2002); Gary Miron and Christopher Nelson, *What's Public about Charter Schools? Lessons Learned about Choice and Accountability* (Thousand Oaks, Calif.: Corwin Press, 2002). Figures for Texas come from Francis X. Clines, "Re-educating the Voters about Texas Schools," *New York Times*, June 3, 2003, p. A30.

40. Monte Whaley, "Owens Signs School Voucher Bill," *Denver Post*, April 17, 2003. New Zealand is a country with a national system of education in which local school trustees run individual schools (as of 1990) and parents can send their children to any schools they wish (as of 1991). Two researchers have explored this national experiment and found mixed results: general satisfaction among parents with the reform, polarizing of social classes in

various schools, teacher dissatisfaction, and deep concern among national policymakers over poorly performing schools. To what degree researchers and policymakers can apply the New Zealand experience to the United States is unclear, but the decade-long experiment suggests caution, at a minimum. See Edward Fiske and Helen Ladd, *When Schools Compete: A Cautionary Tale* (Washington: Brookings Institution Press, 2000); Helen Ladd and Edward Fiske, "Does Competition Improve Teaching and Learning? Evidence from New Zealand," *Educational Evaluation and Policy Analysis* 25, no. 1 (2003): 97–112.

41. An earlier venture by private-sector firms to operate public schools occurred in the mid-1960s, when companies contracted with school districts enrolling large percentages of low-income minorities to improve reading and math skills in particular schools. See Tyack and Cuban, *Tinkering toward Utopia,* pp. 117–120.

42. Alex Molnar, Glen Wilson, and Daniel Allen, "Profiles of For-Profit Education Management Companies, Fifth Annual Report, 2002–2003" (Tempe: Arizona State University, Commercialism in Education Research Unit, 2003); this report documents the mortality of business firms running schools in the early 1990s. "Edison Schools: The First Decade," advertisement, *New York Times,* November 14, 2002, p. C5. Also see Lynn Schnaiberg, "Seeking a Competitive Advantage," *Education Week,* December 8, 1999, pp. 1, 12–14; Mark Walsh, "Report Card on For-Profit Industry Still Incomplete," *Education Week,* December 15, 1999, pp. 1, 14–16; Carrie Lips, "'Edupreneurs': A Survey of For-Profit Education," Policy Analysis no. 386 (Washington: Cato Institute, 2000).

43. I draw these ideas from a manuscript by Craig Peck and Larry Cuban, "Good for Business, Good for Education?" (April 2002). Craig Peck coined the word "businessification."

44. There are charters in first-ring suburbs of big cities enrolling high percentages of minority students (New York, Washington, Chicago). As state and local school budget retrenchment occurred in 2002 and 2003, tensions between charters and regular schools competing for the same dollars escalated. See Josh Barbanel, "Charter Schools Grow in Suburbs Uneasily," *New York Times,* May 3, 2003, pp. A1, 18. Also see Clines, "Re-educating the Voters about Texas Schools," p. A30.

45. See, e.g., Susan Snyder and Dale Mezzacappa, "Report Shows Progress

in Edison's Test Scores," *Philadelphia Inquirer,* February 28, 2003, *www. philly.com/mld/inquirer/news/local/5280809.htm?* Edison Schools advertisement, *New York Times,* November 14, 2002; Mark Walsh, "Reports Paint Opposite Pictures of Edison Achievement," *Education Week,* March 5, 2003, p. 5; Gerald Bracey, "The Market in Theory Meets the Market in Practice: The Case of Edison Schools," (Tempe: Education Policy Research Unit, College of Education, Arizona State University, 2002).

46. General Accounting Office, "Public Schools: Insufficient Research to Determine Effectiveness of Selected Private Education Companies," October 2002, GAO-03-11.

47. Mark Walsh, "Education Stocks Sag as Markets Stay in Bearish Mode," *Education Week,* September 4, 2002, 8.

48. Brian O'Reilly, "Why Edison Doesn't Work," *Fortune,* December 4, 2002. Edison posted its first-ever quarterly net income gain of $10.2 million in September 2003. *www.fortune.com/fortune/articles/0,15114,395208,00. html.* Daniel Gross, "Edison's Dim Bulbs," *Slate,* September 10, 2002, *slate.msn.com/?ed=2070329;* Diana Henriques, "Edison Schools' Founder to Take It Private," *New York Times,* July 15, 2003, p. C9. Liberty partners bought Edison for $174 million in July 2003; see *www.edisonschools.com/ news/news.cfm?ID=157.*

49. *www.ed.gov/nclb/landing.jhtml.*

50. Michael Fullan, *The New Meaning of Educational Change* (New York: Teachers College Press, 1991), pp. 88–93; Kay Moffett, "Making Waves While Learning to Swim: New Teachers in Reforming Schools" (Doctoral diss., Stanford University, 1999).

51. Most journalists have had so little direct experience in inner-city schools as students, teachers, or daily observers that it is too much to expect them to write of the complex trials of life in these settings and connections to neighborhood and larger community as crucial factors in determining the quality of teaching and learning. Exceptions are Sam Freedman, *Small Victories* (New York: HarperCollins, 1990); Jonathan Schorr, *Hard Lessons* (New York: Ballantine, 2002); Leslie Baldacci, *Inside Mrs. B's Classroom* (New York: McGraw-Hill, 2004); and Alex Kotlowitz, *There Are No Children Here* (New York: Anchor, 1992). If journalists had to live in the community for a few months and serve as teachers, coach teams, or work with school

clubs, the complexities of students' lives, the community, and their daily schooling would become far more apparent. I suspect that their subsequent writing would reflect the deeper knowledge (and anger) that schools are surely important institutions but can hardly transform academic and behavioral performance alone.

52. Rothstein, "The Myth of Public School Failure." Levin and Kelley, "Can Education Do It Alone?"; Henry Levin and Clive Belfield, "Families as Contractual Partners in Education," *UCLA Law Review* 49, no. 6 (2002).

53. See Sarah Deschenes, David Tyack, and Larry Cuban, "Mismatch: Historical Perspectives on Schools and Students Who Don't Fit Them," *Teachers College Record* 103, no. 4 (2001): 525–547. A number of state court decisions involving equitable funding of public schools have occurred recently in New Jersey, Kentucky, and elsewhere. See, e.g., Al Baker, "Education Advocates Urge Quick Action by Albany on School Financing," *New York Times,* July 3, 3003, p. B7.

54. James Fallows, "The Age of Murdoch," *Atlantic Monthly,* September 2003, pp. 82–98; quotation p. 92.

55. For a useful point-counterpoint debate about similarities and differences between schools and businesses, see John Chubb and Henry Levin, "The Profit Motive," *Education Next* 1, no. 1 (2001): 6–15.

56. There are many writers who have tried to define the similarities and differences between the public and private, between the public good and the private interest. Sources that have been helpful to me are Jane Mansbridge, "On the Contested Nature of the Public Good" (pp. 3–19), and Craig Calhoun, "The Public Good as a Social and Cultural Project" (pp. 20–35), in Walter Powell and Elisabeth Clemens, eds., *Private Action and the Public Good* (New Haven: Yale University Press, 1998). For an example of questioning the public-ness of public schools, see Frederick Hess, "Making Sense of the 'Public' in Public Education," PPI Policy Report (Washington: Progressive Policy Institute, 2002). For a spirited analysis of the private and public in schooling, see Martha Minow, *Partners, Not Rivals: Privatization and the Public Good* (Boston: Beacon Press, 2002).

57. Some educators have challenged the comparison of schools and business over the decades. For a typical example of an educator writing to demonstrate that little if anything can be learned from business, see Marvin

Marshall, "Business: A Poor Model for Learning," *Teachers.Net Gazette, teachers.net/gazette/AUG03/marshallprint.html.*

58. Lowell Rose and Alec Gallup, "The 32nd Annual Phi Delta Kappa/ Gallup Poll of the Public's Attitudes toward the Public Schools," *Phi Delta Kappan,* September 2000, p. 47.

59. Mark Moore, "Privatizing Public Management," in John Donohue and Joseph Nye, eds., *Market-Based Governance* (Washington: Brookings Institution Press, 2002), pp. 298–301.

60. See David Labaree, "Public Goods, Private Goods: The American Struggle over Educational Goals," *American Educational Research Journal* 34 (1997): 39–81. Also John Rury, "Democracy's High School? Social Change and American Secondary Education in the Post-Conant Era," *American Educational Research Journal* 39, no. 2 (2002): 307–336.

61. For a scorecard of corporate scandals between 2000–2002, see Penelope Patsuris, "The Corporate Scandal Sheet" *Forbes.com,* August 26, 2002, *www.forbes.com/home/2002/07/25/accountingtracker.html.*

62. Quotation from Floyd Norris, "A Small Move to Shareholder Democracy," *New York Times,* July 16, 2003, p. C1. On the Apple resolution and its outcome see James Surowiecki, "To the Barricades," *New Yorker,* June 9, 2003, p. 44.

63. For instances of cheating in schools, see Robert Johnston and Michelle Galley, "Austin District Charged with Test Tampering," *Education Week,* April 14, 1999, p. 3; Francis Clines, "Cheating Report Renews Debate over Use of Tests to Evaluate Schools," *New York Times,* June 12, 2000, p. A16. A rash of articles on corporate boards of directors granting exorbitant pay packages to their CEOs was implicated in the resignation of the chairman and CEO of the New York Stock Exchange in 2003. See Kurt Eichenwald, "In String of Corporate Troubles, Critics Focus on Boards' Failings," *New York Times,* September 21, 2003, pp. 1, 30.

64. Quotation from Surowiecki, "To the Barricades."; remark attributed to Nell Minow.

65. Jeffrey Henig, *Rethinking School Choice: Limits of the Market Metaphor* (Princeton: Princeton University Press, 1994), pp. 199–200.

66. Larry Cuban, "How Schools Change Reforms: Redefining Reform Success and Failure," *Teachers College Record,* 99, no. 3 (1998): 453–477.

67. Quotation from David Leonhardt, "A Sickly Economy with No Cure in Sight," *New York Times*, May 25, 2003, "News of the Week," p. 1.

68. Moore, "Privatizing Public Management," p. 309.

69. Andrew Porter and John Smithson, "Are Content Standards Being Implemented in the Classroom? A Methodology and Some Tentative Answers," in Susan H. Fuhrman, ed., *From the Capitol to the Classroom: Standard Based Reform in the States*, 100th Yearbook of the National Society for the Study of Education (Chicago: University of Chicago Press, 2001), pp. 60–80, was helpful in my thinking here.

70. Drucker quoted in Rosabeth Kanter and David Summers, "Doing Well While Doing Good: Dilemmas of Performance Measurement in Nonprofit Organizations and the Need for a Multiple-Constituency Approach," in Walter Powell, ed., *The Nonprofit Sector: A Research Handbook* (New Haven: Yale University Press, 1987), p. 156. Richard Murnane compares economic and educational indicators. He examines generic commonalties between the measurement of unemployment and that of educational performance, but he recognizes two key differences. First, local school boards are responsible for raising children's achievement, while local employers and government officials are not held responsible for local unemployment. Second, the decentralized governance of schools heavily influences the choice and quality of indicators, an influence missing from indicators of economic performance. Murnane, "Improving Education Indicators and Economic Indicators: The Same Problems," *Educational Evaluation and Policy Analysis* 9, no. 2 (1987): 101–116. Also see Jack Triplett and Barry Bosworth, "Productivity in the Services Sector," paper prepared for American Economic Association conference, January 9, 2000.

6. Has Business Influence Improved Schools?

1. Sherri Day, "Yogurt Makers Shrink the Cup, Trying to Turn Less into More," *New York Times*, May 3, 2003, pp. B1, B14.

2. I have not mentioned the array of commercial influences that have penetrated the schools, such as corporate-produced curriculum materials, corporate advertisements, Channel 1 television, and similar ventures embraced by many cash-strapped districts. I have omitted this topic for two

reasons. First, I want to show that business influence on institutional structures of schooling goes far deeper and is far more pervasive than teachers' use of materials produced by Pizza Hut or scoreboards funded by Coca-Cola. Second, I want to point out that business influence on organizational structures and institutional processes is limited, not all-powerful as some writers have made it out to be. Moreover, business influence in some instances can be construed as positive.

3. Clarence Stone, ed., *Changing Urban Education* (Lawrence: University Press of Kansas, 1998); Clarence Stone, *Building Civic Capacity: The Politics of Reforming Urban Schools* (Lawrence: University Press of Kansas, 2001); Robert Putnam, *Bowling Alone: The Collapse and Revival of American Community* (New York: Simon and Schuster, 2001); Dorothy Shipps, "Pulling Together: Civic Capacity and Urban School Reform," *American Educational Research Journal* (forthcoming); also Rosyln A. Mickelson, "Corporations and Classrooms: A Critical Examination of the Business Agenda for Urban School Reform," in Karen McClafferty, Carlos Torres, and Theodore Mitchell, eds., *Challenges of Urban Education: Sociological Perspectives for the Next Century* (Albany: State University of New York Press, 2000), pp. 127–173; Charles Handy, "What's a Business For?" *Harvard Business Review*, December 2002, pp. 49–55.

4. For the diversity in teachers' responses to standards-based reform, see Suzanne Wilson and Robert Floden, "Hedging Bets: Standards-Based Reform in Classrooms," in S. Fuhrman, ed., *From the Capitol to the Classroom: Standards-based Reform in the States,* 100th Yearbook of National Society for the Study of Education, part 2 (Chicago: NSSE, 2001), pp. 193–216; Cynthia Coburn, "Collective Sensemaking about Reading: How Teachers Mediate Reading Policy in Their Professional Communities," *Educational Evaluation and Policy Analysis* 23, no. 2 (2001): 145–170; Michael Knapp, "Between Systemic Reforms and the Mathematics and Science Classroom: The Dynamics of Innovation, Implementation, and Professional Learning," *Review of Educational Research* 67, no. 2 (1997): 227–266; James Spillane, "Challenging Instruction for 'All Students': Policy, Practitioners, and Practice," in Fuhrman, ed., *From the Capitol to the Classroom,* part II, pp. 217–241; James Spillane and John Zeuli, "Reform and Teaching: Exploring Patterns of Practice in the Context of National and State Mathematics Reforms," *Educational Evalua-*

tion and Policy Analysis 21, no. 1 (1999): 1–27; Carol Barnes and David Cohen, *Standards Reform in High-Poverty Schools* (New York: Teachers College Press, 2002); Rodney Ogawa, Judith Sandholtz, Marilyn Martinez-Flores, and Samantha Scribner, "The Substantive and Symbolic Consequences of a District's Standards-Based Curriculum," *American Educational Research Journal* 2003, 40, no. 1 (2003): 147–176.

5. Michael Winerup, "Holding Back a Pupil: A Bad Idea Despite Intent," *New York Times,* May 21, 2003, p. A26.

6. Lawrence Kraus, "The Citizen-Scientist's Obligation to Stand Up for Standards," *New York Times,* April 22, 2003, p. D3.

7. Mensah Dean, "Consumer Affairs Chief to Propose Financial Literacy Course for High Schools," *Philadelphia Daily News,* October 8, 2003, p. 17; Dewey quoted in Herbert Kliebard, *Schooled to Work* (New York: Teachers College Press, 1999), p. 219.

8. Gunnar Myrdal, *An American Dilemma: The Negro Problem and Modern Democracy* (New York, Harper and Row, 1944).

9. Many writers have made these points, such as Lawrence Cremin, David Labaree, Tyack and Cuban, and Patricia Graham. For a succinct and typical article, see John Hardin Best, "Reforming America's Schools: The High Risks of Failure," *Teachers College Record* 86, no. 2 (1984): 265–274.

10. Robert Heilbroner, *Twenty-first Century Capitalism* (New York: Norton, 1993), chs. 6–7.

11. The 1910 figures come from David Tyack and Elisabeth Hansot, *Managers of Virtue* (New York: Basic Books, 1982), 109; later figures come from Kevin Phillips, *Wealth and Democracy* (New York: Broadway Books, 2002), pp. 122–123.

12. "Kevin Phillips, Dialogue with James Fallows," part 2, Atlantic Online, July 12, 2002, *www.theatlantic.com/unbound/fallows/jf2002-07-03/phillips2. htm.* Also see Phillips, *Wealth and Democracy,* ch. 8.

13. David Shipler, *The Working Poor: Invisible in America* (New York: Knopf, 2004). Jennifer Hochschild, *Facing Up to the American Dream: Race, Class, and the Soul of the Nation* (Princeton: Princeton University Press, 1995), p. 185. Also see "Can We Give America a Raise?" *American Prospect,* January 2004, pp. 35–62, esp. Christopher Jencks, "The Low-Wage Puzzle," pp. 35–37.

14. Hochschild, *Facing Up to the American Dream;* Douglas Massey and Nancy Denton, *American Apartheid: Segregation and the Making of the Underclass* (Cambridge, Mass.: Harvard University Press, 1993); Glenn Loury, *The Anatomy of Racial Inequality* (Cambridge, Mass.: Harvard University Press, 2002); Christopher Jencks and Meredith Phillips, eds., *The Black-White Test Score Gap* (Washington: Brookings Institution Press, 1998).

15. Richard Herrnstein and Charles Murray, *The Bell Curve: Intelligence and Class Structure in American Life* (New York: Free Press, 1999).

16. For another view of ideologies in education that focuses on the market and public good as competing ideas, see Kevin Smith, *The Ideology of Education: The Commonwealth, the Market, and America's Schools* (Albany: State University of New York Press, 2003).

17. Charles Tilly, *Durable Inequality* (Berkeley: University of California Press, 1998), pp. 22–25. Tilly sums up this view crisply: "We pay a price for concentrating on well-documented outcomes. Recent students of inequality under capitalism have, unsurprisingly, focused on wages, a topic that lends itself both to measurement and to explanation in individual terms. They have neglected wealth, health, nutrition, power, deference, privilege, security, and other critical zones of inequality that in the long run matter more to well-being than wages" (p. 24).

18. William Julius Wilson, *The Truly Disadvantaged* (Chicago: University of Chicago Press, 1987); Loury, *Anatomy of Racial Inequality;* Eduardo Bonilla-Silva, *Racism without Racists: Color-Blind Racism and the Persistence of Social Inequality in the United States* (London: Rowman and Littlefield, 2003). For Individual Development Accounts, see Michael Sherraden, "From Research to Policy: Lessons from Individual Development Accounts," *Journal of Consumer Affairs* 34, no. 2 (2000): 159–181; also see "Wealth in America," *American Prospect,* May 2003.

19. Tilly, *Durable Inequality.*

20. Rona Wilensky, "College for Everyone Is Not the Answer to High School Reform," *HeadFirst Colorado* 1, no. 2 (2003): 26–32. Norton Grubb and Marvin Lazerson, *The Education Gospel: The Economic Power of Schooling* (Cambridge, Mass.: Harvard University Press, 2004), introduction.

21. Kati Haycock, "A New Core Curriculum for All: Aiming High for Other People's Children," *Thinking K–16,* 7, no. 1 (Winter 2003): 2; also see Sarah Deschenes, David Tyack, and Larry Cuban, "Mismatch: Historical

Perspectives on Schools and Students That Don't Match Them," *Teachers College Record* 103, no. 4 (2001): 525–547, for the point that the standards movement, like previous reforms, will have students who fail and will come up with labels for them as earlier generations of reformers have done.

22. For a recent view of vocational education, now called career and technical education, and the melding of it with standards-based reform, see Marisa Castellano and Sam Stringfield, "Secondary Career and Technical Education and Comprehensive School Reform: Implications for Research and Practice," *Review of Educational Research* 73, no. 2 (2003): 231–272.

23. Jeffrey Henig, *Rethinking School Choice: The Limits of the Market Metaphor* (Princeton: Princeton University Press, 1994), p. 13.

24. Anthony Downs, "Up and Down with Ecology—The Issue-Attention Cycle," *Public Interest* 2, no. 3 (1972).

25. Mike Allen, "Tax Cuts Will Do the Job, President Says," *Washington Post*, August 14, 2003, p. AO3; Jared Bernstein, "The Young and Jobless," *American Prospect*, October 2003, p. A17.

26. Krueger quoted from Derek Neal's review of Krueger's book *Education Matters* (Edward Elgar, 2001), *www.educationnext.org/20031/85.html*. A recent RAND study also recommended pilot studies before large-scale reforms: Laura Hamilton et al., "Studying Large-Scale Reforms of Instructional Practice: An Example from Mathematics and Science," *Educational Evaluation and Policy Analysis* 25, no. 1 (2003): 1–29.

27. Committee for Economic Development, *Preschool for All: Investing in Productive and Just Society* (New York: Committee for Economic Development, 2002). Also see Valerie Lee and David Burkham, *Inequality at the Starting Gate: Social Background Differences in Achievement as Children Begin School* (Washington: Economic Policy Institute, 2002).

28. Geoffrey Borman and Gina Hewes, "The Long-Term Effects and Cost-Effectiveness of Success for All," *Educational Evaluation and Policy Analysis* 24, no. 4 (2002): 243–266.

29. PBS, *News Hour with Jim Lehrer*, "School for Success," December 29, 2003, transcript at *www.pbs.org/newshour/bb/education/july-dec03/charter_12-29-03.html*; Parents United for the D.C. Public Schools, "D.C. Public School Funding: Myth and Reality," February 2003, p. 14.

30. Karen Arenson, "What Would Teachers Do If They Had the Chance?" *New York Times*, September 17, 2003, p. A26; New York City Board of Edu-

cation, "Office of Financial Management Reporting on School-Based Expenditures Reports, School Year 2000–2001," January 2002, p. 1.

31. Michael Winerup, "The Lasting Legacy of a Promise of Free Education," *New York Times,* April 23, 2003, p. A26.

32. Pamela Prah, "Education Funding Draws New Lawsuits, Ballot Initiatives," *Stateline.Org,* August 20, 2003, *www.stateline.org/stateline/?pa=story &sa=showStoryInfo&id=321271.*

33. See Business Coalition for Education Reform, "Improving the Quality of Teaching: The Business Role," no date, *www.bcer.org/.* Press release and Gerstner quoted in Greg Winter, "Striving to Improve Those at the Head of the Class," *New York Times,* January 14, 2004, p. A18.

34. See Cynthia Coburn, "Rethinking Scale: Moving beyond Numbers to Deep and Lasting Change," *Educational Researcher* 32, no. 6 (2003): 3–12.

35. Benjamin Barber, "America Skips School," *Harper's Magazine,* November 1993, p. 43.

36. Larry Cuban, *Why Are Good Schools So Hard to Get?* (New York: Teachers College Press, 2003).

37. Quoted in Roland Marchand, *Creating the Corporate Soul* (Berkeley: University of California Press, 1998), p. 166.

38. Ibid., pp. 359, 363.

39. Clarence Stone, Jeffrey Henig, Bryan Jones, and Carol Pierannunzi, *Building Civic Capacity: The Politics of Reforming Urban Schools* (Lawrence: University Press of Kansas, 2001).

40. Jamie Vollmer, presentation he made in Graves County, Kentucky (no date given); *www.graves.k12.ky.us/news/district/rethinking_ed.htm.* I expand on the many kinds of "good" schools in Cuban, *Why Is It So Hard to Get Good Schools,* ch. 3.

41. Nan Stone, "Does Business Have Any Business in Education?" *Harvard Business Review,* March-April 1991, pp. 6–7.

42. Ibid., pp. 11–12.

43. Ibid., p. 12.

44. An early study that provides a research base for the anecdote about Vera is Melvin Kohn, *Class and Conformity: A Study in Values* (Homewood, Ill.: Dorsey Press, 1969); see chs. 1–4, 9–11.

ACKNOWLEDGMENTS

In nearly half a century as an educator, I have read many accounts of the relationship between schools and businesses, ranging from the polemical bashing of business leaders as exploiting innocent teachers and children to uncritical and admiring tributes to unselfish CEOs for extending a helping hand to needy schools. I found little in those accounts that fit my experiences in schools as a teacher, superintendent, and professor.

Four years ago the president of Teachers College, Columbia University, asked me to give three lectures on school reform. One of the lectures concerned the links between business leaders and school reformers over the past century. Writing and delivering that talk made me want to know more about the degree to which business leaders initiated and shaped school reform and about what actually occurred in schools as a result of business-inspired efforts. So I decided to delve more deeply into the topic of the role of business leaders in school reform between the 1890s and the present. This book is the result of that research and reflection.

As with all of my work, I have been most fortunate in family, friends, and colleagues who pitched in to help me complete this book. First, I thank readers who gave graciously of their time to comment on portions of a draft or the entire manuscript: Martin Carnoy, Sondra Cuban, Hank Levin, Gary Lichtenstein, Susanna Loeb, Ray McDermott, Dick Murnane, Anne Newman, Dorothy Shipps, and David Tyack. I am most grateful for their extensive comments and critiques. Two anonymous reviewers for Harvard University Press offered helpful comments. I also thank Elizabeth Knoll for encouraging me to write this book.

INDEX